A Journey in Three Acts: The Story of Horatio Ward

By Horatio Ward

Ward Publishing

2025

i

Published by **Ward Publishing**

ISBN: 979-8-9932238-1-0

Cover design: Horatio Ward

Book design: Horatio Ward

Printed in the United States of America

2025

Dedication

To my father, **Hugh Valentine St. Aubyn Ward** — Though your candle burned too quickly, its light has never gone out. I carry your name, your promise, and your love in every step I take.

To my mother, **Mama (Marva),** whose unwavering strength and selfless love have guided every chapter of my life — from the dusty lanes of Denham Town to classrooms across three continents. Your sacrifices, wisdom, and fierce determination laid the foundation upon which I have built my dreams.

To my children, **Jilisha and Rhys** — your love, laughter, and boundless curiosity have been my greatest joy and inspiration. You gave purpose to every cross-Atlantic journey and remind me of the legacy I want to leave behind.

To **Sharon** — thank you for your enduring presence, your patience, and for seeing me through seasons when I didn't always make it easy. I know I was a challenge, but you stood firm.

To my brother **Wayne (Roos),** my first and best friend — your loyalty, humor, and quiet strength have been constants in a world of change.

To my **Aunty Bar and Aunty Patsy** — your love, guidance, and humor filled my childhood with warmth and belonging.

To my **Uncle Basil** — your calm wisdom and steady presence helped shape the man I have become.

To my sister **Shema** — your quiet strength, thoughtful words, and ever-supportive presence have meant more to me than you'll ever know.

To my cousins **Nadia, Kaydean and Oneil** — thank you for the love, laughter, and shared memories that made growing up feel like an adventure.

To my sixth-grade teacher **Mrs. Dunn**, who saw in me a light I hadn't yet recognized and opened the first academic door that led to St. George's College. Your belief was a turning point.

To **Ms. Dorrett Campbell**, my brilliant college English lecturer at The Mico Teachers' Collegee, whose passion for literature and unwavering standards taught me that language is not only power — it is purpose. Your influence echoes in every classroom I've ever taught in.

My journey, in all its beauty and complexity, belongs to all of you. Your spirits walk with me on every page, every lesson, every triumph.

"A child who reads, grows into an adult who thinks."

Horatio Ward

Table of Contents

ACT I

Chapter I: The Roots
My Father's Legacy
The Strength of Mama
17 Tulip Lane
The Siblings

Chapter II: Coming of Age
St. George's College
Manchester United
Iniko in Portmore
The Outlaws
The Rhythm and The Fight

Chapter III: Becoming
Paycheck
The Mico
Uncle Basil
Cometh The Teacher
Sharon

ACT II

Chapter 1: The Crossing
Beckoning
London
Jilisha: The Arrival
The Teacher in London

Chapter II: Becoming More
The Woman Who Would Not Bend
The Girl Who Would
His Name is Rhys

Chapter III: Football and Haircuts
Rivalry
One Cake
Sharon Joins
Rhys' Choice
Simply U
The Call

ACT III:

Chapter I: The Harvest
I am Here
Teaching Through Sales
The CBD Shop

Chapter II: Foundations of a Teacher's Journey
The Classroom
First Days
Legacy

Chapter III: Growth Takes Hold
Home
Back To The Building
AVID

Chapter IV: New Ground
LAMS
Beyond The Classroom
The Faculty Class
AVID Beyond English
Service

Chapter V: A Rising Voice
Onwards
The Rise of Ahead of The Class
Honors and Grief
The Quiet Legend

Chapter VI: Breakthroughs
Beginnings
The Movement

2024- Facing Change
The Classroom as Sanctuary
BSI-Lemuel Teal
The Return

Chapter VII: 2025
Mango Tree Years
Florida Does Florida
Seeds We Scatter
Letting Go
The Classroom Legacy

Epilogue: The Fruit Still Grows
As I Live Act IV

Act I

Chapter I: The Roots

My Father's Legacy

Born in the foothills of Denham Town in 1969, I was the first of two boys. My father, **Hugh Valentine St. Aubyn Ward,** a quiet, intelligent man with a passion for books and football, (soccer) died tragically young—just nineteen—just after graduating from Jamaica College. The loss reverberated through the generations. My mother, Marva — known to all as Mama — was just seventeen, yet even at that tender age, Mama was a whirlwind of strength and grace, balancing discipline with affection, and raising her sons with a fierce belief in the power of education.

Though I never had the chance to know my father in the way a son longs to know his dad, the stories about him became my inheritance. They were carried in whispers from family members, in laughter-filled anecdotes from friends, and in the quiet pride on Mama's face whenever his name was spoken.

"Val," as he was affectionately called, was remembered not simply as a young man who left too soon, but as a figure of promise — a flame extinguished just as it was beginning to burn brightly.

People always said he was a man ahead of his years. Though barely out of boyhood, he carried himself with a maturity that made others take notice. His drive was evident in the way he attacked his studies at Jamaica College, pouring over textbooks late into the night, determined not only to pass but to excel. He was a thinker, a strategist, a dreamer who paired ambition with discipline. Football was his great love after books, and he was said to have been graceful with the ball at his feet, moving with the kind of quiet authority that earned respect rather than demanded it. To him, football wasn't just a game — it was a discipline, a place where character revealed itself.

But beyond his achievements, what made my father memorable to those who knew him was his decency. In a community where bravado often substituted for respect, my dad was known for his honesty, his sense of fairness, his refusal to compromise on what he felt was right.

Relatives often said, "*Yuh father was a gentleman,*" (Your father was a gentleman) and not in the casual way people use the word. They meant it — he was deliberate with his manners, respectful to elders, protective of the vulnerable, and always mindful of the dignity of others.

His honesty was both a compass and a shield. He would rather face difficulty than cut corners. It was said he once walked miles back to a shop to return a small item he hadn't paid for by mistake.

"It nuh belong to me," (It does not belong to me) he told the shopkeeper, brushing off her astonishment.

That story was told and retold not because of the money involved — it was insignificant — but because of the principle. Even as a teenager, my dad lived with a kind of moral clarity that inspired those around him.

And, of course, there was the matter of his good looks. My father was tall and slim, with a confident stride that seemed to mark him as someone bound for great things. He had sharp features softened by an easy smile, and eyes that carried warmth even when his face was serious. Aunty Bar would often remark on how handsome he was, shaking her head wistfully at the tragedy of his short life. Mama never needed to say much on that subject — her choice to be with him at such a young age spoke volumes about the pull he had. He was the kind of man people noticed, but he never carried himself with arrogance. His good looks were simply part of who he was, matched by an even greater inner beauty.

What moves me most in the stories is the way he loved my mother. They were young — too young, some would say — but their love was genuine, full of fire and tenderness. Friends would say they were inseparable, walking the lanes of Denham Town and nearby Hannah Town hand in hand, sharing plans for the future that life never allowed them to realize. Mama would sometimes speak of him in fragments, her eyes softening, her voice lowering:

"Your father loved deep. He treated me with care, with respect. He believed in us."

That love, though cut short, was powerful enough to endure. It became a legacy in itself, woven into the fabric of how Mama raised me — with the conviction that love must be strong, honest, and never halfway.

His death at nineteen left a wound that time could never fully heal, but it also left a challenge: to live up to the name "**Hugh Valentine St. Aubyn Ward**" to carry forward the decency, the honesty, the drive that defined him. I often wonder what life might have been like had he lived — whether he would have coached me on a football pitch, or pressed books into my hands with the same insistence Mama did or simply sat with me under a mango tree and shared his quiet wisdom. That wondering shaped me too. It made me hungry to embody the qualities I had only heard about, to let his absence become a guidepost rather than a void.

My father's absence was never just a silence in our house — it was a contrast etched into every corner of my boyhood. At St. George's College, I would watch fathers arrive to cheer their sons at football matches. They stood tall along the sidelines, shirts tucked in, voices carrying over the field. A boy could miss a goal and still look up to see his father clapping, reminding him that effort mattered as much as outcome. That presence was an anchor, and it gave boys a confidence that could not be taught in classrooms.

For me, that anchor was missing. On Manning Cup afternoons, with the chants of *"Hess Tee Gee Cee"* (STGC) echoing across Sabina Park, I found myself glancing at the stands, searching for a face I knew would never be there. I imagined him — Val, tall and slender, his confident stride carrying him through the crowd, his eyes burning with pride. I gave him a voice in my head, cheering, calling my name. I stitched that presence out of absence because every boy wants his father to see him.

Yet when she could, Mama substituted for him. Dressed in her Sunday best even on a weekday afternoon, she made her way to the football field. Her voice did not carry like the other men, but it carried something else: a determination that her son would not feel alone. I can still see her clapping furiously beside me in the grandstand at Sabina Park, during the 1983 Manning Cup final against Tivoli Gardens High School. Her face lit with pride as though my every effort in my devotion as a fan — was a victory worth celebrating. She could not replace my father's absence entirely, but she filled the gap with love, with presence, with a fierce insistence that I was not alone.

That wound of absence, however, followed me into adulthood. I eventually found out where my dad was buried — Shooter's Hill Cemetery in Bull Bay — but for nearly thirty years I never went. Life's busyness, distance, and my own hesitation delayed the moment. Yet as the years wore on, the pull grew stronger and stronger: I had to find him, had to stand where he lay, had to confront the silence. I had to meet my dad again.

On a hot morning, I went with my lifelong brother, Alva Taylor in his new Suzuki Swift motor car. We drove through the winding roads of Kingston, the sea breeze from Bull Bay and Harbour View carrying salt and memory. Shooter's Hill Cemetery spread before us, wild and unkempt. Graves lay hidden beneath tall grass and stubborn bush; the order of the place had been lost to time. Machete in hand, we pressed forward, sweat soaking our shirts, insects buzzing around us.

For a while, I feared we wouldn't find him. Then, through the overgrowth, we saw it: a headstone, weathered yet defiant. And there, carved clear despite the years, was the name:

9

"**Hugh Valentine St. Aubyn Ward.**"

My father.

I swallowed. I stared, transfixed. I froze. The years collapsed into that instant.

I knelt and brushed away the weeds, my hands trembling as if I could reach through stone and time. His name had endured where his body had not. Tears welled, and the words slipped out:

"*Daddy, mi deh yah.*" (Daddy, I am here.)

The world narrowed to the rasp of my breath and the whisper of grass against the stone. Sun pressed on the back of my neck, hot and insistent, and somewhere a bird scolded from a tamarind tree. The air smelled of dust and cut stems. I traced the letters again—carefully, almost reverently—like a child sounding out the alphabet, hoping the name might open into a voice. In the chipped corners and hairline cracks I saw all the breaks we never mended: birthdays missed, stories never told, the old arguments we never had, laughter that was never shared.

I thought of his hands — scarred, steady — and how they could have taught me to hold a hammer, a pen, a promise. I thought of his laugh, that I could not remember. *"Mi agoh tek care of yuh name,"* (I am going to take care of your name), I quietly whispered and decades later while sitting in Starbucks in Lehigh Acres, writing this chapter and remembering that moment, my throat tightened and the tears flowed silently down my cheeks, landing softly on my laptop's keypad.

"I carried you with me," I whispered. "Through cities, through winters, through rooms that never knew your voice." The breeze shifted. Leaves ticked like a clock. I pressed my palm flat, as if to sign my name beside his.

"Daddy, mi deh yah," I said again, steadier this time. *"An' mi nah go nowhere, yuh always agoh deh inna mi heart."* (And I'm not going anywhere. You will always be in my heart).

11

Beside me, Alva placed a hand on my shoulder, his silence heavy with understanding. We stood there in the wild cemetery, two men facing the permanence of death and the persistence of memory.

Years later, the past reached for me in a way I could not ignore. I still remember the dream—June 30, 2014—clear in 2025 as the night it found me. In the dream, I was in Florida, living at Aunty Bar's house, and he appeared: a tall man with his right foot bent at the knee on a hassock, his elbow resting on his thigh, fingers enveloping his chin, staring back at me—the exact pose I'd struck as a boy in a photo studio on Duke Street. The likeness hit like lightning, one still frame echoing another across decades. He stood very still, staring at me, the air thick as if time itself held its breath. His eyes said what his mouth did not:

"I am so sorry, my son."

I woke with my heart pounding and my palms open, as if receiving a benediction, I'd waited on since boyhood. I called Mama the moment I could breathe again and told her,

12

breathless, what I had seen. She grew quiet, and in that hush, I heard every room we had walked through without him, every birthday with one chair unfilled. The apology did not erase the absences, but it softened their edges, and the sorrow in that gaze pierced me deeper than any voice could. When I woke, the feeling lingered, heavy and raw, as though he had truly crossed time to find me.

After that, every small choice became a way of answering him back: I hear you. I'm still carrying the name you gave me.

So, while I never walked beside my father in this life, I carried him in my steps. Every act of discipline, every choice to pursue education, every attempt to live with decency and honesty, every refusal to compromise my integrity — I did these things with his face in my memory, his name in my chest. He was my first silent teacher, the man whose love for Mama and whose promise as a son of Jamaica left a mark that even death could not erase.

But carrying my father was not a passive thing — it was deliberate. As a boy, I sometimes walked the streets of Denham Town with a quiet determination, telling myself I had to walk straight because Val's son could not stumble carelessly.

If a neighbor called me, "*the pickney weh Val leave behind*" (The child who Val left behind), I straightened my back a little more, as if to prove that the son of Val must carry himself with honor. I did not have his hand on my shoulder, but I had his name, and names have weight.

Even in small choices, I felt him watching. When tempted to follow boys who strayed into trouble, I would hear the whispers of stories about my father's honesty — of returning the shopkeeper's money after being given too much change. That story lived in me like scripture. It taught me that integrity was not about grand gestures but about the small decisions that revealed character when no one was looking. So, I, too, tried to live in a way that would make people say, "Yes, Val's son is just like him."

And in books, I felt closest to him. Family members told me my father loved to read, that he could lose himself in pages even when noise filled the yard. Whenever I opened a book and let words carry me beyond Tulip Lane, I imagined I was walking with him, sharing the same path of curiosity and imagination. His passion became mine, and though death had stolen his presence, it could not steal the inheritance of his mind.

At night, I would sometimes stare at the one photograph of him we kept close — a young man, slim and confident, with eyes that seemed to look beyond the camera into a future he never lived to see. I would trace his features with my eyes, comparing them to my own in the mirror, wondering which parts of me were his. Did I inherit his stride? His smile? His way of thinking? In those questions, I found both sorrow and strength. Sorrow because I would never truly know; strength because the very wondering pushed me to make sure that if anyone ever saw my dad in me, it would be in my decency, my effort, my resilience.

The Strength of Mama

If my father's life was a candle that burned too quickly, my mother's was the lamp that stayed lit through storm and silence, steady and unyielding. But where my father's life was a spark, brief and brilliant, Mama's was the steady flame. His absence might have been my wound, but her presence was my healing. She became both anchor and sail—holding me steady while pushing me forward. Mama did not just tell stories of my father; she embodied the very qualities people said he had—discipline, faith, dignity, and resilience. Through her, I saw the continuation of his love, stretched across time and circumstance.

If my father's legacy was the blueprint, Mama's strength was the foundation. Together, they became the twin roots that held me upright in the rocky, oftentimes treacherous soil of Denham Town, Hannah Town and Tivoli Gardens. His story gave me something to live up to; her story gave me the daily strength to survive. And it was in that fusion—his silent guidance and her relentless presence—that I first learned what legacy truly meant.

Legacy is not just the inheritance of wealth or land. It is the passing down of values, of faith, of resilience. My father left me honesty, intelligence, and love—wrapped in memory. Mama gave me survival, sacrifice, and unshakable devotion—wrapped in flesh and blood. Between them, I was raised by both presence and absence, both memory and endurance.

Marva, known to all as Mama, was just seventeen when my dad died, yet from that tender age she carried herself with the bearing of someone twice her years. She was thrust into adulthood with a baby on her hip and grief in her chest, but she refused to bow. Where others might have broken, Mama bent—only to spring back with even more determination.

Mama's strength was forged in sacrifice. She had been a promising student in high school, sharp with words and quick to learn. Teachers told her she had the potential to go far, but life had other plans. With me already in her arms and her future abruptly rewritten by grief, she made the heartbreaking decision to leave school before finishing. For many, that choice would have meant surrender. But for Mama, it was not an end—it was a pivot. She never saw it as dropping out; she saw it as stepping up, taking responsibility, and shouldering the weight of survival for both her and her son.

Work came quickly, and it was no easy work. Mama began at Kingston Public Hospital (KPH), one of the busiest hospitals in Jamaica, where suffering and resilience collided every day. It was a place where you learned fast, or you sank. Mama thrived. Though barely more than a teenager herself, she moved through the wards with a maturity that earned the respect of nurses, doctors, and patients alike.

At KPH, in the X-ray department, working alongside older staff members like Mr. Gilzene, Ms. Biggerstaff, Bredda G, Ms. Holding, Ms. Henry, and later, a young Peaches (Stewy), she cared, she carried, she tended. She did the jobs no one glamorized—the heavy lifting, the long hours, the thankless tasks. Yet she did them with dignity. Family members would say, *"Marva have pride in everything she do"* (Marva has pride in everything that she does) and it was true. Even scrubbing floors or delivering meals to patients, she carried herself with the grace of someone who understood that every role, no matter how small, was part of a larger purpose.

Her natural compassion soon became evident. Mama couldn't pass a suffering patient without offering a kind word, a gentle touch, or a prayer whispered under her breath. Though she was not a nurse by title, she nursed by nature. Her colleagues said she had a way of easing tension, of bringing calm to the chaos of crowded wards. And at the end of long shifts, when she returned to 17 Tulip Lane, she carried none of the bitterness that hard work and little pay might have justified. Instead, she poured her energy into me and my brother.

Her strength was not only physical but moral. Mama was determined that we would not see her sacrifice as excuse but as example.

"Mi never finish school," (I never finished school) she would say, "but you will."

Those words carried weight because they came from a woman who had traded her own dreams for ours. When she corrected us over homework or scolded us for laziness, it wasn't just discipline—it was her way of demanding that we use the opportunities she had been denied.

KPH became more than just her workplace. It was her training ground, teaching her resilience, discipline, and compassion that she would later pour into us. She worked alongside people from every walk of life, witnessing both human frailty and human courage. And in her quiet way, she absorbed those lessons and carried them home, instilling in us the belief that every life had value, that no work was beneath us, and that dignity was found in effort, not in title.

Mama

Yet Mama was more than her labor. She was beautiful, striking in her youth, with a presence that turned heads and a sense of humor that was second to none. But she never let beauty distract her from purpose. She was courted, admired, and could have chosen an easier path by leaning on others. Instead, she chose independence. She raised us not as a

21

woman waiting for rescue, but as a warrior determined to prove that she could hold her family together with her own two hands, and held us together, she did: with dignity, with determination and with courage.

Her faith was the other pillar that carried her. After long shifts at KPH, she still found time for praise and worship, still bent her knees in prayer. She believed deeply that God had not abandoned her, that every test was also a lesson. And she raised us in that belief. We learned to pray before bed, to give thanks even when cupboards were nearly bare, and to carry ourselves with integrity because, as she said,

"God watching even when people not."

She summed up her philosophy one evening, when the weight of her choices pressed hardest and yet her spirit remained unbroken:

"If my children are to survive, I have to survive — and survive I will."

That line, simple yet fierce, became her mantra, and by extension, mine. It was not just a statement of endurance; it was a vow to life itself. She refused to let despair claim her, because to give up would have meant giving us up too.

Through all these chapters and acts — Bustamante, KPH, Mico — Mama remained a constant. Marva, the girl who had become a mother at seventeen, never stopped moving forward. She had been barely more than a child herself when she first cradled me in her arms, yet she carried the weight of motherhood with a determination that defied her years. Now, her hair has grayed, the silver strands catching the light like threads of wisdom. The lines on her face have deepened, not from defeat but from the countless hours spent working, worrying, and loving. Her eyes, though, never lost their light, or the humor contained — that unwavering spark of laughter, faith and fight still live and brightly they burn.

It was during one of her shifts at Kingston Public Hospital that she faced her deepest sorrow. She had walked the corridors countless times, yet on that day her steps slowed when she noticed a stretcher in the hallway, a body covered by a plain white sheet. At first, it was just another patient, another anonymous form among many. She passed it again later, unease tugging at her spirit. After several times, a colleague pulled her aside. The words fell like stone:

"It's your baby father."

The corridor swayed beneath her. She turned back, staring at the body she had walked past without knowing. The outline of his shoulders was unmistakable, the height of him even in death. Her chest heaved as she reached toward the sheet, her hand trembling. And there, in the open hallway, my mother collapsed, hitting the bleach cleaned, tiled floor of the X-ray department's narrow hallway — the love of her life laid on that stretcher-lifeless, gone, her world cracked open.

Mama

But my mother did not crumble. She rose from that grief with her sons, her faith, and her dreams for us as her only riches. Every certificate, every graduation, every small step forward became her reward. Mama wore our victories like badges of honor, proof that her sacrifice had not been in vain, and that love could build a legacy even when life had stripped so much away.

I understood this more as I got older. At Mico, when I walked across the stage to receive my teaching diploma, I looked into the crowd and saw her — small in stature but unmissable in spirit — clapping so hard her hands must have stung. I remembered the sacrifices: the days she went without food, so that her children could eat, the times she told us, *"Wi agoh dweet, dis anoh the end"* (We will do it. This is not the end) with a smile that masked her own worry.

Mama's pride was never boastful. She wasn't the type to shout her son's achievements from the rooftops, but when someone asked, her face would light up and her voice would warm. "My son is a teacher," she would say simply, but in those words was an entire history — the hardships, the perseverance, the prayers whispered in the quiet hours of the night.

Even in her later years, when work grew harder and her steps slowed, she remained the anchor. She kept her Bible close, often marking verses she believed applied to her sons. She prayed not just for our success but for our safety, our wisdom, our hearts. And when life tested me — in my career, in my personal struggles — Mama's counsel was steady. *"Remember weh you come from,"* (Remember where you come from).

In her presence, I always felt both grounded and lifted. Grounded by the values she had instilled in me — hard work, humility, compassion — and lifted by the certainty that, no matter the storm, there was always someone in my corner who believed I could weather it.

Mama was more than a mother. She was proof that you didn't need formal titles or academic accolades to be extraordinary. Her legacy was written not on paper, but in the lives of her children — and in the lives of everyone who had been touched by her quiet strength.

When I walked into classrooms later in life, chalk in hand, or stood before students urging them to value education, I was really echoing Mama. I was carrying forward the lesson she taught me from the tender age of seventeen: that sacrifice is not the end of dreams but the soil in which new ones can grow.

17 Tulip Lane

From my father's brief but brilliant spark and Mama's steady flame, my own journey began in Denham Town. Home was 17 Tulip Lane, a place as rough as it was rich with memory. I was born at Victoria Jubilee Hospital on May 15, 1969 and attended St. Anne's Infant School on North Street, before progressing to St. Anne's Primary School on Bond Street. It was on the roads of Tulip Lane, Bond Street, Regent Street, North Street, Chestnut Lane, Rose Lane, Matthews Lane, Oxford Street, and Wellington Street that I first learned the music of laughter mixed with the harsh notes of struggle and the tantalizing scent of jerk chicken: where football matches played in dust-filled yards gave way to dreams bigger than the lane itself, and where Mama's discipline was tested daily by two energetic boys.

Life was never easy, but it was never empty. Our home at 17 Tulip Lane in mid Kingston, Jamaica, was a modest tenement yard, a place that pulsed with activity from dawn till dusk. The air was always thick with voices, laughter, the clang of pots, the succulent smell of jerk chicken, the bark of distant dogs. It was a shared world — a close-knit, noisy village bound not by walls, but by love, respect, and obligation.

17 Tulip Lane after the yard was ravaged by fire in 2011

My two grand aunts, Aunt Amanda and Aunt B, elderly pillars of the family, ruled the compound with quiet dignity. They kept order and held memory. Their presence was calming but never passive. Aunt Amanda, with her silver bun and wise eyes, was the resident historian, storyteller, and judge. Aunt Beatrice, a little plumper and sterner, had a way of folding her arms and pursing her lips that could silence even the most rebellious child.

The yard echoed daily with laughter and mischief. Mama had sisters Pauline (Aunty Bar) and Patsy (Aunty Patsy) — and each added her own energy to the place. Their voices intertwined with the patter of feet and the shrieks of children: Nadia, Oneil, Manda, Hurry, Kaydean, Sandra, Beverly, Dennis, and Juliet. They were cousins in name but siblings in heart.

Meals were often sparse but shared. Everyone got a piece of something — breadfruit, fried dumplings, callaloo, jerk chicken. Salt mackerel and green bananas were stretchable commodities, and on Sundays, if the pot was big enough, even the neighbors could taste the stew.

At age ten, I was a somewhat plump and bright-eyed boy with an insatiable curiosity, and I had a favorite hideout beneath Aunt Amanda's towering double-decker bed. The cool, dusty space was my fortress of solitude. There, lying on a piece of cardboard or flattened flour sack, I'd stretch out with a stack of Spiderman, Superman, Batman and Captain America comics, Hardy Boys adventures, and Nancy Drew mysteries. The scent of wood polish, old clothes, and mothballs surrounded me, but none of it mattered. The only world that existed was the one in my books.

Stories consumed me. I loved how words could build entire worlds, take me to foreign places, introduce me to brave heroes and cunning villains. That was where I learned English — not from a chalkboard or school, but from dialogue bubbles and plot twists. I read aloud in whispers, mimicking accents, practicing new vocabulary, imagining myself solving mysteries with Frank and Joe or swinging through skyscrapers like Peter Parker in his Spiderman suit.

Cousin Kaydean

My passion didn't go unnoticed. By the age of ten, I was already beating Mama at crossword puzzles from the afternoon newspaper, *The Star*. I could fill in ten-letter words before Mama had read the clue properly. Aunty Bar would shake her head and say, *"Dat boy sharp like razor!"* (That boy is sharp like a razor).

My mind was a sponge, absorbing not just words but meanings, rhythms, and nuance. In the yard, I became known as the boy with the big words. I'd use phrases like "astonishing" and "melancholy" in conversations about marbles or mangoes, leaving the other children giggling or confused. But even they admired me. I had a way of turning a simple story about a missing pencil into an epic tale of betrayal and redemption.

Cousin Oneil

My sixth-grade teacher, Mrs. Esmine Dunn, was the first formal educator to recognize my abilities. A tall, dark-skinned woman with a penchant for floral blouses and exacting standards, she spotted something in me that felt urgent. She began feeding me extra books, longer writing assignments, early morning private lessons, and subtle nudges toward excellence.

One day, after a particularly well-written composition on the topic of "My Greatest Hero," she pulled me aside and said, "Horatio, you don't just write stories. You write truth. That's a gift."

Mrs. Esmine Dunn

It was Mrs. Dunn who recommended me for the Common Entrance exam — the high school qualifying test that could open the gates to elite schools. Most boys living in and around the Tulip Lane area attended St Anne's Secondary School or dropped out entirely. But I had a chance. I studied by kerosene lamp at night, propped up on my stack of Hardy Boys books, eyes burning but mind alive. Mama supported me every step of the way — ironing my uniform, packing my book bag, praying beside me.

On that sunny Thursday afternoon in July 1981 when the results of the Common Entrance Examination came in, it was my brother, a nine-year-old Wayne, who galloped excitedly up Tulip Lane, with his head cocked to his left, eyes brimming with tears, The *Daily Gleaner* newspaper in hand shouting repeatedly,

"Mama, Lance pass! Mama, Lance pass!"

17 Tulip Lane erupted. I had passed the exam with flying colors and my name was listed in the daily newspaper. And not just that — I had earned a place at St. George's College, one of the most prestigious Catholic boys' schools in Jamaica. Mama cried. Aunt Amanda clapped and muttered a prayer. Aunty Bar walked around the yard, arms raised, shouting,

"Mi tell unu! Di bwoy a genius!" (I told you all, the boy is a genius).

Cousin Nadia

For me, it was more than a pass. It was a passport. A doorway. A promise. That day, as the sun dipped behind the buildings and the hibiscus folded into sleep, I sat quietly beneath the guinep tree at the back of the yard, *The Gleaner* in hand. I looked up at the stars just beginning to twinkle above the rust-colored roofs of Tulip Lane.

Something had begun. Something big. Something beautiful. And I was ready.

Aunty Bar, cousin Aiden, Aunty Patsy, cousin
Avant, Cousin Jameika in front

Sibling Love

And always by my side—sometimes quiet, sometimes mischievous—was Wayne, my younger brother. Wayne had grown into his own: quick-witted, mechanically gifted, fiercely loyal. Where I lived in my head and heart, Wayne was hands-on. He could fix a bicycle with a spoon and a piece of wire, rewire a radio without instruction, and charm his way out of any trouble. Together, we were a team, moving through childhood like a two-man crew with an unspoken code.

One night, not long after Aunt Amanda had passed, ten-year-old Wayne and I—twelve at the time—found ourselves heading home far too late after watching *The Man from Atlantis* by Tulip Lane's gully, inside Madda Mack's (Mother Mack's) house. Madda Mack, a stalwart of Tulip Lane's history, had the only TV on the lane, and as boys we would gather at night in her living room to watch our favorite shows—*The Incredible Hulk*, *The Six Million Dollar Man*, and, of course, *The Man from Atlantis*. That night the lane was unusually

41

quiet, shadows stretching like long fingers beneath the weak streetlights, and the air felt thick with that uneasy stillness that comes after midnight. Aunt Amanda had warned us countless times about staying out late. Her voice was sharp, almost prophetic:

"Mi tell unu already, nutt'n good nuh deh a road after dark. Unu fi come home to bed!" (I told you both already, that nothing good is on the road after dark. You must come home to bed!).

Those words, once irritating, suddenly took on new weight that night.

As we neared 17 Tulip Lane's gate, Wayne froze. His eyes widened, and when I followed his gaze, my heart nearly leapt out of my chest. There she was — or so it seemed. A tall, stern figure, standing motionless, angrily glaring at us with that same disapproving look she wore in life. For a moment, neither of us breathed. The hairs on the back of my neck stood like soldiers on parade.

Then instinct took over. Without a word, simultaneously, as if we could read each other's mind, Wayne and I bolted. We sprinted down Tulip Lane as if Usain Bolt himself was chasing us, our sandals slapping the pavement like gunshots. We cut the corner hard, onto Chestnut Lane, and I swear we broke records that night. My lungs burned, but fear was a better coach than any PE teacher. Wayne, smaller in body and usually slower, was suddenly right at my side, his face twisted in terror and determination. And we sprinted and sprinted out of pure unadulterated terror. In our little developing minds, Aunt Amanda's duppy (ghost) was chasing us.

Wayne

By the time we reached Cousin Sandra's house, we were drenched in sweat, panting like dogs after a long chase. We didn't even bother to knock politely — we banged on the door and literally bawled out our guts until Sandra came,

44

bleary-eyed and confused. We tumbled inside, talking over each other, trying to explain that Aunt Amanda's duppy (ghost) had been waiting for us in the lane, glaring us back into obedience and chasing us.

Sandra laughed until tears rolled down her cheeks, but Wayne and I weren't laughing then. We planted ourselves on her floor and flat-out refused to go back home that night. Sleep came in fits, interrupted by every creak and shadow. Looking back now, it's funny—two young boys sprinting for their lives, chased not by duppies, but by the guilty weight of Aunt Amanda's warnings. Still, in our hearts, we were sure she had the last word that night. And if nothing else, she managed to teach us the value of coming home early—even from beyond the grave.

But we were not only two. Our younger sister, Shema, rounded out the crew and gave our childhood its balance. Shema was pretty and sharp-tongued yet tender, quick to laugh and quicker to tell you when you were wrong. She was the one who could mock Wayne for being covered in grease from tinkering with a

45

bicycle, then turn to me and tease, "*Yuh always deh inna yuh book dem like yaah old man.*" (You're always in your books like you're an old man).

She carried her own spark, a mix of boldness and wit, and though she was younger, she often acted like the referee in our daily adventures.

Our life on Tulip Lane was tight — a constant mix of laughter, quarrels, and the unrelenting rhythm of downtown Kingston. Yet even in the crush of poverty and politics, we found joy. The gully at the edge of Tulip Lane was our universe. For most outsiders, it was just a concrete channel carrying dirty rainwater through the city. But to us, it was a world of endless possibilities. Wayne and I knew every inch of that gully like the backs of our hands. We would easily scrambled up and down its 20ft high concrete banks with the ease and gracefulness of Olympic level gymnasts, with wooden sticks in hand, imagining ourselves as warriors on patrol or secret agents on a mission. Shema, sometimes following behind, rolled her eyes at our dramatic poses but always watched with interest. When we turned scraps of board into boats and raced them down the water after a rainfall, she was the one who kept score, shouting which "ship" had won and clapping as if it were a real regatta.

Shema

When the three of us weren't in the gully, we were in the dusty patch at 6 Mahoe Drive in Olympic Gardens playing marbles. The earth was cracked from the sun, perfect for the small circles we carved with sticks. Wayne had his sneaky angles, I had my steady shot, and Shema was the commentator, her high voice narrating the drama like a radio announcer:

"Family showdown — who going win dis time?" (Family showdown, who will win this time?).

Even if she didn't play, she was part of every game.

Snacks sealed the ritual. Coins clinking in our pockets, we hurried to the corner shop for banana chips or sweetie, returning with little crinkly bags that disappeared too quickly. Shema always ate hers slowly, taunting Wayne and me as we licked the salt and grease off our fingers.

"Unnu too greedy," (You are both too greedy) she'd say, before finally sharing her last chip.

Evenings brought the glow of the television set, its antenna wrapped in foil for better reception. *The Six Million Dollar Man* was our king. Steve Austin, with his bionic arm and slow-motion leaps, was proof that men could be rebuilt stronger, faster, better. Wayne reenacted his every move, running across the yard in exaggerated slow motion, making the famous "ch-ch-ch-ch" sound.

I provided the narration:

"Steve Austin… the man barely alive… but rebuilt into the world's first bionic man!"

And Shema? She laughed until her sides hurt, calling Wayne:
"Bionic fool!"

We were just as captivated by *The Man from Atlantis*. Patrick Duffy, with his underwater powers, fascinated us. Wayne and I practiced the dolphin-like swimming stroke in the basin, daring each other to hold our breath. Shema was the timer, counting dramatically, shouting,

"Yuh drown already!" (You drowned already?).

Then she'd pour water on us for added effect. She wasn't just an observer — she was the spark that turned our games into the experience.

On weekends, karate movies ruled. Bruce Lee, Carter Wong, Fu Sheng, Bolo, and Silver Fox became our masters, the gully our dojo. Wayne and I sparred until our knees were bruised, shouting: "Hi-yah!"into the dusk. Shema clapped from the edge, laughing at our clumsy kicks, sometimes trying a stance of her own before running off to tell Mama.

"Dem gwine mash up demself again." (They are going to hurt themselves again).

Wayne's gift was always mechanical. Bicycles, pushcarts, radios — he had the magic touch. By the time we moved to Ridgeway Road in Meadowbrook Estate, Wayne already carried the title of "the driver." Even before he was of age, he handled cars with a calm confidence that left neighbors stunned. Driving and mechanics became his language, shaping his professional life in ways that mirrored the curiosity of his youth.

Shema, though, was different. Where Wayne was fascinated with machines and I was consumed by books, Shema loved people and their stories. She had a natural sense for humor and a talent for turning everyday life into performance. She could mimic a teacher's voice perfectly, reenact Mama's scoldings until we doubled over in laughter, or compose whole skits out of our quarrels. If Wayne and I were the builders and fighters, Shema was the storyteller. She kept our world colorful and alive, giving us perspective when our rivalry threatened to get too serious.

No matter the house — Tulip Lane, Mahoe Drive, Ridgeway Road, Cumberland — the rhythm between us stayed the same. We shared secrets, snacks, victories, and quarrels. When I passed the Common Entrance exam and earned my place at St. George's College, Wayne shouted the news as though it were his own success. When he earned his place at St Andrew Technical High School, I boasted of his skill to

51

anyone who would listen. And Shema, never left behind, was there to remind us that her own achievements would shine just as brightly.

Even when we argued — over shoes, over who ate the last dumpling, over which cassette tape to play — the love never broke. Arguments ended as quickly as they began, replaced by laughter or the next scheme. Tulip Lane had given us many things: resilience, street smarts, resourcefulness. But the greatest gift it gave was each other.

Together — Wayne, Shema, and I — were a trinity of survival and joy. The driver, the dreamer, the storyteller. No move, no hardship, and no distance could undo the bond we built in the gullies, the dust, and the laughter of Kingston.

Chapter II: Coming of Age

St. George's College

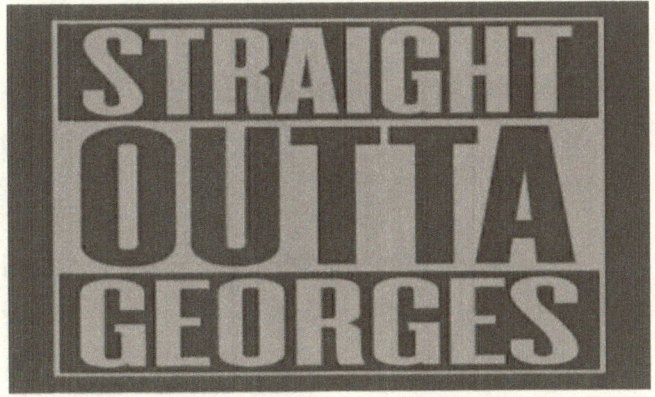

In September 1981, I proudly walked through the gates of St. George's College for the first time as a student — not realizing I was crossing into a tradition that would shape the rest of my life. As the years went by, I was no longer just a student navigating lessons and exams—I became part of something greater, a brotherhood that shaped me as much as the classrooms did. It was a bond forged in faith, strengthened by loyalty, and colored with the kind of laughter that echoed through corridors long after the day had ended. My George's brothers held each other to a standard, unspoken yet deeply understood, a shared code of honor that bound us together in ways that time could never erase. What started as schoolyard companionship evolved into a fellowship that carried us through challenges, victories, and the ordinary rhythms of life, leaving me with a sense of belonging that no textbook could ever teach.

The school's majestic buildings, cloaked in ivy and memory, stood like sentinels over Winchester Park, keeping watch over generations of boys becoming men. For me, stepping through the gate each morning was stepping into a world that demanded more of me — but also gave me more in return.

That brotherhood — etched in classrooms and carved on football bleachers — rested on the foundations of trust and love. Brothers like Lascelle Powell (Andypow), whose homework I copied so often that once I actually copied his name on my paper and handed it in to the teacher; Ainsworth Beckford (Becky), who later became my teaching colleague; Warren Grant

(Bug), who tried to teach me to breakdance in Meadowbrook Estate; Clifton Brooks (Cheva), who spent countless nights with me in some of Kingston's "gentlemen's strip clubs"; Caliph Delmohammed (Zellie), whose family owned Turbo Cruiser—the bus on which I met Iniko; the measured decency and honesty of Clive Scarlett (Sam); Terrence Beach (TiBeach), another with distinct grace and honesty; my *"bredrin"* (brethren) Paul Tomlinson (Tommy); Robert Hall (Ratty), our skilled Manning Cup footballer; the ever-wise Delroy Smith (Smelly); Clayton Osbourne (CJ), our resident Michael Jackson lookalike and later a teaching colleague; and Alva Taylor, who also became my teaching colleague and who taught me to drive in his Suzuki Swift—weren't just classmates and friends. They were lifelines. Each one brought a different rhythm to the song of adolescence—some loud, some reflective, some mischievous. Together, we were unstoppable. And decades later, our voices still echo in the digital corridors of our WhatsApp group, "StGC Class of '86," where we are joined by Travis (Trey, Kwame, Sankofa). The teasing, prayers, memories—arguments with Zal, COVID-vaccination arguments with Dennis (Gyallis), US-politics debates with Knox (Nax) — and advice continue to bind us like brothers of the same womb.

We laughed through punishments, shared bun and cheese at break time, and defended one another like lions when needed. It was Zal and my mother in 1983, after St. George's College won the Manning Cup final against Tivoli Gardens High School, who prevented injury or worse to me and a group of St. George's College students who were attacked by fans of Tivoli Gardens High. There was a hierarchy of friendship, yes, but it was tempered by deep respect. If you were in trouble — whether with a teacher, a rival schoolboy, or your own demons — these were the boys who had your back. Always. Without question.

That brotherhood was stitched together in countless small moments that, at the time, seemed ordinary but in hindsight revealed themselves to be extraordinary. We laughed at the absurdity of punishment, using spoons to weed out the grass on our sacred Winchester Park, or standing in lines under the blazing

Kingston sun, shirts damp with sweat, waiting for the prefect's command. Even when the discipline came swift and stinging — the ruler across the palm, the laps around the field — it somehow brought us closer. We would exchange knowing looks, biting our lips to keep from grinning, and then burst out laughing the moment backs were turned. The punishment never seemed to matter as much as the company we endured it with.

Break times were feasts in disguise. A single piece of bun and cheese could stretch across three or four of us, divided with care, passed from hand to hand. We would sit out in the school yard, in the shadow of the Abe Issa Auditorium, legs stretched out, uniforms dusty, and trade not just food but dreams. Ratty, Fisha and Norris spoke of football glory, others of becoming lawyers, doctors, pilots, or teachers. And though our ambitions varied, there was always an unspoken belief that we were all in this together, that the success of one was the pride of all.

Robert Hall about to tackle for the ball

The defense of one another was where our loyalty shone brightest. Rivalries between schools were fierce in those days, and it was not uncommon for heated words or flying fists to erupt after football matches as happened on the dusty pitch of Kingston College in the mid-eighties. Again, it was Zal, joined by Roger (Mullo) who had our backs. If one of us was cornered, the others stepped in without hesitation. We moved like a pack, watching each other's backs, knowing instinctively that no one was ever left to fight alone. Even beyond the schoolyard battles, there was defense of spirit. If a friend was struggling—whether it

58

was trouble at home, heartbreak, or a heavy burden carried silently — we formed a wall around him, offering jokes, advice, or simply presence. Sometimes the greatest defense was just sitting quietly, saying nothing, but making sure he knew he wasn't alone.

And yes, there was a hierarchy of friendship, as there always is in groups of boys. Some led with natural authority, others followed with quiet loyalty. But even within those layers, there was a balance — a respect that ensured no one was dismissed or diminished. Each of us had a place, a role, a value. It was this balance that kept the brotherhood intact, that allowed laughter and loyalty to coexist with order and discipline. Looking back, I realize that what we built was more than camaraderie. It was training for life. The laughter taught us resilience — that joy could be found even in hardship. The shared bun and cheese or Miss. Chin's patty and coco bread taught us generosity — that no one should go without if you had even a little to give. The defense of one another taught us courage — that strength was magnified when it was shared. And the hierarchy taught us humility — that leadership was not about dominance, but about responsibility.

These boys, my brothers, became the mirror in which I saw myself grow. With them, I learned what it meant to belong, to be accountable, to carry others and be carried in return. Time has carried us in different directions—some to distant shores, some to quiet lives, some no longer with us at all—but the code we lived by lingers still. It whispers in my memory every time I think of those days: laughter ringing through corridors, bun and cheese split into careful portions, fists raised not in anger but in protection, and above all, loyalty that needed no words. We were more than students. We were a brotherhood. And though years and miles have stretched between us, the truth remains—once you belonged, you belonged forever.

To my brothers who have journeyed on before me—**Fitzgerald Johnson (Fitzie), Peter Lue, Roland Layne (Bingy), Elvis Penny, Dalton Benjamin (Benjy), Paul Howell (Lippy), Michael Edwards (Fisha), Kenneth Smith, David Waugh, Mervin Jarrett, Richard**

Linton, Clinton Kates, Robert Seaton and Damian Feany King — stay blessed, I salute you all.

Each of you carried a spark that lit up our time together, a laughter, a presence, a bond that no passing can erase. Though your voices have grown silent, and your steps no longer echo alongside ours, your memory remains alive in every story told, every corner of our shared past.

I think of you often, not just in moments of sorrow, but in the ordinary rhythms of life — in the music we once moved to, in the games we played, in the streets where we walked and dreamed together. Your absence is felt, but so too is your enduring presence, woven into the fabric of who I am.

Rest well, my brothers. Your names are not forgotten, nor your lives lived in vain. You are part of my foundation, my history, my unbroken chain of belonging. Until we meet again, I honor you, with love, with respect, and with gratitude for the time we shared.

With Ainsworth Beckford (Becky), Florida, 2025

It wasn't just academics and brotherhood that captured my heart at St. George's. From September to December each year, the pulse of Kingston shifted. The entire city was baptized in schoolboy football fever. Manning Cup season transformed ordinary high school boys into demigods and Sabina Park and Stadium East into sacred grounds. Uniforms were ironed with extra care on match days. Students spoke in tactical analyses like armchair coaches. And parents, vendors, taxi drivers—all seemed to rearrange their lives around match fixtures.

1983 Triple Champions (Manning Cup, Walker Cup and Olivier Shield Champions)

For me, there was and still is only one allegiance—the blue and white of St. George's College. As always, the fervor began with morning devotion, where prayers were whispered not just for spiritual guidance, but for victory over archrivals like Kingston College, Calabar, or Jamaica College. There was a sacredness to the ritual—tying our shoelaces just right, making sure our socks were pulled high, brushing a speck of dust from our Clark's shoes—and heading to school knowing that, win or lose, we were backing George's.

I wasn't a player. My gifts weren't found on the field. But my devotion made me part of the team's spiritual core. I knew every player's nickname, position, and history. I could quote the number of goals Richard Strachan scored in the 1983 season, recite the way Christopher Ziadie curved a free kick in the 84th minute against Charlie Smith, or describe the precise moment Robert Hall silenced the KC crowd with a goal that seemed blessed by the football gods.

Afternoons were spent at Winchester Park, watching training sessions with the intensity of a scout. I, and others, would sit on the Winchester Wall, discussing strategies, cheering tackles, and dreaming in chants. Coach Dennis Ziadie's voice became a backdrop to our lives. Coach Ziadie wasn't just a coach—he was a general, a philosopher, and a father figure to many. His words—sharp, sometimes poetic, always purposeful—carried weight in a young man's life.

Captain Richard Strachan holds the Manning Cup trophy aloft in 1983

Halftime Manning Cup final 1983

**Strachan scores against Excelsior High School
in Walker Cup final 1983**

Match days were spiritual. The sun hung
lower, the air thick with anticipation. Hundreds
of students from Georges would gather — Roger
Mcfarquhar with the bugle, iron pipes, and
beating hearts in tow — marching like pilgrims
to Sabina Park or Stadium East. The chants rang
out long before kickoff:

*"Hess Tee Gee Cee, Hess Tee Gee Cee, Hess
Tee Gee Cee!"* (STGC, STGC, STGC)

"Blue and white forever!"

"If yuh nuh ready, move from round wi'!" (If you're not ready, move away from us).

My pride in StGC's football team went deeper than sport. It was cultural. It was resistance. In a city sometimes fractured by politics, class, and post-colonial tension, schoolboy football gave voice to the dreams and rage of the youth. It was a space where poor boys could become legends, where unity trumped division, where beauty — raw, athletic, spontaneous — could still win.

The George's team wasn't just eleven boys on a pitch. They were avatars of the school's legacy. Richard Strachan's goal scoring exploits and his strength and fierce shot were poetry in motion. Christopher Morgan's wily commanding presence on the forward line was the stuff of myth. The Ziadie brothers, Nicholas and Christopher, played like twins tethered by telepathy. Andrew Price's calm at the back, Michael Forbes' relentless drive in goal, and Robert Hall's almost telepathic vision made every game a narrative that I never tired of retelling.

And oh, how sweet it was and still is to beat Kingston College.

Kingston College (KC), a traditional powerhouse, came with the swagger of money and history. But when George's beat them, it was more than three points — it was symbolic. It was like David slinging Goliath, it was an underdog's roar, it was the kind of triumph that made boys believe in the impossible. To beat KC was to remind the world that heart could outmatch privilege, that spirit could humble swagger.

ST. GEORGES COLLEGES   KINGSTON COLLEGE

But in 1981, there was no such triumph for us. That year, Kingston College marched into the Manning Cup clash with the confidence of kings, and they dismantled St. George's College 4–0. The scoreline haunts me to this day. It wasn't just a loss — it was an annihilation. And as the goals poured in, so too did my tears. I was only a boy, but in that moment, the weight of generations of rivalry and pride fell squarely on my shoulders. I wept uncontrollably, the salt of my tears mingling with the dust on my uniform collar. Around me, boys tried to hold back their emotions, some burying their faces in their hands, others turning away to hide their shame. But I couldn't. I sobbed openly, chest heaving, as if each KC goal had been scored against me personally.

It was the first time I felt that football could break more than just a team's defense — it could break your heart. And out of that heartbreak, a seed of eternal hatred took root. From that day on, Kingston College became my sworn enemy. I despised the smirk of their supporters, the chants that echoed through the stands, the air of entitlement that seemed to cling to them like a second skin. And most of all, I despised their color — purple, even to this very day.

You have to understand, this wasn't just dislike. This was the kind of loathing that made me cross the street if I saw a KC boy in uniform, the kind that made me hiss under my breath whenever I spotted a purple tie on a Kingston bus, the kind that made me not walk on the other side of the road that KC was on. If someone showed up at a party in lavender, I'd immediately give them the side-eye. To this very day, I cannot even drink grape soda or eat purple grapes, and I own nothing purple, nor do I have anything colored purple in my house. It's as if that color no longer exists to me.

The KC supporters seemed to take pride in rubbing it in. Their chants weren't just chants; they were like needles in the skin, sung with a smugness that said, "We know we're better, and we're going to let you know it, too." I swear some of their boys didn't even like football — they just liked seeing us lose. The way they strutted around after a win, you would think they had personally scored every goal, invented the sport, and been knighted by the Queen all in one afternoon.

Meanwhile, we George's boys nursed our wounds in silence, replaying matches in our heads, wondering how on earth we could have let them get the better of us. Losing to anyone else was bad, but losing to KC was like being forced to eat a plate of cold callaloo without salt — insulting and hard to swallow.

And yet, in the middle of my chest-beating hatred, there was humor too. Because looking back, the sight of me, a scrawny schoolboy, vowing eternal war on an entire institution of purple-clad teenagers was a little ridiculous. But in that moment, I meant every word. I swore that KC and I were enemies for life. Even now, decades later, when I catch sight of purple curtains in someone's house, a part of me wants to pull them down and set them on fire.

That's the madness of Jamaica's schoolboy football — it digs its way into your heart and refuses to leave, even if it means you'll be waging a private war against a color for the rest of your days.

And yet, that hate did something else. It sharpened my love for St. George's. Every time George's faced KC after that, it was personal. The matches were not just fixtures on the calendar; they were battles for dignity. When we beat them, the victory was sweeter than sugar cane, the chants louder, the joy almost holy. It was vindication. It was resurrection. To topple KC was to restore balance, to remind ourselves that history was not destiny, that heart could conquer heritage.

A defining moment in Jamaica's schoolboy football for me, came in the 2011 Walker Cup final where we mercilessly beat Kingston College 2-1. This was one of those victories that seemed to echo far beyond the ninety minutes. St. George's College came into that match with fire in our boots and history on our shoulders. KC, draped in their eternal purple, carried themselves with the swagger of kings, but George's had no intention of bowing. Fresh from our triumph in the Manning Cup final only four days earlier, our boys pressed, tackled, and surged forward with the kind of rhythm that makes football feel like poetry. The goals came, the crowd erupted, and when the final whistle sounded, we had toppled the giants.

The Walker Cup was ours, and it wasn't just a win — it was vindication. The smirk on KC faces was gone, replaced with stunned silence. On North Street, it felt like a national holiday. We sang until our throats were raw, and the cup gleamed under the lights as proof that purple could bleed. That night, the rivalry tilted in our favor, and it was glorious.

But football has a long memory, and KC bided their time. Fast forward to the 2018, Manning Cup final, and the two schools faced off again. The game was everything a rivalry match should be — tense, breathless, fierce. St. George's led, 2-1, with only three minutes to go. We could almost taste the glory. Supporters were already lifting voices, imagining the celebration, ready to write a new chapter of triumph.

And then, the cruel twist. Our forward missed an empty goal, which would have given us a 3-1 lead and surely the trophy, but immediately from that missed sitter, KC found an equalizer, snatching the air out of our lungs. It was 2-2 after 90 minutes and in injury time the purple wave roared back to life, and before we could steady ourselves, they struck again. The final whistle was a blade across our hopes —

victory turned to heartbreak in the blink of an eye. KC had won 3-2, snatching victory from the jaws of defeat, and they lifted the Manning Cup. Their chants thundered through the stadium, a reminder that football can be merciless.

Those two finals—2011's joy and 2018's agony—show the essence of the St. George's-KC rivalry. It is never just a game; it is history, pride, and identity colliding on the field. To beat KC is to touch the heavens, and to lose to them is to feel the ground collapse beneath you. Together, those moments remind me why I love the game and why the rivalry will never die.

For me, those wins were never simply about football—they were spiritual. They were life lessons dressed in jerseys and boots. Beating KC was about proving that no matter how small you seemed in the eyes of the world, no matter how rich or powerful your opponent might be, with enough courage and unity, you could rise. It was proof that David's sling still worked.

The brotherhood I shared with my schoolmates was deepened by that rivalry. We stood shoulder to shoulder not just in laughter and mischief, but in the heat of those clashes, voices hoarse from shouting, bodies tense with hope and fear. The shared memory of 1981 made every subsequent meeting with KC carry more weight. It wasn't just about winning three points — it was about reclaiming pride, rewriting the script, healing the wound of that bitter day.

Looking back, I realize those emotions were bigger than football. They were about belonging, about identity, about finding something worth fighting for. The tears of 1981, as humiliating as they felt, were also the tears that bound me to St. George's for life. And the hate that grew for KC, irrational though it may have been, kept me fiercely loyal to my own colors — blue and white. Because for every flash of purple on the horizon, there was always the reminder that brotherhood, heart, and faith were stronger than swagger.

I remember another particular match in 1985 like scripture. KC had dominated the first half and had St. George's under relentless pressure. The purple tide surged forward with chants and bravado. But George's, disciplined and daring, flipped the script in the second half. Antonio Demessa weaved past three defenders like they were shadows, passed to Robert Hall, who volleyed it straight into the net. The stadium erupted. I leapt so high my glasses flew off. Cheva caught them midair.

"Dem cyaan hold wi!" (They cannot hold us) I screamed.

That night, no homework was done. No chores remembered. We met at Cheva's yard, still dressed in our uniforms, and replayed the match a hundred times in words and gestures.

"Yuh see di pass yute, mi tell yuh Forbes a di king!" (Did you see the pass youth; I told you Forbes is the king!)

"Mi lose mi voice star, caah KC a bug side!" (I lost my voice my friend, because KC is not a good team!)

These weren't just moments. These were memories engraved into soul and sinew.

**Legends Andrew Price and Christopher
Morgan 1983 and 1984 triple champions**

Yet, Georges was never just football. The
Jesuit tradition meant that I was also pushed
intellectually and morally. There was Father
Ryan, stern but fair, who taught English with a
cadence that made the old language sing. Mrs.
Barrett, the English teacher, who told me that I
had a gift with words. Mr. White (Señor Blanco),
who ran the Spanish department with military
precision, and taught boys to stand tall —
physically and spiritually.

With Clayton Osbourne, Orlando 2025

There were quiet, contemplative moments too—moments that balanced the noise of competition and the thrill of brotherhood. I remember lunches under the almond tree by the chapel, the branches casting a lace of shadows across our uniforms as we unwrapped our bun and cheese or shared a soda, stretching small meals into feasts through conversation and laughter. There were confessions whispered on the chapel steps, where the sacredness of the place seemed to invite honesty — fears about grades, frustrations with teachers, or the simple mysteries of growing up that none of us could quite explain but all of us felt. Even the air seemed charged with meaning: the scent of polish rising from the freshly cleaned halls, the powder of chalk lingering on our fingers, the unmistakable fragrance of ambition in a school that demanded the best.

But life at George's carried its share of painful lessons too. There were crushes for Alpha girls that went unreturned, the sting of rejection teaching us that not every story ended with the happy ending we imagined. There were friends who vanished quietly, boys who once sat beside us and then were gone — pulled away by hardship, family struggles, or choices that closed the door to their futures. Their absence was a reminder that the brotherhood was precious, and that not all of us would march together into adulthood. There was discipline too — swift, sharp, and sometimes harsh. The crack of a ruler, the embarrassment of standing before a class, the laps around the field that left lungs burning. Those moments left their mark, yet they also carved resilience into us, shaping us into men who could bend without breaking.

And perhaps the hardest truth was the awareness that not all dreams would come true. Some of us spoke of glory — of football careers, of medical school, of escape to lands far beyond Kingston — but life had its own rhythm, and not every boy's melody reached its chorus. Still, George's never let go of its sons. The school left an imprint that went deeper than wins or losses, punishments or accolades. It laid down a blueprint, etched a rhythm into our hearts, a cadence of faith, discipline, and loyalty that followed us long after we walked out of those gates.

Years later, as grown men, my brothers and I still greet each other with the phrase, *"Big up, knight."* (Hello knight). It isn't just a nod to the school. It is a nod to a shared DNA. Through weddings and funerals, job losses and triumphs, the Class of '86 would remain tethered — not just by WhatsApp chats and voice notes, but by those foundational years when we were boys becoming men under the watchful eye of Father Brodley and the looming walls of that grand Jesuit cathedral.

Brotherhood, Travis, me and Terrence, London 2025

I often thought of George's not just as a school, but as a second mother. She scolded me, challenged me, fed me wisdom, taught me how to think, how to lead, and how to feel. She shaped my language, sharpened my questions, and called me to a higher purpose. She gave me brothers — true brothers — who, even after 40 years, still call to check if I've eaten, still remember which girl broke my heart in fourth form, still remind me who scored the winner against Wolmer's in '85.

And when I walk into a classroom today, Expo marker in hand, or correct a student's essay, or cheer on a local football team, there is something of George's still in me.

St. George's was also where I first learned the delicate balance between being led and becoming a leader. As fourth form rolled into fifth, I found myself more involved in student life — not in any grand public way, but in quiet influence. Younger students would come to me for help with math or English, or even how to deal with an unfair teacher. I wasn't the loudest or the flashiest, but I carried an air of assurance that others trusted. The kind that wasn't taught—it was absorbed from hours of observing, of listening, of walking the school's corridors with eyes wide open.

I remember the time when a younger boy named Richard Johnson (Scabbie Diver) was being bullied. The other boys laughed at Richard's stammer, turning it into a cruel game. I didn't make a show of it, didn't throw fists or raise my voice. One afternoon, I simply walked Richard home—shoulder to shoulder. By the next week, the laughter had died down. Respect is sometimes loud, but often, it's quiet and consistent. That kind of moral leadership— simple, strong, and grounded—would become a hallmark of my adult life. But its seeds were planted right there, beneath the rain trees and stone archways of George's.

And then there were the rituals—rites of passage unique to the school that bonded boys in mischief and memory. The trek across North Street to get patties at Miss Chin's shop. The debates in Form 5I about whether Mr. Bucknor or Miss Stafford was the stricter English teacher. The way everybody paused in silence when "Prayer Before Class" played over the PA system, even if someone had just been joking seconds earlier.

Assemblies were events in themselves. When Father Hose took the podium, a hush would fall like a velvet curtain. His presence was commanding, yet somehow kind. His messages weren't laced with fire and brimstone—they were calls to integrity, to purpose, to compassion. He spoke of being "a man for others," a mantra the Jesuits held dear. At the time, I didn't fully grasp the weight of those words. But years later, as a teacher myself, standing in front of my own class, I would whisper them silently before my lessons began.

"A man for others."

It wasn't a slogan. It was an identity.

Outside the gates of the school, the world sometimes raged. The 1980s were not gentle in Kingston. Political unrest simmered. Poverty pinched at the margins of dreams. Gunshots were not unheard. But inside George's, there was a kind of sacred bubble—a place where learning could still be sacred, where boys could still be boys, with books under their arms and hope in their stride.

Some days, I stayed back late—not because I had to, but because I didn't want to leave. I would walk past the chapel and hear the choir rehearsing Latin hymns. I'd watch as the late afternoon sun poured gold onto the stained-glass windows. There was beauty in these moments. Beauty in silence. Beauty in belonging.

In my final year, when it came time to select a prefect body, my name was whispered by many, but I wasn't chosen—not that year. Perhaps because I never courted popularity, or maybe because I challenged certain norms with too much of an adverse attitude. But it didn't sting for long. In my heart, I knew leadership wasn't about a badge. It was about bearing.

On graduation day, the tears came quietly. Boys who had once wrestled and argued now hugged tightly, promising to stay in touch, to never forget. And while many of those promises would fade with time, a few would hold fast, like the men of the StGC Class of '86—my forever brethren, now scattered across the globe, but stitched together by memory and faith.

One particular message in the WhatsApp group will always stay with me. It was sent by Zellie on a random Tuesday:

"You ever realize seh all of we still trying to be the kind of man George's trained us to be?" (Did any of you ever realized that all of us are still trying to be the kinds of men that George's trained us to be?").

That line hit different.

Because it was true. Every man in that group—whether now a businessman, a pastor, a mechanic, a teacher, or an artist—still carried George's in our marrow. Still tried to live up to those impossible, beautiful standards set by men like Father Hose and Dennis Ziadie.

And for me, that legacy lived on every time I step into my own classroom. When I speak with compassion to a struggling student, or corrected one who needed guidance, or took a few minutes to talk football with a boy who felt unseen—I was passing on the spirit of St. George's College. Because George's wasn't just about books and football. It was about vision. And voice. And becoming.

When I later told my own son, Rhys, about my school days, I didn't just talk about wins and grades. I spoke of friends who became brothers. Of teachers who saw more in me than I saw in myself. Of a boy who learned how to dream.

I would end those stories with one simple truth:

"Mi never born with plenty, but Georges mek mi feel like mi did have the world." (I was not born with a lot, but George's made me feel like I had the world).

Manchester United

My love for football that came into being from me watching my Uncle Neily play on

Wellington Street, extended far beyond the island. From the first moment I saw Diego Maradona weave his magic on a grainy black-and-white television during the 1982 World Cup in Spain, I was even more hooked. It was a humid June afternoon in Kingston, and Tulip Lane had gone unusually quiet. Someone had dragged an old TV — precariously on a wooden crate — onto a verandah so the entire yard could watch. The picture flickered with static, the commentary switching between Spanish and English depending on which station picked up the feed. But none of that mattered when Maradona got the ball.

There he was—stocky, low to the ground, every step calculated but full of flair. He would take on three defenders at once, the ball glued to his left foot like it was born there. I watched, wide-eyed, as Maradona twisted and turned, sending defenders the wrong way. Even when Argentina lost that year, the magic had already done its work. I wasn't just seeing football; I was seeing poetry, mischief, and genius all rolled into one. From that day forward, Argentina was my team—at least until 2014, when politics and shifting allegiances tested that loyalty.

That same year, Tulip Lane was a mini-World Cup of its own. Every evening, as the sun dipped low and the zinc fences glowed orange in the light, the boys would turn the street into a pitch. The "goals" were two battered school shoes on either side of the road, and the ball was often just a cheap plastic one from the corner shop, patched with electrical tape to keep it from splitting. I would take on Wayne, Manda, and half the neighborhood, pulling off moves I'd just seen Maradona do hours earlier—at least in my mind. A stepover here, a cheeky nutmeg there, the crowd of barefooted kids cheering like they were at Old Trafford.

It wasn't just about skill—it was about heart. The uneven asphalt taught me; the crowded games taught me vision. Every time I heard the "thunk" of the ball against the zinc fence, it was another lesson in resilience. The games would stretch past dusk, broken only by the smell of Mama's dinner calling me home.

Years later, another football love would claim my heart—Manchester United. That bond was born out of Sunday afternoons watching Big League Soccer on JBC TV and cemented during my first visit to England and staying with my grandfather, who lived within walking distance of Aston Villa's stadium. I would sit in the old man's living room, sipping tea and listening to stories of English football from the days before sponsorships and million-pound transfers. The rain would patter against the window, and my grandfather's voice would carry tales of muddy pitches, standing terraces, and players who played for pride as much as pay.

But long before I learned to chant United's songs or knew the names of the greats, the fire had already been kindled in my bloodline. My grandfather had been a lifelong Manchester United supporter. In the era when radios carried matches across the Atlantic crackle by crackle, he had chosen his side, and once chosen, he never wavered. He would tell me about the Busby Babes as if he had known them personally—about Duncan Edwards, whose promise was cut short in Munich, and about the way Bobby Charlton carried himself with dignity even after tragedy. His eyes always seemed to glisten when he spoke about Sir Matt Busby, as though the man was not just a manager but a symbol of perseverance itself.

That loyalty seeped into my mother. She grew up in a house where United's victories were celebrated like national holidays and defeats were mourned like personal losses. She may not have followed every match or memorized every squad number, but she absorbed the faith. It was in her DNA, passed down from her father, wrapped in the memories of listening to games on the crackling BBC World Service and watching snippets of match highlights that arrived late on Jamaican television. When she became a parent, that quiet loyalty became part of my inheritance.

Me and Mama watching Man Utd vs Real Madrid in Miami in 2018

By the time I came of age, it felt inevitable. Football was everywhere in Kingston—played barefooted on dusty pitches, argued about on verandas and debated in taxis. But when I leaned toward Manchester United, it wasn't just because of the glamour of red shirts or the brilliance of players like Bryan Robson and later Eric Cantona. It was because I was stepping into a lineage, a tradition that tied me not just to a team but to my family. Supporting United was like carrying a torch passed hand to hand from my grandfather in England, to my mother in Jamaica, and then to me.

Sitting in my grandfather's living room, I began to understand what that torch really meant. Football, for him, was never only about the scoreline. It was about resilience—the way United rose from the ashes of Munich in 1958 to climb again, to conquer Europe a decade later. It was about community—the feeling of standing shoulder to shoulder in a stadium, or thousands of miles away, still belonging to the same tribe. And it was about loyalty—choosing a side and standing by it, win or lose, because that's what family and football demanded.

I carried those lessons back with me when I returned to Jamaica. The late-night games on TV, the whispered commentary so I wouldn't wake the house, the joy of seeing United rise under Sir Alex Ferguson—it all felt like an extension of those tea-scented nights in my grandfather's home. United wasn't just a club; it was a thread connecting three generations, stitching together stories of sacrifice, survival, and belonging. And every time I pulled on a red shirt or saw the crest glint beneath the lights, I felt that connection—an inheritance not of wealth, but of passion, pride, and undying loyalty.

My heart belonged to Old Trafford. I fell for United's grit, their drama, their refusal to give in. George Best's artistry, Bryan Robson's leadership, Eric Cantona's swagger, Dwight Yorke's Caribbean pride, Paul Scholes' quiet genius, and Cristiano Ronaldo's relentless drive all became part of my personal pantheon.

Back in Jamaica, Sunday mornings were sacred. The streets might still be asleep, but I would be up, eyes glued to the TV. Sometimes I would pace, other times I would sit on the edge of my chair, muttering tactical advice as though Sir Alex Ferguson could somehow hear me across the Atlantic. A United win meant a good day; a loss could sour my mood until Monday.

Even now, thousands of miles from Kingston, the ritual remains. My living room becomes my stadium with the chants from Stretford End. The game has taught me strategy, patience, and how to find beauty in struggle. And while Manchester United may lose more often than they win these days, for me, loyalty isn't about the scoreboard — it's about the story. And the story, like my own life, is still being written.

Iniko in Portmore

In 1985 our small family, Mama, me, Shema and Wayne, moved to our own home on Kirkbride Avenue, in Cumberland, Portmore. For Mama, it was more than a change of address; it was the fulfillment of a long-held dream. After years of struggle and sacrifice, she finally had a place she could call hers, a house where her children would grow without the constant shadow of uncertainty. I remember the day we carried our few belongings through the front door. The house was modest, its walls still smelling of fresh paint, the floors echoing with our footsteps. But to us, it was a castle.

Portmore itself felt like another world. The air carried the salt of the nearby sea, and the streets buzzed with the energy of families like ours—people carving out a life beyond Kingston's crowded lanes. Wayne and I explored every corner, riding bikes through the developing schemes, playing football on open lots until dusk painted the sky orange. At night, the sound of crickets mixed with the distant laughter of neighbors, a new rhythm that quickly became home. 1060 Kirkbride Avenue wasn't just a house; it was a new beginning. It gave Mama peace, and it gave us space to dream bigger than ever before.

It was while living in Cumberland and attending St. George's College that I met Iniko. She was radiant, skin the color of roasted almonds, eyes like deep pools of quiet determination, and a smile that seemed to rise just a second before it reached her lips. There was a grace to the way she carried herself that felt beyond her years—poised but playful, confident without being loud. She walked as if she knew where she was going, even when no one else did. And when she looked your way, you felt seen—not just noticed, but understood.

I was already known for my charm, quick wit, and expressive eyes, and I was no stranger to admiration. But Iniko was different. She didn't giggle or melt at my compliments like some of the other girls did. Instead, she smiled knowingly, like someone who had read the ending of a novel you were still halfway through. It intrigued me. It disarmed me. It humbled me.

We met by chance. It was a cool Tuesday morning on the way to school in a bus called Turbo Cruiser, which was owned by my school mate Zellie's family. We were both standing in a crowded aisle, but only a few feet away from each other. I stole a quick glance at her as I did every single morning, but this time, she glanced back. And she smiled.

I literally melted right there on the spot — hands trembling, breath growing shallow, chest rising and falling as though I had just run a marathon. It was the kind of smile that disarmed you, that left your carefully rehearsed words scattered like leaves in the wind. I had imagined talking to her a hundred times before, had practiced clever lines in my head, even rehearsed casual nods in the mirror. But in that moment, none of it mattered. Her smile stripped me of every defense, every mask.

It was not just the curve of her lips — it was the light in her eyes, the warmth that seemed to say, "I see you." And in a world where young boys often felt invisible, that look was enough to undo me completely. My knees wobbled, my fingers twitched, my heartbeat stumbled into a rhythm all its own.

I tried to steady myself, to will my body into calm, but it was no use. I was suspended in that moment, caught between boyhood wonder and the terrifying awareness that this was something bigger than a schoolyard crush. Her smile carried the weight of possibility—the chance that my feelings might not be one-sided, that perhaps she, too, felt a spark flicker in the silence between us.

Every detail around me faded: the chatter of passengers, the hum of the bus's engine, even the ironic base of Shabba Ranks' 'Mr. Loverman' playing through the bus's speakers became a dull hum. All I could hear was the rush of blood in my ears and the whisper of a future I dared to dream about. And though I knew nothing was promised, that smile planted itself in my memory like a seed, destined to grow into something unforgettable.

That was the power of first love—not grand gestures or sweeping declarations, but a single smile that had the strength to melt a boy

100

and make him believe, for the first time, in magic.

My brother, Wayne, standing beside me, looked at me inquisitively and asked,

"Yuh arite yute?" (Are you ok youth?).

And I nervously swallowed and nodded. But unbeknownst to me just like that, the rhythm of my world shifted with grace and elegance.

Iniko and I began spending time together. First in groups, then walking home from school events, and soon—on long, unhurried strolls through Portmore's gentle streets. Friends, seeing us always hand in hand or shoulder to shoulder, dubbed us the "Prince and Princess of Cumberland." The name started as a joke, but it stuck—because it felt true.

We exchanged cassette tapes like love letters. I would spend hours recording mixtapes on my twin-deck stereo, carefully curating each song—Luther Vandross, Maxi Priest, Air Supply, and every now and then, a Bob Marley track with a message just for her. Iniko would return the favor, her handwriting on the labels always neat, looping the words "For You" at the top with a heart beneath.

We would listen together in the park or on her veranda, sharing a single pair of headphones. I would close my eyes during the instrumental breaks, imagining a future that felt just within reach: A small house in the hills. Books lining the walls. Children with her smile.

It was young love, yes, but it was real.

We talked for hours—about music, school, dreams, and the world we wanted to create. Iniko was fiercely intelligent and could debate anyone into silence, including me. She challenged me to read more, think deeper, feel harder. Under her influence, I began keeping a small journal, writing down my thoughts, my poems, and my heartbreaks. It was the first time I truly examined my own inner life. She awakened my introspection.

There are moments that last. There are loves that blaze hot and fast, burning out quickly. And then there are the slow, glowing embers — quiet, steady, unforgettable. Our love was the latter. Even decades later, I can still remember the exact scent of her hair — mango and coconut oil. The way she laughed, head tilted back, eyes closed. The softness of her voice when she called me "Ratio."

We had favorite spots: Carib, Regal, and State movie theatres, and watching George's play Manning Cup. But love, as they say, is not always enough.

By late 1989, the personal pressure and expectations began to pull us in different directions. Iniko started working at a local bank, while I accepted a job at Bustamante Children's Hospital. The movie dates became less frequent. The conversations, more strained. And slowly, almost imperceptibly, life began to fill the spaces where we had once existed as a "we."

We tried to hold on. Then on a cool Friday afternoon in March of 1990, on Mama's floral sofa, the breakup happened. We hugged, long and deep. There were no angry words, no accusations — just a quiet acceptance that sometimes, life writes different stories for people who once dreamed together. She kissed my cheek and whispered,

"Don't forget me, Mr. Horatio Ward."

I never did. But I was devastated. I was rocked to the core.

Years later, time passed. Life moved on. I loved again. I had children. I changed countries, careers, homes. But Iniko always remained somewhere in my heart, untouched by the years.

To me, Iniko was part of my origin story — the first chapter that made all the others possible. She was my first muse, the one who taught me how to love, and perhaps more importantly, how to lose with grace.

In moments of silence — late at night, grading papers in the quiet hum of a Florida living room — I would sometimes hear a song from our mixtapes. I would smile, close my eyes, and feel the Caribbean breeze of 1986 on my skin again. The scent of Iniko's coconut oil. The soft brush of her fingers again.

The Outlaws

In 1984, my cousin Manda and I joined a breakdancing group called The Outlaws. We weren't just a group—we were a movement, at least in our own eyes. Denham Town was alive with the sound of boom boxes, the smell of jerk chicken on the corner, and the sight of young men spinning, twisting, and popping in every available space. Breakdancing was the latest cultural export from America, brought into the community by cassette tapes, VHS videos, and travelers returning from the States with stories of the Bronx and Brooklyn.

The Outlaws practiced religiously, sometimes in the cracked concrete yards between zinc fences, sometimes in the wide, dusty expanse of the community center. Our dedication bordered on obsession. The windmill, the backspin, the head glide—we drilled each move until it became muscle memory. The cardboard we used as a dance surface would wear thin within days, forcing us to scavenge for new sheets from grocery stores or hardware shops. Every practice session was equal parts competition and collaboration; each dancer wanted to outdo the others, but we also pushed each other to be better.

I had a natural fluidity, a rhythm that seemed to flow from deep inside me. I wasn't just hitting moves—I was telling a story with my body. The crowd could feel it, and The Outlaws knew we had something special in me.

Our big break, so to speak, came at a neighborhood barbecue hosted by a local business owner. The sound system was blasting Ninjaman and Run-D.M.C., and the crowd had already been warmed up by smaller dance crews. When The Outlaws took the floor, there

106

was a different energy — calm at first, then electrifying. I stepped forward, the music hit, and I moved like my life depended on it. Every twist, every spin, every freeze landed perfectly. By the time I hit my final pose, the crowd erupted. People were screaming, stomping, banging on zinc fences.

The next week, the Portmore News ran a small feature on the event, complete with a blurry black-and-white photo of The Outlaws mid-performance. For the first time, I saw myself in print. It was a small thing to most, but for a boy from Denham Town, it felt like monumental proof that my talents could take me beyond the narrow borders of my neighborhood.

Mama was in the audience that day, standing near the front, clapping and screaming herself hoarse.

"*Go deh, Rambo!*" (Go there Rambo) she yelled, her voice cutting through the music.

After the barbecue, things shifted. We weren't just The Outlaws anymore—we were local celebrities. Kids started mimicking our moves in schoolyards. Shopkeepers nodded at us with pride. Even the elders, who had once dismissed breakdancing as "foreign foolishness," began to see it as a form of expression, a way for youth to reclaim space and voice. We were rewriting the narrative of Denham Town, one spin at a time.

We started getting invitations to perform at birthday parties, school events, even church fundraisers. Each performance was a chance to refine our craft, to push the boundaries of what our bodies could say. I began choreographing routines, blending traditional Jamaican dancehall steps with breakdance fundamentals. The fusion was electric. It felt like bridging two worlds — Kingston and the Bronx, zinc fences and subway stations.

But it wasn't just about the moves. It was about the message. We danced to tell stories — of survival, of joy, of resistance. We danced to honor the boys who never made it past sixteen, the girls who carried too much too soon, the mothers who prayed over us with trembling hands. Every performance was a tribute.

One evening, after a particularly powerful show at the community center, an older man approached me. He was quiet, dressed in a neatly pressed shirt, and carried the air of someone who had seen too much. "Mi see yuh," (I see you) he said simply. *"Yuh remind mi of mi bredda.* (You remind me of my brother). *"Him used to dance too, before di streets tek him."*

(He used to dance too before the streets took him). He didn't say much else, but his eyes held a depth that stayed with me. That moment reminded me that our art was more than entertainment — it was memory. It was healing.

The Outlaws eventually disbanded, as life pulled us in different directions — school, work, migration. But the rhythm never left me. It lived in my walk, in my teaching, in the way I held space for others. Breakdancing taught me how to move through the world with intention, how to fall and rise with grace. And though the cardboard is long gone, the story still spins.

The Rhythm and the Fight

The nickname — Rambo — had been born a few months earlier, during a far less joyful moment. A fight had broken out near the market, and I'd stepped in to defend my brother. I didn't throw the first punch, but I threw the last. Word spread quickly, and by the next morning, the name had stuck. "Rambo," they called me — not just for the fight, but for the fire. It wasn't a name I chose, but it was one I grew into. In a place like Denham Town, names carried weight. They were armor, reputation, prophecy.

On that hot, memorable afternoon, Wayne, my younger brother, was ambushed by a group of older boys. It started with teasing, then escalated into shoving, then fists. By the time I arrived, Wayne was on the ground, clutching his side, and the boys were circling. Something in me snapped. I didn't hesitate. I grabbed the nearest thing at hand—a broken Dragon Stout bottle from the gutter—and stepped in between Wayne and his attackers.

It wasn't a fair fight, but I didn't care. My only goal was to get Wayne out of there in one piece. Shouts, threats, and the glint of broken glass were enough to send the older boys scattering. When the dust settled, I helped Wayne to his feet and walked him home, adrenaline still pounding in my ears.

To me, it wasn't an act of heroism—it was simply what a big brother was supposed to do. But to the rest of the community, it became legend. Friends started calling me Rambo, half in jest, half in respect. The name stuck, following me into every corner of my life. It wasn't just about physical bravery — it became a symbol of my role as a protector, someone who stood up for the people I loved, even at personal risk.

Mama didn't like the nickname at first. She worried it glorified violence, that it would follow me into places I didn't belong. But that night at the barbecue, when she saw me dancing — saw me transform that name into something powerful, something poetic — she embraced it. "*Go deh, Rambo!*" wasn't just cheerleading. It was a blessing. A release. A recognition that her son had found a way to turn struggle into art.

These were foundational years for me. Life in Denham Town wasn't easy — it was raw, sometimes dangerous, always unpredictable. But it was also vibrant and full of meaning. There were moments of beauty tucked between the hardships: the laughter of friends playing dominoes under the almond tree, the smell of curry goat wafting through the alleyways, the sound of gospel choirs competing with sound system clashes on Sunday afternoons.

My famous Rambo hat

Books and bruises defined this period of my life. During the day, I devoured novels and poetry collections borrowed from the small but determined local library. At night, I navigated the realities of a neighborhood where survival often depended on quick thinking and quicker reflexes. My reading habits confused some of my peers—how could the same boy who could outdance anyone in the yard also spend hours lost in *The Count of Monte Cristo*? But to me, there was no contradiction. The physical discipline of dance and the mental discipline of reading fed the same hunger: the need to master something, to create, to be more than what my surroundings tried to dictate.

My breakdancing crew gave me an outlet, but it also taught me structure. The Outlaws weren't just freestyling in the streets — we set practice schedules, planned routines, and strategized how to impress judges at local talent shows. That discipline mirrored the commitment I showed in my studies. I began to understand that success, whether in art, academics, or life, wasn't just about talent — it was about showing up, again and again, even when no one was watching.

The nickname Rambo followed me into those rehearsals, shouted by kids leaning against fences or by friends daring me to try a new move. Sometimes I played into it, striking mock action-hero poses before dropping into a perfect backspin. Other times, I shrugged it off, focusing instead on the beat and the flow. Still, deep down, I understood the weight of it. Rambo was more than a nickname—it was a reminder of who I was to my family, especially to my brother.

Wayne, for his part, took pride in his brother's reputation. He would tell the story of *"The bottle and the bullies"* with embellishments that grew wilder over time, until I barely recognized the tale. But I never corrected him. It was Wayne's version, and in Wayne's version, his big brother was a hero.

Through all this, I began to feel the stirrings of something bigger. Dance was thrilling, but it wasn't enough. I wanted to leave a mark, to create a story worth telling—not just in the moves I made on the dance floor, but in the choices I made in life. Denham Town was both a cradle and a crucible, shaping me into someone who could navigate chaos while holding onto dreams.

I knew the dangers: the boys who got pulled into gang life, the friends who drifted into hustles that promised quick cash but carried even quicker consequences. I saw too many faces vanish from the neighborhood, some to prison, some to violence, some simply disappearing without explanation. I didn't want that path. I wanted something else — something that felt like forward motion.

And yet, I loved my community fiercely. It was where Mama's voice echoed from the veranda, where Wayne's laughter filled the narrow yard of 17 Tulip Lane, where my aunts and cousins brought joy to street corners, and where neighbors shared food and gossip in equal measure. The contradictions didn't bother me. Denham Town could be dangerous and beautiful, harsh and full of love — all at the same time.

By the end of 1984, I felt like my life was opening into multiple directions. Dance, academics, brotherhood, and street reputation all swirled together in a complicated but exhilarating mix. I didn't have a clear map yet, but I knew that I was moving toward something greater.

And through it all — whether on a dance floor, in a library, or standing between Wayne and trouble—I carried one unshakable belief: My life was a story worth telling, not because it was perfect, but because it was mine to tell. And the first chapters were just beginning.

Chapter III: Becoming

Paycheck

Needing to make ends meet after leaving St. George's and before enrolling in college, I took a job as a cashier at Bustamante Children's Hospital. It wasn't glamorous work — but it was deeply human work, the kind of job that quietly shapes the way a person sees the world. My days began early, often before the Kingston sun had fully stretched itself over the Blue Mountains. The air in the hospital was a mix of antiseptic and quiet tension, broken occasionally by a burst of laughter from a nurse's station or the cries of a child.

My post was just outside the pediatric ward, where parents shuffled in with tired eyes and wrinkled clothes, clutching their children and their hopes in equal measure. Some came for routine visits — checkups, vaccinations, the occasional cough that just wouldn't quit. Others came in panic, clutching babies with fevers or injuries that had turned the night into a blur. I handled invoices, payments, and paperwork, but my work was never just about numbers or receipts. It was about being the steady, calm voice in a moment when someone else's world was spinning.

I learned very quickly that money was not the only currency in those corridors — patience, kindness, and compassion were traded just as often. Parents who couldn't afford certain medications would linger after transactions, hesitant, their pride wrestling with desperation. More than once, I found myself quietly covering small shortfalls from my own pocket, never announcing it, never expecting thanks.

In between transactions, I would watch the ward. The nurses were like silent generals, leading a war against time and disease. The doctors, though sometimes brusque, carried the weight of decisions that could shift a family's entire future. But it was the children who taught me the most. They were fighters — tiny, fragile, but filled with a resilience that humbled me. I saw bald heads from chemotherapy treatments,

119

casts scribbled over with colorful doodles, and eyes that seemed far older than the small bodies they belonged to.

There was one little boy, probably no more than five, who visited regularly for asthma treatments. Every time he came, he would run straight to my desk, not for the candy I sometimes kept in my drawer, but to show me his latest drawing. *"One day, mi a go be a big artist,"* (One day I am going to be a big artist) the boy would say, puffing out his small chest. I pinned each drawing to the side of my desk until it was a makeshift gallery of stick figures, suns, and clumsy rainbows.

The work was often emotionally heavy. There were days when parents left without their child, and the corridors felt like they had swallowed all the light in the building. Those were the nights I went home quiet, lying in bed staring at the ceiling, thinking about how fleeting everything could be. It was in those moments that I began to write more — short stories scribbled on the backs of used forms; poems jotted in the margins of duty rosters. My writing became both an escape and a way to process what I was witnessing daily.

After some time at Bustamante Hospital, I moved to Kingston Public Hospital (KPH), and the pace was even more relentless. If Bustamante was about tender hope, KPH was about the raw, unvarnished reality of life in a city where accidents, violence, and illness collided daily. The emergency room there never slept, sirens blaring outside, gurneys rushing in, nurses barking orders, and the constant hum of fluorescent lights overhead.

KPH taught me a different kind of endurance. Bustamante had been about holding onto hope; KPH was about navigating chaos without losing yourself. As a cashier there, I was stationed in a high-traffic area, handling payments for a variety of departments — X-rays, surgeries, prescriptions. I saw the toll that poverty took on health. I saw injuries from car accidents on Halfway Tree Road, gunshot wounds from turf wars in Tivoli Gardens, machete cuts from rural disputes that had spilled into the city.

But even in the madness, there was humanity. I saw elderly patients clasping hands like newlyweds, children who brought their parents flowers after surgery, strangers who pooled their money to help someone pay for urgent medication. And through it all, I was there—sometimes as a silent observer, sometimes as a small comfort in the form of a reassuring word or a patient explanation.

It was at KPH that my understanding of empathy deepened. I realized that empathy wasn't just feeling sorry for someone—it was stepping into their world long enough to truly understand their struggle. It was the difference between saying, "I hope you feel better" and saying, "I understand what this means for you, and I'm here in whatever way I can be."

The suffering that I saw at KPH didn't harden me — it sharpened my ability to listen, to look past the surface. I began to see patterns in people's eyes — the mix of fear and trust when they handed me their paperwork, the subtle relief when I explained a process clearly, the gratitude that came not from grand gestures but from small acts of respect.

This was the training ground for my later work as a teacher, though I didn't know it yet. At KPH, I learned to read people the way some read books—to pick up on the unspoken, to adjust my tone depending on the audience, to know when someone needed efficiency and when they needed patience. These skills, though developed in hospital corridors, would later become my greatest tools in the classroom.

I also learned about the fragility of human life. The line between "everything is fine" and "everything has changed forever" was often just a heartbeat, a traffic light, or a stray bullet away. It made me value the small victories: a patient discharged after a long stay, a family smiling together in the waiting area, a nurse finally taking a coffee break after hours on her feet.

Outside of work, my writing took on a sharper edge. I began to explore themes of survival, resilience, and dignity in my short stories. My characters were often composites of people I had seen in the hospital—mothers carrying two jobs and a sick child, men haunted by mistakes they couldn't undo, young people navigating a world that seemed determined to break them.

By the time my acceptance letter from Mico Teachers' College arrived, I was more than ready to leave the hospital world behind — but I carried it with me in ways that would shape my identity forever. Mico would give me the formal training to be a teacher, but Bustamante and KPH had already given me a masterclass in humanity.

When I finally walked onto Mico's campus, textbooks in hand, I wasn't just another student chasing a diploma. I was a man who had seen life in its rawest form, who had sat across from grief and joy in equal measure, who understood that every person carried a story that was bigger than their outward appearance.

Later, in my own classroom, when a student came in with a clouded expression or restless energy, I would think back to those hospital corridors. I would remember that everyone is carrying something unseen. And that memory made me gentler, more patient, more willing to find a way to reach them.

Bustamante had taught me how to comfort the fragile. KPH had taught me how to survive chaos. Together, they had taught me how to teach — not just lessons, but life.

The Mico

After graduating from St. George's College, I faced a question that haunts many bright Jamaican youths even to this very day: what next? University was a dream, but not yet a reality. The cost was too steep, and time seemed too short. But teaching? That felt natural. That felt like purpose.

I enrolled at The Mico Teachers' College later known as The Mico University College, in September 1991. Mico, a historic institution nestled along Marescaux Road in Kingston, was a place where boys and girls became educators — leaders in the making — and where traditions ran deep. Mico wasn't easy. The work was rigorous, and the expectations high. But I thrived.

I found kinship among fellow students like Orson Nelson (Nello), Lennox Christie (DJ Lennox), Michelle Needham (Michieboo), Joel Findlay, Karen Miller, Aston Shaw (Stretch), Dennis Davis (PJ), and many others. It was a melting pot of ambition and camaraderie, with debates on politics over patties, group projects that turned into sleepovers, and evenings spent studying in the hush of the library.

At Mico, the bonds I formed were deep and lasting. Orson "Nello" Nelson was my debate partner—a fiery soul who argued politics like a seasoned lawyer. Michelle "Michieboo" Needham was the voice of reason, always offering hugs, hard truths, or her last beef patty. Dennis Davis, known as PJ, was the joker who somehow aced exams without opening a book.

We studied together, struggled together, dreamed together. Sometimes, late into the night, we would lie on our dorm beds with the windows open, talking about the kind of teachers that we wanted to be. "Mi nah just teach fi get a paycheck," (I am not teaching for a paycheck) I once said. "*Mi want teach fi save soul.*" (I want to teach to save souls).

"*You think you a Jesus?*" (Do you think you are Jesus?) PJ teased.

"Nah," I grinned. "*Mi just know seh the right word at the right time can change a man whole life.*" (I just know that the right word at the right time can change a man's whole life).

Under the guidance of passionate lecturers—especially Ms. Dorrett Campbell—I emerged as one of the most promising English students in the Class of 1994. Ms. Campbell, sharp-eyed and no-nonsense, taught Use of English, and she saw in me what few others did:

128

not just a love for words, but an instinct for using them—cleanly, purposefully, and with care for the reader. Where others praised my metaphors, she reached for my verbs. Where I chased grand conclusions, she hunted for the missing premise in the second paragraph. "Language is the first tool of liberation," she would say, setting her pencil on my draft. "Use the tool correctly, and you can build almost anything."

Her classroom ran on three questions, always written on the board: What do you mean? How do you know? Why does it matter? Those questions stripped my sentences of decoration. A claim without evidence limped. A paragraph without purpose felt dishonest. When I hedged, she drew a firm line through the adverbs and handed back the page. "You're not in trouble," she'd say. "You're in revision." Then came the drills: identify the subject and finite verb in every sentence; test pronoun reference; check parallelism like a carpenter checks a frame. She made grammar feel less like a maze and more like a set of reliable joints that keep a structure standing when the roof is heavy.

We wrote for audience and purpose until those words lived under our skin. One week we turned the same information into a notice, a memo, and a letter of complaint. Another week we summarized a 1,000-word passage in exactly 120 words, then again in 60, then in one sentence. "Brevity is not starvation," she said, "it's clarity on a budget." She taught us to make topic sentences function like promises and paragraphs like contracts. If the body did not deliver what the topic sentence offered, she circled the whole block and wrote, simply, "Breach."

Her feedback was a legend of abbreviations: CS for comma splice, MM for misplaced modifier, AGR for subject-verb agreement, AWK for awkwardness that only a rewrite could cure. When I asked why a semicolon worked in one place and failed in another, she drew two short ladders: one with sturdy rungs (two independent clauses) and one with a missing rung (a dependent clause pretending to be grown). "A semicolon is a bridge," she said. "Do not build it over a swamp." I have never misused one since.

Ms. Dorrett Campbell

What Mrs. Dunn had started years earlier—the courage to write at all—Ms. Campbell refined into craft. She taught me how to plan before the page: quick outlines made of claims, reasons, and evidence; transition words chosen on purpose; a final sentence that settled accounts instead of firing fireworks. She made us hear the difference between active and passive constructions, not because one is always better than the other, but because a writer should choose. When we overused heavy nominalizations, she sent us hunting for the hidden verb. "Let the verb carry the weight," she insisted. "It has the muscles."

In Use of English, we also learned the ethics of accuracy. She insisted on attribution even in small assignments and introduced us to citation long before any research seminar. "If a thought is borrowed," she said, "return it with thanks." She trained us to paraphrase without losing the pulse of the original and to summarize without smuggling in our opinions. When we wrote arguments, she taught the rhetorical triangle—ethos, logos, pathos—and warned us not to lean on pathos like a crutch.

"Feeling can open a door," she said, "but evidence pays the rent."

Because we were Caribbean students, she honored register and code-switching. "You are bilingual even if you think you're not," she told us, moving between Jamaican Patois examples and Standard English constructions. "Know which room you're in and speak accordingly. Both languages deserve respect; both have rules." She would not let anyone despise the mother tongue, nor would she allow us to use it as an excuse for sloppiness. That balance—dignity for home, discipline for school—became a compass I still use in my own classroom.

Her tutorials were small workshops in clarity under pressure. She timed our summary writing with the gentle cruelty of a coach: ten minutes left, pencils down, read it aloud. She made us listen to the sound of a sentence and feel where it caught. "If you run out of breath," she'd say, "your reader will run out of patience." She was allergic to padding. "Cut twenty percent," she'd challenge, handing back a draft. Panic would bloom—and then relief, when we realized the piece was better without its ornaments.

But Ms. Campbell was not all red pen. She praised precision with the same gravity she used to correct. After a class debate on the use of statistics in editorials, she closed my notebook and said, "You kept your verbs honest." It was the kind of compliment that anchors a young writer. Later, when I presented a workshop on cohesion devices—repetition with variation, lexical chains, pronoun reference—she nodded once and wrote "clear and useful" on the margin of my handout. I still keep that page.

The course spilled beyond the classroom. She sent us to the writing center to tutor first-year students, insisting that teaching someone else how to find a thesis will expose the weak joints in your own. She made us edit campus notices and draft letters to real offices so we would feel the weight of clarity in public life. Once she assigned us to rewrite a policy paragraph so that any parent could understand it in one read. "Plain language is not plain thinking," she said. "It is a gift."

When I drifted toward purple prose, she tugged me back to reader needs. "Who is your reader at this moment?" she would ask. "What does this reader need next—definition, example, or concession?" If I could not answer, the paragraph changed. She taught me to signpost without condescension and to use concision as kindness. In her class I learned that revising a sentence is a kind of hospitality: you move the furniture so your guest can walk through without bruising a shin.

One afternoon I turned in a piece that I thought was brilliant: a fierce conclusion wrapped in lyric sentences. She slid it back with a single question penciled in the margin: "Where did you prove this?" I went hunting and discovered I was trying to cash a check I hadn't written. That day I learned to earn my endings, and I have been cashing only covered checks since.

By the end of the year, Use of English had changed more than my essays; it had changed my habits. I started carrying a small list at the front of every notebook—Audience, Purpose, Tone, Evidence, Structure—and I ticked them off like a pilot before take-off. I learned to draft with generosity and edit with discipline, to trust a topic sentence and interrogate a transition, to treat the colon and dash as tools instead of decorations. When the awards came — small campus certificates, a commendation from the department — they felt less like applause and more like confirmation that I was learning to carry language responsibly.

Years later, when I stood in my own classroom teaching AVID students how to craft a claim, how to summarize without stealing, how to argue without shouting, I could hear Ms. Campbell in every mini-lesson. The Cornell notes format I love works because Use of English taught me to divide a page into ideas, evidence, and reflection. The tutorials I run succeed because she showed me that questions are more powerful than answers when they are precise. When I tell my students that discipline is the bridge between dream and destiny, I am echoing her insistence that sentences are not just pretty; they are ethical.

Mrs. Dunn lit the first match in sixth grade — she made reading feel like a doorway you could open with bare hands. Ms. Campbell kept that flame honest. She taught me to use English — to choose a register, to build a paragraph, to repair a comma splice, to let verbs do the work, to respect the reader's time. If anything I have written has helped a student find the next step, or helped a parent understand a policy without a translator, or helped a colleague make a clearer argument, it is because two women shaped the same boy at different times. Mrs. Dunn gave me permission. Ms. Campbell gave me precision.

But more than texts and terms, Mico solidified my love for teaching. It was in those lecture halls that I realized storytelling wasn't just art — it was survival. Literature and Religious Education had saved me in the quiet corners of Denham Town. Now, I wanted to offer that same lifeline to others.

It was at Mico that I finally stepped into the fullness of my potential. I didn't just survive there — I soared. I joined the debating society, wrote articles for the school paper, and even helped to organize the college's annual literary festival, a celebration of Caribbean voices that

137

included poetry readings, dramatic monologues, and guest lectures from published authors and cultural critics.

Mico was also where I became political — not in the sense of party loyalty, but in a deeper, more personal way. I began to see education not merely as a job but as a tool for transformation. I would sit for hours at Heroes Circle, just outside campus, reflecting on the struggles of ordinary Jamaicans, on the neglected children in the ghettos, the boys in khaki uniforms who could barely read, and the girls who dropped out because of early pregnancies. I began to write about these things — not for class assignments, but because I had to, because they haunted me.

During my final year, I completed a practicum placement at Norman Manley High School in Kingston. It was a notoriously tough school — underfunded, overcrowded, and plagued by violence. But I was undaunted. Armed with a box of chalk, a heart full of purpose, and my ever-present folder of poems and stories, I stepped into the classroom. I didn't lecture. I engaged. I met the students where they were—mentally, emotionally, and culturally. I rapped Shakespeare. I dramatized Caribbean folktales. I turned grammar drills into games. And the students responded. They came alive.

There was one student, in particular, a wiry, sharp-tongued youth named Devon, who had already been suspended three times. He entered my class with a scowl and a warning:

"*Mi nah do no bookwork, teach.*" (I won't be doing any book work teach).

But I, unfazed, handed him a copy of Oliver Twist and said,

"*Try dis. Mek mi know if di bwoy remind yuh of anybody yuh know.*" (Try this and let me know if the boy reminds you of anybody who you know).

Devon ended up reading the whole book and writing a two-page essay comparing Oliver's hunger to his own childhood struggles. For the first time, Devon passed English that term. That was the moment I knew that I was exactly where I was meant to be.

By the time I entered my second year at The Mico Teachers' College, I was no longer the quiet observer with wide eyes and a heart full of Denham Town. I had grown into myself — confident, purposeful, and surrounded by a tribe of unforgettable characters who helped shape the man I was becoming. Chief among them were best friends Nello and Karen Miller.

The Mico Religious Education class of 1994

Nello, real name Orson Nelson, was as loyal as they came. Born on Nelson Road,

140

Kingston 13, Nello had a smile that could disarm the sternest lecturer and a charisma that made him a natural crowd-puller. He and I clicked immediately, both drawn to deep conversations, raucous laughter, and an abiding love for football. But beyond the surface, Nello was introspective—a thinker. He often quoted Bob Marley or Malcolm X in casual conversation but always twisted the meaning in humorous ways.

He called me "the poet with boots," and I called him "the general without a rank."

Karen Miller was different—sharp, focused, a future leader long before the world caught on. She walked the campus with purpose and often reminded the boys that ambition without discipline was wasted potential. Karen became both confidante and sparring partner to me—challenging me to think critically, organize my time, and even improve my grammar. She once corrected a love letter I wrote to Michelle and told me, "You can't say you love a woman and spell 'beautiful' wrong. Fix it."

Together, the trio of me, Nello, and Karen formed a kind of triumvirate. We studied late into the night, argued about politics over bun and cheese, and supported each other through academic challenges, financial hardship, and heartbreak. We weren't just classmates — we were kin.

But if our trio was the heart of my Mico experience, then Christopher Landell — Baydie — was its rhythm. My roommate for two years, Baydie was the kind of presence that made a room feel lived in. He had a laugh that started in his belly and ended in the hallway, and a way of telling stories that made even the mundane sound like folklore. Baydie was from St Ann, and he carried that energy with him — part historian, part comedian, and always a brother.

Our room was more than a shared space — it was a sanctuary. Between the scent of Baydie's fried dumplings and my stack of poetry books, it was a place where ideas bloomed, and secrets were safe. He'd often stay up late, humming old-school reggae while ironing his khakis, and I'd be scribbling verses by lamplight. We respected each other's rhythms, and when life got heavy, we knew how to lighten it—whether with a spontaneous game of cards or a deep, soul-searching talk about legacy and love.

Baydie had a gift for grounding me. When I was overwhelmed by deadlines or distracted by heartbreak, he'd say,

"Boss, yuh writing like yuh vex wid di paper. Go walk, come back, and write like yuh love again." (Boss you are writing like you're vex with the paper. Go walk, come back, and write like you love again).

And somehow, that always worked.

He was also the unofficial fixer of our dorm block—patching up broken fans, smoothing over roommate disputes, and even helping one student recover a lost scholarship form by retracing steps like a detective. Everyone knew Baydie, and everyone trusted him. He had a way of making you feel seen, even when you didn't know you needed it.

Between Nello's fire, Karen's precision, and Baydie's warmth, I was held in a constellation of care. They didn't just shape my college years — they shaped my understanding of friendship, accountability, and the quiet power of showing up.

And when I think back on those days — the laughter echoing through the halls, the scent of curry drifting from the canteen, the late-night debates about Marcus Garvey and Miss Lou — I know that I wasn't just growing into myself. I was being grown by the people around me. People like Nello, Karen, and Baydie. People who saw me, challenged me, and loved me into becoming.

Then there was Joel Findlay — a wiry, mischievous spirit from Ewarton, who could talk his way into — or out of — anything. Findlay was the kind of friend my mother warned me about, but who always somehow made life more interesting. He had a grin that could disarm a security guard and a laugh that echoed down alleyways like a dare. His pockets were always empty, but his mind was full of schemes, shortcuts, and stories that blurred the line between truth and legend.

Our adventures were legendary. One infamous weekend, we sneaked out after lights-out at Mico, scaling the back fence with the grace of street cats, just to attend a late-night rendezvous with our girlfriends Del and Cynthia in Tel Aviv, a gritty section of Southside. The streets were buzzing with music, boasting, and the clack of tiles on folding tables. I, cautious but thrilled, watched as Findlay danced through the crowd like he owned it. He greeted domino players like old friends, flirted with vendors for extra fried fish, and somehow convinced a man twice his size to lend us his folding chairs.

We navigated the underbelly of Kingston without fear — but not without caution. "*Always walk like you belong,*" he'd say, "even if yuh don't."

That was Findlay's gospel. He wore confidence like cologne — strong, unmistakable, and just a little overwhelming. He taught me how to read a room, how to spot trouble before it spotted us, and how to disappear when necessary.

There were close calls — narrow escapes from territorial youths, the time our cab got stuck in Rae Town during a party-turned-riot, or when we were nearly caught hiding Red Stripe bottles in a Bible bag on campus. That last one nearly got us expelled, but Findlay somehow spun the story into a misunderstanding involving a church outreach program and a mislabeled donation.

But through it all, Findlay was family. He had a sharp tongue and a sharper sense of loyalty. When I was broke or broken, it was often Findlay who showed up with roasted breadfruit and encouragement. He never asked for explanations — just handed me a plate, cracked a joke, and reminded me that "bad times don't last, but bad company does." And somehow, that made everything feel lighter.

One night, after a particularly rough week of exams and heartbreak, Findlay dragged me to a backyard jam in Trench Town. "Yuh need rhythm, not reason," he said, handing me a bottle of Ting and a patty wrapped in newspaper. The music was loud, the bass thumping like a heartbeat, and the air thick with sweat and stories. We danced until our feet ached, until the ache in my chest gave way to laughter. That was Findlay's magic — he knew when silence was needed, and when noise was the cure.

He had a way with people, especially elders. Miss Inez, the neighborhood matriarch, once told me,

"That bwoy have old soul. Mischievous, yes — but respectful."

She'd let him borrow her bicycle, her radio, even her Sunday paper, so long as he promised to return it. And he always did. Late, but intact.

Findlay's charm wasn't just for show — it was survival. Growing up in Ewarton, he learned early how to stretch a dollar, how to dodge trouble, and how to make allies out of strangers. He could barter with a vendor using only compliments, and once convinced a police officer to let us go with a warning by quoting Marcus Garvey and offering him a mango. "Words sweet, but fruit sweeter," he said afterward, grinning.

We had our falling outs, of course. There was the time he borrowed my best shirt and returned it with curry stains, or when he forgot to pick me up for a tutoring gig in Half-Way Tree. I was furious, but he showed up the next day with a handwritten apology and a cassette tape labeled *"Forgive Me Mix."* It had Beres Hammond, Garnett Silk, and a bootleg recording of Findlay singing *"Sorry Seems to Be the Hardest Word."* Off-key, but heartfelt.

Our bond was forged not just in mischief, but in moments of quiet. Like the time we sat on the roof of the dorm, watching the city lights flicker like fireflies.

"Yuh ever wonder if we too wild for this world?" (Have you ever wondered if we are too wild for this world?) he asked.

I shrugged. "Maybe. But maybe the world too tame for us."

He nodded, and we sat in silence, the kind that only true friendship can hold.

Years later, when I started teaching, Findlay was one of the first to show up at my classroom door.

"*Mi come fi see if yuh really serious,*" (I came to see if you were really serious) he joked, handing me a stack of notebooks and a bag of tamarind balls. He stayed for the lesson, chimed in with stories, and left the students wide-eyed and laughing.

"*Yuh teach wid hart,*" (You teach with heart) he said afterward. "That's the only way it stick."

Findlay never stayed in one place too long. He was a wanderer, a storyteller, a collector of moments. But he always circled back — to Mico, to Southside, to me.

Now, when I walk through Kingston, I still hear echoes of our shenanigans. The clack of dominoes, the hum of dancehall, the laughter spilling from corner shops. I see shadows of

Findlay in every bold step, every sly grin, every act of defiance wrapped in love. He taught me that adventure isn't always about distance – it's about depth. That loyalty can be loud, and healing can come in the form of roasted breadfruit and a well-timed joke. That sometimes, the best education happens after lights-out, beyond the fence, in the heart of Southside.

And so, when I tell my students about courage, about friendship, about finding joy in unlikely places, I tell them about Joel Findlay. About the boy from Ewarton who danced through danger, who turned mischief into memory, and who reminded me – again and again – that life is meant to be lived boldly, and never alone.

It was in my second year at Mico that my quiet leadership started to shine. I was named assistant house captain of Lushington House, one of the most spirited and competitive student house groups at the college. The position wasn't just ceremonial – it was earned. I had shown maturity, consistency, and a willingness to serve. Lushington wasn't just a house group—it was a living organism, pulsing with ambition, mischief, and pride. To lead it meant more than wearing a badge; it meant becoming a steward of its spirit.

I organized study groups, mediated roommate disputes, and helped enforce rules that even I had once tried to bend. It was a balancing act—maintaining the trust of students while upholding the standards of the college. I handled it with grace. I learned to listen before speaking, to lead without shouting, and to correct without humiliating. My room became a kind of unofficial office—students dropped by for advice, venting, or just a quiet place to think. I kept a stash of Milo and crackers for those who came hungry, and a stack of borrowed textbooks for those who came unprepared.

By the time final year came around, I had been elected house captain of Lushington. Wearing the title with humility and pride, I led my dorm through academic competitions, cultural nights, and intramural games. I wasn't the loudest captain, but I was respected. I gave rousing speeches before football matches,

151

helped fellow students prepare teaching demonstrations, and stayed up late with those facing mental or emotional strain. I knew that leadership wasn't about being above others — it was about being among them, especially when things got hard.

One of my proudest moments came during the annual Cultural Explosion. Each house was tasked with presenting a showcase of Jamaican heritage, and Lushington was determined to outdo itself. I worked with dancers, poets, and dramatists — many of whom had never performed before. We built a set from discarded wood and painted it with borrowed brushes. I wrote a spoken-word piece that tied our segments together, and when the curtain rose, Lushington shone. We didn't win first place, but we won something deeper: unity, pride, and a standing ovation.

I once stood up to a lecturer who unfairly penalized a Lushington student and was nearly suspended for it. But my defense was eloquent, my position unwavering. I cited policy, precedent, and the student's record. I spoke not just as a captain, but as a brother. The matter was dropped. My legend grew. Students began calling me "Batfink" half in jest, half in reverence. I didn't seek the title — but I honored it.

Leadership at Mico taught me that influence isn't measured in volume, but in impact. That showing up — consistently, compassionately — is its own kind of power. And that sometimes, the most radical act is simply to believe in someone when they've stopped believing in themselves.

Lushington House gave me a stage, but more importantly, it gave me a congregation. And in serving them, I found my voice — not just as a leader, but as a builder of belonging.

**Standing: Badger, Sheldon, Bruce, Tyme.
Front: Horatio Nello, Findlay**

When I wasn't studying or leading student house group meetings, I could almost always be found on the football field. Football was breath, rhythm, meditation. It was the one place where my thoughts could run free, where my body could speak in ways my words sometimes couldn't. And St. Andrew Scots Kirk, a modest church near Duke Street, was the canvas upon which many masterpieces were painted.

The field wasn't much to look at — patchy grass, uneven lines, and goalposts that leaned like tired elders — but it was ours. It held the echoes of laughter, the sting of missed chances, and the glory of last-minute goals. There, under the afternoon sun and the gaze of a few street vendors and curious onlookers, I played alongside Nello, Findlay, Bruce Webb, Gauntlet Gordon (Badger) and my George's brothers Andypow and Cheva. We weren't professionals — but we had chemistry. We moved like a unit, each player tuned to the rhythm of the others, each pass a conversation, each goal a poem.

Gauntlet, a striker with lightning pace, was all flair and fire. He had a signature move — a feint to the left, then a burst to the right — that defenders never seemed to learn from. His boots were always the brightest on the field, and his celebrations were theatrical, arms raised like

155

a gladiator saluting the crowd. Beside him up top was Cheva, a cold-eyed finisher who lived for the near-post dart; give him half a yard and he'd tuck it away before you blinked. Bruce Webb, tall and quiet, was the team's wall in defense, always sliding in for the cleanest tackles. He rarely spoke, but when he did, it was usually to say, *"Mi got yuh back."* (I've got your back.) And he always did.

In midfield, Nello played with vision and guts. He saw angles no one else did, threading passes through impossible gaps and dictating the tempo like a maestro. Andypow worked beside him — metronome steady — clean first touch, crisp five-yard passes, and the knack for showing up exactly where the game needed calming. Nello would shout instructions mid-run, quote Bob Marley between plays, and once paused a match to help a vendor pick up spilled oranges. That was Nello — heart and hustle in equal measure. And then there was Findlay, who floated between positions like a jazz musician — erratic, brilliant, unpredictable. One minute he was defending, the next he was scoring. He played with a kind of reckless joy, like the ball owed him something.

156

I played right midfield, fast and fearless, known for my bone-crunching tackles and inch-perfect crosses. I wasn't flashy, but I was dependable. I once scored a 35-yard screamer that hit the crossbar, bounced down, and back out. The ref hesitated. The crowd screamed. The call stood — goal. It became part of local folklore. *"Yuh see Horatio's rocket?"* (Did you see Horatio's rocket?) they'd say in barbershops and betting lounges. "Crossbar still trembling."

Our matches were more than games — they were rituals. We'd arrive early, stretch in silence, and then erupt into laughter as Findlay tried to juggle the ball while reciting poetry. Vendors would drift over, selling bag juice and fried dumplings, and sometimes a curious child would ask to join. We always let them. Football, for us, was community.

After matches, we would sit near the church steps, shirts soaked, passing bottles of Ting between us and discussing everything from Marcus Garvey to who was the best reggae vocalist — Dennis Brown or Beres Hammond. Those were sacred moments — brotherhood sealed in sweat and sun. We'd argue, laugh, and sometimes fall into reflective silence, watching the sky shift from gold to indigo.

One afternoon, after a particularly intense match against a rival team from Cross Roads, we sat nursing bruises and pride. Gauntlet had scored twice, Bruce had saved a penalty, and I had limped off with a twisted ankle. Findlay, ever the dramatist, declared, *"This is what freedom feel like – mud on yuh skin, sun on yuh back, and no one telling yuh what to do."* (This is what freedom feels like-mud on your skin, sun on your back, and no one telling you what to do).

Nello nodded, adding, "Football is the only place where poor man and rich man speak the same language."

We didn't always win, but we always showed up. Rain or shine, exam season or holiday, we played. And in playing, we healed. The field became a sanctuary, a place where we could forget the weight of expectations, the sting of rejection, the ache of homesickness. It was where we reminded ourselves that we were more than students — we were warriors, artists, brothers.

Sometimes, we'd play under the fading light, the church bells ringing in the distance, and I'd feel something sacred in the air. Not religious, but spiritual. A kind of communion. The ball would move from foot to foot, and I'd think of my father's stories, my mother's prayers, and the legacy I was trying to build. Every tackle, every sprint, every goal was a verse in that story.

There were moments of tension too — arguments over missed passes, frustration with referees, bruised egos. But we always found our way back. Bruce once broke up a heated exchange between Gauntlet and Findlay by saying, "*Yuh both wrong. Now pass the ball and hush.*" (You are both wrong. Now pass the ball and hush). And just like that, peace returned.

We played tournaments too — small ones organized by local youth groups or community centers. We'd pile into borrowed vans, boots dangling from windows, and arrive like underdogs with fire in our eyes. We didn't have matching kits or fancy gear, but we had heart. And that was enough. We won some, lost others, but always left with stories.

One tournament in particular stand out. It was held in Spanish Town, and the final match was against a team known for their aggression. The field was rough, the crowd rowdy, and the stakes high. We played like men possessed—Gauntlet scored a header, Nello assisted with a no-look pass, and I cleared a goal-bound shot with a last-ditch slide. We won 2-1. The trophy was small, but the pride was immense. We carried it back to Scots Kirk like it was the World Cup.

Years later, when life scattered us across cities and careers, I'd still pass by Scots Kirk and feel the pull. I'd hear echoes of laughter, the thud of boots on grass, the whistle of wind through goalposts. I'd remember Findlay's wild runs, Bruce's quiet strength, Nello's wisdom, Andypow's skill, Cheva's goals and Gauntlet's fire. And I'd remember myself—young, determined, and full of dreams.

Football gave me more than bruises and glory — it gave me belonging. It taught me discipline, teamwork, and the beauty of shared struggle. It reminded me that greatness isn't always loud — it can be found in muddy fields, in quiet passes, in the way a team lifts each other up.

And so, when I speak of my time at Mico, I don't just speak of classrooms and dorms. I speak of Scots Kirk. Of the field that held our stories. Of the afternoons that shaped our souls. Of the brotherhood that still lives in every step I take.

During my whirlwind of studies and football, I also found myself entangled in a relationship that was both magical and maddening: Michelle Needham. She was a fellow student at Mico — tall, graceful, with cheekbones sharp enough to cut glass and eyes that flickered between fire and ice. Michelle was ambition personified. She was studying to become a school guidance counsellor, and even then, she carried herself like someone already entrusted with the futures of others.

Michelle didn't just walk into a room — she entered with intention. Her notebooks were color-coded, her calendar precise, and her goals written in bold ink. I, with my poetry scribbled on the backs of handouts and my heart tangled in metaphors, was both fascinated and intimidated. "You write poems. I write plans," she once said, not as a dismissal, but as a challenge. And I accepted.

Our relationship was passionate, but not always peaceful. We fought over politics, time, attention, and once — over whether Beenie Man or Buju Banton had better lyrics. That particular debate lasted three days and involved a handwritten list of songs, lyrical analysis, and a surprise mixtape from Findlay, who declared himself the "unbiased judge." Michelle argued for Buju's depth and grit; I defended Beenie's cleverness and charisma. In the end, we agreed to disagree — then kissed under the clock tower like it was a truce signed in moonlight.

The make-ups were worth it. Long walks to Devon House. Shared scoops of soursop ice cream. Early morning bus rides to Half-Way Tree just to hold hands in the back row. Michelle had a way of making ordinary moments feel cinematic. She'd tilt her head when she laughed, lean in when she listened, and sometimes, when I was deep in thought, she'd whisper, "Come back to me." And I always did.

She forced me to sharpen myself. Michelle didn't tolerate laziness — not in herself, not in me. She questioned my comfort zones, challenged my assumptions, and once rewrote the conclusion of one of my essays because she said it "lacked conviction." I was furious at first, but when I reread it, I saw her point. She helped me dream wider, think deeper, and articulate my purpose with more clarity.

There were quiet moments too — nights when we sat on the dorm steps, watching the stars, speaking in half-sentences and shared silences. She'd rest her head on my shoulder, and I'd feel the weight of her trust. We talked about legacy, about the kind of educators we wanted to become, about the homes we hoped to build. Michelle believed in structure, in healing, in the power of intentional love. I believed in rhythm, in story, in the magic of presence. Somehow, we met in the middle.

And though the relationship would eventually fade—pulled apart by ambition, geography, and the quiet erosion of time—she left me with a sharper edge, a clearer vision, and a few unforgettable nights under the Kingston moon. Michelle was a chapter I didn't expect, but one I'll never forget. She taught me that love isn't always soft—it can be fierce, demanding, and transformative. And sometimes, that's exactly what we need.

And then there was Charmaine Walker, better known as Ginger—a nickname earned not for the color of her hair, but for her spicy personality. Ginger was unapologetic, raw, and hilarious. She spoke her mind with surgical precision and had zero tolerance for nonsense. *"Mi nuh business if yuh like me,"* (I don't care if you like me) she'd say, *"mi like miself enough fi both of wi."* (I like myself enough for the both of us). She and I had a platonic friendship rooted in respect and mutual laughter. She was one of the few people who could roast me and live to tell the tale. *"You really think yuh have lyrics?"* (Do you really think you have lyrics?) she once teased, *"Mi granny write better love letters dan you.*" (My grandmother writes better love letters than you).

Ginger had timing. She knew when to drop a joke, when to call out hypocrisy, and when to simply sit beside you in silence. She was the kind of friend who didn't need permission to speak truth. If your shirt was wrinkled, she'd say so. If your ego was inflated, she'd pop it. But if your spirit was low, she'd lift it — without fanfare, without fuss.

She had a soft heart beneath the armor. She would check in when I looked tired, slip me an extra patty from the cafeteria, and defend me when others misunderstood me. Once, when I bombed a teaching practice, she met me afterward and said, "So what? Next one better. You still brilliant." And she meant it. Ginger didn't believe in coddling, but she believed in you. Fiercely.

We had a rhythm — banter in the mornings, debates in the afternoons, and long talks on the dorm steps when the campus quieted down. She'd lean back, arms crossed, eyes scanning the stars like she was reading them. *"Yuh ever feel like we bigger than this place?"* (Have you ever felt like we are bigger than this place?) she asked once. I nodded. *"But this place still shaping we,"* (But this place is still shaping us) I replied.

She smiled. *"True. But mi shaping it back."* (True, but I am shaping it back).

Ginger was a force. She organized study sessions, led student protests, and once convinced the canteen staff to extend lunch hours during exam week. She had influence — not because she sought it, but because she earned it. People listened when Ginger spoke. Not out of fear, but out of respect.

Years later, we stayed in touch. Ginger would migrate to Canada, helping hundreds of students find their footing. She became a guidance counsellor, just like Michelle once dreamed of, and her office was known as a safe haven for newcomers, misfits, and dreamers. She sent me photos of her desk — cluttered with affirmation cards, Jamaican flags, and a mug that read *"Queen of Real Talk."* She hadn't changed. Just expanded.

And so I do. For Ginger. For the fierce and the fearless. For the friend who taught me that truth is love, and love is never quiet.

Looking back, those years at Mico weren't just about teacher training or lectures on Bloom's Taxonomy. They were about becoming. About transformation through the alchemy of friendship, football, failure, and love. Mico was more than a college — it was a crucible. A place where raw potential met fire, and where the heat of experience forged something lasting.

Lushington House molded my leadership. It taught me that authority without empathy is hollow, and that true influence is earned in the quiet moments — helping a roommate through grief, staying up late to edit a lesson plan, standing firm when rules felt unjust. I learned to lead not with volume, but with presence. To be the kind of captain who knew every name, every struggle, every triumph.

Scots Kirk strengthened my body and brotherhood. That uneven field, tucked behind

167

the church, became sacred ground. It was where I learned rhythm, resilience, and the beauty of shared struggle. The sweat, the bruises, the laughter — they stitched us together. And in those post-match reflections, passing bottles of Ting between us, I discovered that vulnerability and strength are not opposites — they are companions.

Michelle stretched my heart. She taught me that love isn't just poetry — it's accountability. That being seen is powerful, but being challenged is transformative. Her ambition sharpened mine. Her questions forced me to articulate my dreams. And though our paths diverged, her imprint remained — in the way I held space for others, in the way I dared to dream beyond the familiar.

Ginger sharpened my confidence. She was the mirror that didn't flatter, but always reflected truth. Her humor was a balm, her loyalty a shield. She reminded me that self-worth isn't negotiable, and that showing up for others begins with showing up for yourself. Even now, when I speak truth to power, when I advocate for a misunderstood student, I hear

168

her voice: *"Mi like miself enough fi both of wi."* (I like myself enough for the both of us). And Nello, Karen, and Findlay—my ride-or-die tribe—kept me grounded and soaring at once. They were my compass, my chorus, my co-authors. We built something sacred in those years—a fellowship rooted in laughter, learning, and legacy. We didn't just survive Mico—we made it ours.

Years later, when I now stand before my own students in Florida classrooms, guiding them through essays, emotions, and expectations, I draw from my well. I lead like a House Captain. I care like Karen. I coach like Nello. I listen like Michelle had taught me. I joke like Ginger. And sometimes, late at night, when I reflect on the path behind me, I smile at the memory of a young man chasing a football across a dusty field, chasing dreams under Caribbean skies, becoming something more than I ever imagined. Because Mico didn't just prepare me to teach—it prepared me to love, to lead, and to live with purpose. And that, more than any credential, is the legacy I carry into every classroom, every conversation, every moment of becoming.

The Mico Graduation. June 1994

Uncle Basil

At times when Mama was bogged down by financial constraints, it was my Uncle Basil who stepped in. Quietly, without fuss, he filled the gaps that the untimely passing of my dad and poverty left behind. School fees, exam costs, bus fare when the money just wasn't there — he made sure I could walk through doors that would have otherwise stayed shut. It was Uncle Basil who played an integral role in making my enrollment at Mico Teachers' College possible.

170

Without him, that chapter of my life may never have been written.

Technically, Uncle Basil was my grand-uncle, since he was my father's uncle. But that never mattered. He was my uncle, and that was that. Titles in our family weren't bound by bloodlines alone; they were defined by who showed up, who stood steady when the storms came. And Uncle Basil always did.

His wife, Marcia, was no less a part of that generosity. While Uncle Basil was the one who handled the financial weight, it was Auntie Marcia (Mummy) who gave the support a softer edge—offering a hot meal, a bed for the night, or words of encouragement like when my heart was shattered by my breakup with Iniko. She had a laugh that filled a room, the kind of laugh that told you there was still joy to be found, even when life pressed hard. Together, they made a formidable team: Basil with his steady hand, Marcia with her warmth and joy.

Their children—Lloyd, Rohan, Angie, and Rayon, and Ian, Marcia's younger brother—were cousins to me, though by strict family trees they were a generation removed. But in truth, those lines blurred; we grew together, loved together, and sometimes argued like siblings. We belonged to one another in the way only family shaped by both closeness and necessity can.

Lloyd carried himself with a certain quiet responsibility, so much like his father, always seeming older than his years. Even as boys, he had a steadiness that made you trust him. That quality never left him, and in adulthood it became one of the anchors of our bond. Today, we live less than a hundred miles apart in Florida, and that closeness has allowed our relationship to deepen in ways I never take for granted. Lloyd is more than a cousin; he is a brother in every sense that matters.

I remember when he visited me in April of 2025. The day was unremarkable by the calendar, but it became one of those rare, sacred afternoons that you carry with you. We sat for hours, talking as if time itself had stretched just for us. The conversation ebbed and flowed — childhood memories, family stories, the weight of responsibility, the strangeness of growing older. And all the while, green Heineken bottles clinked between us, the laughter spilling as freely as the drink. There was something deeply healing about it, as if each sip washed away a little of life's exhaustion, as if each shared story stitched our bond tighter. We talked and drank as though our lives depended on it, not in desperation, but in the kind of communion that only family forged through trials can understand.

Rohan, by contrast, was always the spark of mischief. Quick-witted, ready with a joke or a clever twist, he had a way of keeping us all on our toes. His energy could turn an ordinary day into something unexpected, his humor a balm when things were heavy.

Angie, meanwhile, had a gentleness that reminded me so much of her mother. She carried Marcia's warmth in her voice, her gestures, her way of seeing the good in people. In fact, Angie and I attended Mico Teachers' College at the same time, though I was two years ahead of her. I remember the sight of her walking across campus with her books pressed against her chest, her quiet determination

173

evident in every step. To share that season of our lives — our family's sacrifices paying off in the pursuit of education — was something special. It connected us not just as cousins, but as fellow dreamers shaping futures with the tools given to us.

Lloyd, Uncle Basil. Rayon, Rohan

And then there was Rayon, the youngest, the perpetual live wire. His energy was inexhaustible, his spirit irrepressible. He could turn even the dullest day into laughter, his spark infectious to anyone who came near. He carried the joy of youth into every space he entered, a reminder that sometimes resilience is found in refusing to let life's weight snuff out your laughter.

Alongside them was Ian, Aunt Marcia's younger brother. Though not Uncle Basil's child, Ian was woven into the life of their household in such a way that he felt inseparable from the family fabric. He was the kind of uncle-cousin who could drop in with a story, a joke, or a word of advice just when it was needed. Ian had an easygoing presence, a way of putting people at ease, and when he was around the house, there was always an added hum of life. For me, Ian became part of the extended circle that reminded me that family wasn't only blood, but bond, memory, and shared laughter.

A Young Uncle Basil

Together, the four children and Ian formed a constellation around Basil and Marcia. With Lloyd's steady presence, Rohan's wit, Angie's kindness, Rayon's spark, and Ian's easy warmth, I felt surrounded by a net of support that made me believe I could withstand whatever life threw at me. And even now, decades later, those ties endure — not just across states and seas, but in the everyday gestures, the

176

visits, the phone calls, and the laughter we still share.

Looking back, I realize that their home was more than just a place to visit—it was an anchor. When Mama's pockets were empty, when stress pressed down on her shoulders, when the weight of raising us alone threatened to crush her spirit, it was Uncle Basil and his family who helped carry that load. They did it without boasting, without ever making us feel like charity cases. Their help came wrapped in dignity, a reminder that family was supposed to be a safety net, not a scoreboard.

When I think about my own journey, about standing in front of students as a teacher, about the pride I feel in that role, I know that the foundation was laid not just by Mama's sacrifices, but also by Uncle Basil's steady hand. He and Mummy believed in education, not just as a path to survival but as a way to rise, to become more than your circumstances.

"Schooling will carry you further than strength ever could," she once said, her voice firm, her eyes steady. I didn't fully grasp it at the time, but those words have never left me.

It wasn't just money that my uncle gave. It was belief. The kind of belief that tells a young boy from Denham Town that his dreams are not too fragile, not too far-fetched. He invested in me as though he already saw the man I might become. And with Marcia's laughter in the background, with Lloyd's quiet nods, Rohan's teasing, Angie's kindness, and Rayon's sparks of humor, I felt surrounded by a chorus of support.

Now, as I look back, I see that my path to Mico Teachers' College was not walked alone. Every book I bought, every lecture I attended, every degree I earned—my uncle's fingerprints are on them. Marcia's spirit is stitched into them. Their children's echoes are woven into that story, too. They remind me that success is never solitary; it is built on the sacrifices, the gifts, and the unheralded generosity of others.

And so, when I speak of Uncle Basil, I speak not just of a man who paid school fees and gave me money. I speak of a man who understood legacy, who lived out the truth that family means stepping in when it matters most. Grand-uncle by name, uncle by heart, and family in every sense that counted.

Commeth The Teacher

In 1994, teaching diploma in hand, I returned to my alma mater, St. George's College — this time not in khaki uniform as a wide-eyed student, but in pressed long sleeves and polished shoes as a teacher of English and Religious Education. Walking through the school gates that first morning was surreal. The scent of freshly cut grass on the football field mingled with the faint tang of chalk dust drifting from open classroom windows. The same colonial-era buildings that had once towered over me as a teenager now seemed a little smaller, but they carried the same echoes of laughter, shouts, and the ever-present clatter of boys on the move.

The classrooms were cramped — often packed with over forty restless boys squeezed into wooden desks designed for thirty. The air was always thick: part heat, part the energy of teenage boys who were still learning how to focus their wild, brilliant energy. Some were noisy, some sat slouched with an almost artistic level of disinterest, and others stared back at me with eyes that revealed potential waiting to be unlocked. The blackboard became my battlefield, the chalk my weapon of choice. But I had something even more potent than lesson plans or exam rubrics. I had passion.

I refused to teach English like a dry list of rules and assignments. Instead, I made it a living, breathing thing. Shakespeare was not left to wither in the pages of Elizabethan English; instead, I gave Macbeth a Kingston backstreet swagger, turning "Is this a dagger which I see before me?" into "*Is dis a dagger mi see before mi?*" delivered with such theatrical conviction that even the boys who usually slept in the back row leaned forward, grinning.

Chaucer's Canterbury Tales didn't stay in medieval England either. I reimagined the characters as market vendors, minibus drivers, and sound system selectors, their journeys transformed into a trek down Half Way Tree Road. I brought *The Psalms* to life by reading them over a slow reggae beat, my voice carrying the rhythm of a dub poet.

It was unorthodox, but it worked. Students who had dreaded literature began to engage, not because they suddenly loved school, but because they could see themselves in the stories.

181

When it came to *To Kill a Mockingbird*, I guided them through its themes of justice and prejudice, but through the lens of Jamaica's own social issues. The discussions moved beyond Rema, Jungle, into Trench Town, Tivoli, and Constant Spring. We debated real-life court cases from the *Daily Gleaner*, drawing parallels between *Harper Lee's* fictional trial and the headlines that made the evening news.

My Religious Education classes were equally transformative. I refused to be the kind of teacher who merely drilled scripture into students' heads. Instead, I broadened their horizons. We learned about Islam, Sikhism, Buddhism, Judaism, Christianity, Hinduism, and Rastafarianism, exploring the rituals, histories, and philosophies that shaped each faith. I made it clear that spirituality wasn't confined to pews and altars — it could be found in the rhythms of Nyabinghi drumming, in the chants at a dancehall stage show, or in the quiet of a fisherman's early morning prayer before heading out to sea.

The boys responded. They asked questions — real, thoughtful questions. They debated respectfully (and sometimes not-so-respectfully, because teenage boys will be teenage boys), but the important thing was that they were thinking. They were making connections between the classroom and the world around them.

By 1995, the results spoke for themselves. My GCE Religious Education class achieved a 79% pass rate — a school record that has yet to be matched. But more than numbers, it was the stories of transformation that mattered most to me. Among those I taught were Dr. Azizi Seixas, who would become an internationally recognized public health researcher and professor, and Dr. Parris Lyew Ayee, who would rise to prominence in geospatial technology and innovation. These were boys who had once sat in those cramped desks, who had laughed at my Shakespeare-in-patois, and who had absorbed the lessons of both text and life.

Still, teaching at St. George's wasn't without its challenges. The resources were limited — old textbooks missing pages, chalk that crumbled in my hands, and classrooms that could turn into ovens in the afternoon heat. Distractions were constant. Sometimes it was the sound of a football match outside pulling half the class's attention through the windows. Other times it was the hum of downtown life drifting up from North Street — music, shouting vendors, and the occasional blaring of a car horn. But I had learned early on that the key wasn't to fight these distractions — it was to harness them.

If the boys were restless, I got them moving — group activities, role-plays, debates where they stood in front of the class to defend their ideas. If a commotion outside interrupted the lesson, I wove it into the teaching: "Gentlemen, that shouting you hear? That's conflict. Now, how do we resolve it without losing our humanity? Let's talk about Atticus Finch again..."

Beyond academics, I saw myself as a mentor. Many of the boys came from challenging circumstances — single-parent homes, communities where violence was an everyday reality, or households struggling financially. I made it my mission to be more than "just" a teacher. I stayed after school to run extra tutoring sessions. I walked boys to the bus stop if they were worried about passing through a rival neighborhood. I even helped a few of them prepare for job interviews, teaching them how to shake hands firmly and make eye contact.

One of my most enduring memories was of a boy named "R," who had been labeled a troublemaker by almost every teacher in the school. R's grades were poor, and his attendance was spotty, but I noticed something: whenever the class read aloud, R's voice carried a certain rhythm, almost like a deejay toasting over a beat. I encouraged him to write spoken word pieces in patois, then translate them into English. By the end of the term, R wasn't just passing English — he was performing his poetry at the school talent show and would go on to becoming reggae music sensation Iyah Tear.

Moments like that confirmed what I had always believed: teaching was about seeing the human being in front of you, not just the student number on the roll call.

I also became deeply involved in extracurricular life. I coached the debating team, assisted coaching of the School's Challenge Quiz Team, ran the school's cultural club, and occasionally stepped in as a football team mentor. On Fridays, I would host "Literature & Lyrics," an informal lunchtime gathering where boys could bring in song lyrics, poems, or short stories to share and discuss. Everything from Bob Marley to Buju Banton to Pablo Neruda was fair game, as long as they could explain the meaning and the craft behind the words.

By the end of my time teaching at St. George's, I had left more than academic success in my wake. I had instilled a culture of curiosity, creativity, and respect for the power of words. Former students would often stop me on the street years later — some in suits heading to work, others in uniforms serving in the army or police force — to say, "Sir, you probably don't remember me, but you taught me English in 1994. You made me like reading. You made me believe I could pass."

I would smile and nod, often pretending to remember the specific face, but knowing deep down that it didn't matter. What mattered was that they remembered me — not for the grades, but for the way I made them feel capable, seen, and valued.

Teaching at my old school had been a full-circle moment — one that challenged me, shaped me, and reaffirmed my calling. I wasn't just delivering lessons from a curriculum guide. I was shaping futures, one cramped classroom, one Shakespeare soliloquy in patois, and one reggae-backed *Psalm* at a time. And in doing so, I had carved a legacy that would live on in every student who walked out of St. George's gates with a little more confidence, a little more wisdom, and a belief that their story, too, was worth telling.

Sharon

It was during one of my evening adult education classes that I met Sharon. She came in on the second week of the term, slipping into the room with a quiet confidence that made her stand out from the moment she took her seat. Her hair was pulled back neatly, her books stacked with care, and her eyes carried a sharpness that suggested she wasn't there to make up numbers. She had purpose. She had presence.

I noticed her before I even realized I was staring. The world in that small classroom seemed to dull around her. Chalk scraped across the blackboard, chairs creaked, pens scratched across paper, but Sharon carried her own atmosphere—something steady, almost magnetic. She didn't seek attention, yet attention bent toward her all the same.

The first time our eyes met, it wasn't dramatic—it was subtle, a flicker of recognition, as though she had looked straight through my skin and found something I didn't even know I was carrying. I felt the jolt in my chest like a hand tapping me awake. There was no smile, no nod, no exchange of words. Just a glance that lingered a second longer than necessary. But that was enough to etch itself into memory.

As the weeks passed, I found myself measuring time not by the ticking of the clock, but by her presence in the room. I began to anticipate the moment she would slip through the door, sometimes rushing in with a pen clutched in hand, other times gliding in with an ease that made me wonder if she even knew how beautiful she looked when she was unbothered. My penmanship improved; my notes grew sharper. I sat straighter, listened closer, laughed easier. Sharon, without saying a word to me, had already changed the way I inhabited the room.

One evening, during a break, I worked up the courage to speak to her. My heart thumped like a bass drum, loud enough, I thought, for her to hear. She was sitting on Winchester Wall and talking to my childhood friend Alva Taylor.

"You're really serious about your studies," I said, my voice cracking slightly.

She looked at me with a cold stone faced, unreadable expression, then replied.

"Isn't that why we're here?"

I smiled awkwardly, but inside I was reeling. It was such a simple exchange, yet her voice lingered in my mind like the echo of a song.

After that, our conversations grew — small at first, about assignments, the teacher's quirks, the crowded bus rides home. But in those conversations, I found an openness, a wit, a kindness that pulled me in. She laughed softly, never too loud, and when she did, her eyes carried the laughter long after her lips had quieted. That laugh — gentle, melodic — became the melody that scored my evenings.

Sharon was not like anyone else I had ever met. There was no pretense about her, no attempt to dazzle. She didn't have to. Her confidence came from someplace deeper, a quiet river of assurance that ran beneath everything she did. She reminded me of poetry — not the kind printed in books, but the kind lived out in flesh and breath, where every movement, every glance, every word carried rhythm.

190

Soon, I realized it wasn't just admiration I felt—it was a stirring of something far greater. I would drive home after class with her image imprinted on my mind, the way she held her pen, the way she tilted her head when thinking, the way her presence calmed the chaos of the day. She had become, in those weeks, both the question and the answer I didn't know I was looking for.

Meeting Sharon in that modest classroom was like stumbling upon a flame in the dark. It was steady, bright, and warm. And as much as I tried to tell myself to take it slow, my heart had already leapt forward, carried by something both terrifying and exhilarating: the beginning of love…again.

Sharon was ambitious, but not the kind that announced itself loudly. She carried it in her discipline—the way she took notes with tidy precision, the way she asked questions that cut straight to the heart of the topic, the way she stayed behind after class to clarify a point, never wasting a moment. I had seen plenty of students in my years teaching—some there out of obligation, some out of boredom, some chasing

191

a certificate without caring much about the journey. But Sharon... Sharon was different. She wasn't there to play games or waste time. She was there to rise, and rise she did.

At first, I kept it professional. I admired her drive from a respectful distance. I questioned Alva relentlessly about her. I noticed how she listened intently, never distracted by the chatter around her. I saw the way she encouraged her friends Analia and Dorothy, offering quiet help without ever condescending. But over the weeks, that professional admiration softened into something warmer. I found myself looking forward to her presence, glancing toward the door in those first few minutes of class to see if she had arrived.

Outside of class, our conversations started casually — a remark about the lesson, a comment on the weather, a shared laugh about the chaos of Kingston traffic. But soon, those moments stretched longer. We would linger after class, talking about books, music, the state of Jamaica's politics, and the weight of ambition when resources were scarce. Sharon had opinions — well-reasoned, firmly rooted in experience — and she spoke to them without apology. I liked that. It was refreshing.

Our first unofficial "date" wasn't even meant to be a date. One evening, after class ended early, I offered her a ride to Half Way Tree, where she could catch her bus home. I sneakily took the long way, slowly driving past street vendors selling roasted corn and boiled peanuts, past the endless stream of minibus drivers calling out their routes, past school children in rumpled uniforms making their way home. The city was alive — horns blaring, music spilling from corner bars, the smell of jerk chicken drifting through the air. And somewhere along that ride, we discovered we shared the same dry humor, the same love for late-night conversations, the same stubborn refusal to settle for less than we dreamed. Somehow, I still am unable to explain how it happened, we ended up at Carib Cinema and watched *Speed*, a movie starring Keanu Reeves and Sandra Bullock.

From there, things unfolded naturally. Long walks became a habit. We would wander through Devon House gardens eating ice cream — pistachio for her, grapenut for me — or sit by the waterfront at Victoria Pier, eating Black Forest cake and watching the ships in the distance and imagining far-off destinations. Sometimes we stayed in, cooking together in her small kitchen in Pembroke Hall, Sharon seasoning the meat while I chopped vegetables, music playing low in the background. Our affection grew not through grand gestures but through consistency — the little things, the shared laughter, the quiet understanding.

By late 1995, we were a couple in every sense of the word. And soon, our love took on a new dimension with our daughter, Jilisha. From the moment she came into the world, Jilisha was a force—brilliant, sassy, and wide-eyed, as if she had been born already curious about everything around her. I was smitten. I loved being a father in a way I hadn't anticipated. I saw it as my greatest calling yet, a responsibility that both humbled and inspired me.

Fatherhood made me more patient in some ways. I could spend hours just watching Jilisha sleep, her tiny chest rising and falling in rhythm. I loved making her laugh — silly faces, exaggerated voices, bouncing her on my knee. I wanted to give her everything: security, opportunities, and the kind of love that left no room for doubt. But fatherhood didn't erase the struggle.

Teaching during the day was already demanding, but to make ends meet, I took on evening school classes at St. George's College. Those sessions were filled with men and women determined to grab hold of education after long days of their own — factory workers, clerks, apprentices, young mothers. They came tired but hungry for knowledge, and I gave them everything I had. And sometimes, Jilisha came with me.

Sharon would hand her to me at the school gates, bundled up against the Kingston night air, and I would walk across Winchester Park with her tiny fingers gripping mine. My students smiled when they saw me arrive with her — some chuckling, some shaking their heads in disbelief.

"Teacha, yuh bring di baby tonight?" (Teacher did you bring the baby with you tonight?) they would ask.

I would nod, smiling, and reply, "She's auditing the class."

I'd set her up at the back of the classroom with a blanket or in her stroller, her eyes bright and alert. At first she'd coo and babble, as if adding her own commentary to my lessons, and the class would laugh softly. Sometimes she would sit quietly, fiddling with a toy while I explained English grammar or guided students through comprehension passages. And sometimes — especially on the long nights — she would fall asleep to the sound of chalk scratching across the blackboard, her breathing steady like a lullaby that kept me going.

The students, many of them parents themselves, adored her. During breaks, they'd gather around, peeking into the stroller or holding her tiny hands. One woman told me,

"Sir, mi respect yuh. Yuh teach whole day, then whole night, and still bring yuh pickney. Dat is

love." (Sir I respect you. You teach the whole day, then the whole night, and still bring your child. That is love). Her words stayed with me.

It wasn't always easy. There were nights when she grew restless, and I'd have to pace at the back of the classroom, rocking her gently while still explaining a concept to my students. Other times, I wrote notes on the board with one arm while cradling her in the other. I was exhausted, stretched between fatherhood and teaching, but strangely, those evenings never felt like a burden. They felt like a calling.

I realized that Jilisha wasn't just my daughter—she was also my motivation, my symbol of why education mattered. When I told my evening students that they were investing in their children's futures by sitting in that classroom, I knew it wasn't just a line. I was living it. Jilisha was right there, watching me teach, absorbing lessons before she could even read.

Looking back, I see those nights as a holy fusion of my two callings: fatherhood and teaching. George's, the school that had once raised me, now held me as a young teacher and young father, carrying chalk in one hand and a baby bag in the other. I was determined to succeed at both.

And though Jilisha was too young to remember those evenings, I believe a part of her carries them still. The rhythm of chalk, the hum of a classroom, the sight of her father standing steady before a group of students — those were her first lessons. She taught me resilience, and I taught her, without words, that learning and love could share the same space.

Fatherhood, I soon discovered, wasn't just about raising a child — it was also about raising myself. Every day with Jilisha pressed me into becoming a better version of the man I thought I already was. She stretched my patience, sharpened my priorities, and deepened my empathy.

In the classroom, I began to notice the difference. I taught with a softer edge, listening more closely when a boy's excuses seemed flimsy. Instead of only seeing laziness or indiscipline, I started to wonder about the child behind the excuse: Did he have a baby sister he rocked to sleep at night? Was he hungry? Did he have a father waiting at home? That shift—seeing my own daughter in the faces of my students—transformed the way I carried myself as a teacher.

Jilisha also taught me time. A child does not wait for your convenience. She needed me in the moment—whether I was exhausted, grading papers, or still in my shirt and tie from school. That urgency spilled into how I approached lessons. I stopped putting off the important things—like encouraging a struggling student, calling out potential when I saw it, or taking a few minutes to really listen. I learned that delay can be its own kind of neglect. So, I tried to show up for my students the way I wanted to always show up for my daughter: fully present.

There were nights when I returned home after evening school, Jilisha asleep in my arms, and I would whisper prayers over her tiny form. I promised her that no matter what struggles we faced—financial, emotional, or otherwise—I would never stop learning how to be her father.

And quietly, those prayers became vows to my students too. If I could hold one child with such tenderness, why not extend that same spirit of care to the dozens I met every day?

Fatherhood also taught me humility. I quickly realized that babies don't care about titles, degrees, or reputations. They don't care if you've published an article or coached a winning team. They just want to know you're there. That truth reset my compass. It wasn't about how much applause I received in public, but about how consistently I could love in private—at home with Jilisha, and in the classroom with my students.

And perhaps the greatest lesson was endurance. The juggling act of fatherhood, teaching, and evening schoolwork wasn't easy. But I came to see that consistency—showing up day after day, night after night—was a kind of love in itself. Jilisha didn't remember the exhaustion etched in my eyes, only that I was there. My students didn't always grasp the sacrifices I made to teach them, only that I kept showing up.

Looking back, I realize those early years of fatherhood trained me in ways no teacher's college ever could. They taught me that education is not just instruction — it is love practiced in daily, ordinary, and often exhausting ways.

I was still young, still figuring life out. My temper, that old companion from my teenage years, sometimes flared when stress ran high. Money was always tight. Kingston, for all its beauty, was also relentless. The cost of living scraped every dollar thin. A sudden increase in bus fares, an unexpected medical bill, a broken fridge — any one of these could throw the household into crisis.

The pressure gnawed at me. I was teaching, yes, but teacher salaries in Jamaica at the time barely stretched far enough to cover essentials. Rent, utilities, food, school expenses — it all added up faster than pay could come in. I took on extra work where I could, tutoring in the evenings, marking papers late into the night. But even that sometimes wasn't enough.

It was in those moments of desperation that I sometimes veered into decisions I would later regret — impulsive, short-term solutions to long-term problems. I wasn't proud of all of them. There were times I'd spend money earmarked for bills on something fleeting, chasing the comfort of instant gratification after weeks of grind and worry. There were moments I leaned too heavily into Kingston's hustle culture, making quick deals that skirted the edge of propriety. "*Egregious acts,*" I would later call them — half in jest, half in shame.

And yet, Sharon stood by me. She didn't excuse my mistakes, but she understood the pressures that fueled them. She pushed me to be better, not through nagging or ultimatums, but through example. Sharon was disciplined with money, meticulous in planning, and unshakable in her commitment to building a better future: something I would eventually learn from her, years later. She believed in hard work, yes, but also in working smart — in knowing when to say no, when to wait, when to save.

Our home life was a mix of joy and challenge. Weekends were for family outings —

trips to Hope Gardens, picnics at Fort Clarence Beach, visits to relatives where Jilisha was fussed over and spoiled with treats. But weekdays could be tense, especially when bills loomed or when I came home worn out and short-tempered from a long day. Arguments flared, cooled, and flared again, usually about me wasting money or time — two things we never seemed to have enough of.

Despite the friction, there was an undercurrent of resilience. We shared the same dream: to give our daughter a life beyond constant financial strain, to one day own a home, to travel, to create stability. That dream kept us moving forward, even when the road felt steep.

Kingston itself was both backdrop and character in our story. The city was vibrant — music in every corner, street life spilling into every open space — but it was also unforgiving. Crime was a reality. Jobs were scarce for many. Social inequality was inescapable. Yet, in that same environment, there was community — neighbors who would watch your child if you were late from work, shopkeepers who

203

extended credit when pay was slow, friends who would share a meal without expecting anything in return.

Sharon taught me a lesson, sometimes the hard way, that love wasn't just about romance or passion. It was about partnership. It was about weathering the rough patches without losing sight of each other in the process. She taught me that consistency mattered more than charm, that sacrifice was sometimes the purest form of love, and that building a life together meant facing the uncomfortable truths as much as celebrating the victories.

As 1995 gave way to 1996, we stood at a crossroads — not in our love, but in our future. The challenges weren't going away, and I knew something had to shift. I wanted to be more than just a good teacher and a loving father. I wanted to be a provider in the fullest sense, someone who could give Sharon and Jilisha the stability they deserved. That desire, that gnawing need to rise above the constant edge of financial worry, would eventually set in motion the next chapter of my life — one that would take me far beyond Kingston's shores.

Act II

Chapter I: Beckoning

London

In the early 2000s, an opportunity came. A door cracked open: a chance to travel, to study further, to experience teaching beyond Jamaica's shores. The UK beckoned, with its cold winters, old architecture, and complex classroom dynamics.

It wasn't an easy decision. Jamaica was home. My roots were deep in Tulip Lane, in St. George's, in Mico, in Cumberland. My brothers and sisters in education, my family, my friends—they were the threads that made the fabric of my life. But I also felt the tug of something bigger. I had begun to sense that my calling as an educator could not be contained within the borders of one island. I wanted to see how education was practiced in other places, to learn their systems, to test my own resilience and adaptability in unfamiliar waters.

Leaving Jamaica was as much an act of faith as it was a professional step. The skies above Norman Manley International Airport were tinged with grey, a mirror of the unknown I was about to face. Kingston faded into the clouds. My island — its warmth, its culture, its unfiltered honesty — disappeared beneath me as I crossed the Atlantic with little more than a suitcase, a stack of books, and the spirit of Tulip Lane.

My first stop was Birmingham, where I stayed with my grandfather in a small house nestled just a few blocks from Villa Park, home of Aston Villa Football Club. The roar of the crowd on match days carried through the narrow brick lanes like a war cry, and the locals wore claret and blue with the fervor of Jamaican evangelists. My grandfather, a tall, stoic man with kind eyes, introduced me to Britain with patience and precision. He taught me how to dress for the damp, how to read the bus timetables, how to stretch a pound in Tesco. Evenings were spent with the BBC murmuring in the background as I tuned my ear to clipped vowels and unfamiliar idioms. In the drizzle of quiet walks, I prayed for a sign.

It came in the form of a newspaper ad: Teaching vacancies in London schools. The very word "London" hummed with both possibility and fear.

By mid-August, I had made up my mind. I packed my suitcase again and boarded a National Express coach to the capital. Southgate was my destination, a suburban district in North London, quieter than the heart of the city but alive with energy. I crashed with a friend of my mother while I sent out CVs, knocked on school doors, and enrolled with teaching agencies.

Navigating London was a battle at first. The Underground — with its tangled lines, color-coded maps, and constant delays — felt like a test designed to break me. But necessity is a relentless teacher. I bought a foldable Tube map and studied it religiously until the Victoria, Piccadilly, and Northern lines ran through my veins. Soon I was hopping boroughs with confidence, a book always in hand. Derek Walcott, James Baldwin, Maya Angelou — they kept me company as I memorized the rhythm of stations. Each stop became a symbol: Seven Sisters was survival, Finsbury Park was frustration, King's Cross was courage.

Eventually, persistence bore fruit. I landed my first teaching position at St. Thomas More RC School in Wood Green, a diverse secondary school not far from Southgate. The corridors buzzed with students from Somalia, Nigeria, India, Bangladesh, Poland, the Caribbean — children who, like me, carried multiple worlds within them. Many were first- or second-generation immigrants, straddling cultures with unsure feet.

Teaching in London was unlike teaching in Jamaica. At Mico, I had honed resilience and creativity. In Denham Town, I had learned adaptability. In Kingston hospitals, I had learned discipline. All of it came into play now. A Shakespeare passage came alive when set against a reggae lyric. A history lesson found new weight when tied to Jamaica's colonial struggles. Even the most reluctant student perked up when I linked football tactics to essay structures.

The challenges were sharp. Classroom management required diplomacy and grit. Students tested boundaries more boldly than I had ever experienced. Cultural gaps loomed like canyons. Yet trust slowly grew. My accent, once a curiosity, became a badge of authenticity. My stories — of St. George's, of Tulip Lane — became lessons in resilience and identity.

Some days were hard. I remember afternoons when a lesson collapsed into chaos — students talking over me, paper airplanes sailing across the room, tempers flaring. On those days, I walked home with shoulders heavy, wondering if I had made the right

210

choice. But then there were the breakthroughs: the student who stayed behind after class to say thank you, the boy who discovered a love of poetry after comparing it to rap, the girl who handed me her essay with trembling hands and said, "Sir, this is the first time I think I've done something good." Those moments reminded me why I was there.

Life outside the classroom began to settle too. With my first paychecks, I saved carefully, and one grey November afternoon I bought my first car: a maroon Volvo 440, boxy, dependable. I named it Faith. That car gave me freedom — weekend drives into the countryside, easier grocery runs, and rainy-day pickups for Jilisha at Grange Park Primary. Each trip reminded me that I was slowly building a life, brick by brick, mile by mile.

Meanwhile, I pushed myself academically, enrolling at Middlesex University. Balancing study with teaching was grueling, but the long nights of reading and writing felt like echoes of kerosene-lamp evenings back in Tulip Lane. When I walked across the stage in 2006, degree in hand, it was more than a certificate. It was proof that my journey—from Kingston tenement yards to London lecture halls—was valid, worthy, unfolding exactly as it should.

London tested me. It stripped me of certainty, demanded resilience, and offered no safety net. But it also revealed the global nature of education. Teaching was never just about one classroom or one country—it was about preparing young minds to inherit a complicated world.

And so, I became not just a Jamaican teacher abroad, but a citizen of education. The world had beckoned, and I had answered. My roots did not weaken in foreign soil; they deepened, stretched, and bore new fruit.

Jilisha: The Arrival

Just three months into my new life, I welcomed my daughter, Jilisha, to England. She was six now—clever, inquisitive, Jamaican to the bone. She brought a kind of grounding that even poetry couldn't provide. Her arrival turned the rented room in Southgate, a leafy suburb in the northern fringes of North London, from a bachelor's holding bay into something more sacred: a father's first true home in a foreign land.

She stepped off the plane bundled in layers, her little pink Dora the Explorer suitcase bumping along behind her, eyes flicking nervously around Heathrow Airport like a frightened kitten in a strange room. Then came that Bolt-like burst of speed — arms flung wide, pure joy lighting up her face — as she raced forward and let out a shriek of "Dadday!" before crashing into me, the two of us collapsing to the floor in a laughing, tear-filled heap.

Her accent was thick, her questions endless.

"Daddy, why dem people no smile?" (Daddy why don't these people smile?).

I laughed, scooping her up in a bear hug. *"Dis a London, babygirl. Dem smile on the inside."*

(This is London baby girl, they smile on the inside).

For the first time in months, I felt whole. Her laughter echoed in the corners of my soul that had grown quiet since I left Kingston. She followed me everywhere—Cineworld movie theatre, the local Tesco, the job center. People thought she was shy, but I knew she was simply watching, absorbing this strange new world of grey skies and train delays. At night, curled beside me, she would whisper, "Daddy, tell me one more story 'bout Denham Town." And I always did.

Nine months later, Sharon arrived—tired, determined, and beautifully familiar.

The house in Southgate wasn't glamorous. It was a shared three-bedroom council house with creaky floorboards, mismatched furniture, and a window that coughed in the wind. But it was home.

Over the years, the house buzzed with life. Sharon quickly made it warm with her homemade curtains and potted plants. The smell of curry chicken and rice and peas wafted into the hallways every Sunday. On Saturday mornings, the sound of Dennis Brown or Whitney Houston filled the space while Jilisha helped clean, her tiny hands dragging a wet mop across the linoleum floor.

Sharon and I juggled life the way immigrant families did — stretching paychecks like elastic bands, dodging late fees, navigating endless paperwork, and learning the unspoken rules of a society that didn't always welcome us.

Bills came like clockwork, but paychecks were never quite enough. My teaching salary covered most essentials, but there were times I rode the bus to save on petrol. Sharon took on part-time jobs while enrolling in night courses, often commuting two hours across London to attend her lectures.

Sharon took no shortcuts. After long days of spreadsheets and tight deadlines, she would tuck Jilisha in, iron my shirts, and then sit at the kitchen table reviewing her ACCA materials.

Her dream was simple—to become a fully qualified accountant. But getting there meant burning the candle at both ends. She studied on buses, on trains, in waiting rooms. She memorized financial reporting standards while stirring the pot on the stove. I often watched her with quiet awe.

"Yuh a superhero," (You're a superhero) I would say.

She'd laugh, tired but resolute. "Superheroes don't get no sleep."

Our evenings were a dance of resilience. Jilisha would sit at the dining table doing her spelling homework, Sharon would have Excel open on one side of her notebook and a calculator on the other, and I would be marking Year 10 essays, red pen in hand. Occasionally, someone would stop and say, *"Lord, mi tired,"* (Lord I am tired) and we'd all laugh, because tired was constant—but so was love.

Jilisha flourished in school. Her accent softened, but her spirit didn't. She remained inquisitive, always asking about home—real

216

home—where mangoes grew in the backyard and uncles shouted from across zinc fences. She danced in school talent shows, joined the choir, and wrote stories that made her teachers pause.

"She's gifted," they told Sharon and me.

"Wi know," we'd answer, smiling like conspirators.

I continued teaching, my reputation growing. Students respected me. Colleagues leaned on me. I became the teacher parents requested by name. And every evening, when I came through the door, tired but full of stories, Sharon would hand me a plate and say, *"Tell me about di pickney dem."* (Tell me about the children).

It wasn't always easy. Winter months were brutal. Money was tight. There were moments when homesickness felt like a weight on my chest, when I would sit by the window with a cup of tea and watch the cold drizzle fall, wondering what Denham Town looked like under the same moon.

But we had each other. And that was enough.

And through it all, Sharon worked. Worked like gravity was trying to hold her back. Like the world was stacked against her and she had no intention of letting it win.

She took a job at Haringey Council as an administrative officer, tucked between departments, answering calls with a calm voice, logging complaints with precision, and sorting mail by hand when the system went down. It wasn't glamorous. It wasn't what she dreamed of. But it was honest work. And it was a foothold.

The hours were long, the demands unrelenting. She was often the first in the office and the last to leave, powering through piles of files, mastering databases she wasn't trained on, and covering for colleagues who left early. She smiled through stress, nodded through meetings, and let her work speak where her accent sometimes betrayed her.

But even that wasn't enough. She knew that to rise, to truly change the trajectory of her family, she needed more than experience — she needed qualifications.

The Teacher in London

As I settled in London, the corridors at St. Thomas More School buzzed with a different energy than in Jamaican schools. The student body was a patchwork of cultures: Somali, Turkish, Jamaican, Irish, Pakistani, Nigerian, and British-born white working class. Accents collided in the hallways. The slang shifted with every conversation. I quickly learned that "*Are you taking the mick?*" (Are you making fun of me?) meant teasing, "*innit*" (Isn't it) ended half the sentences, and "safe" was the word you used when you wanted to seal a deal of trust.

On my first day, I stood at the front of Year 10 English, looking at a sea of skeptical eyes. Some students slouched low in their chairs; others tapped pens rhythmically on the desk. One boy at the back — tall, hoodie up —

leaned to a friend and whispered just loud enough for me to hear, "He's got an accent, man." The class laughed.

I smiled, remembering similar moments at St. George's. "Yes," I replied, letting the Kingston in my voice pour through, "and so do you. But in here, accents just mean stories — and I hope you've brought yours.". That was the first flicker of connection. By the end of the week, the hoodie-wearing skeptic was reading lines from *Of Mice and Men* with a surprising depth of feeling.

Teaching in London meant adapting. Gone were the days of relying on tropical metaphors and reggae beats alone — here, I blended Shakespeare with grime music lyrics, compared Atticus Finch's quiet dignity to the quiet resilience of immigrant families in Hackney, and used Notting Hill Carnival as a way to talk about cultural identity. In Religious Education, the diversity of the classroom became a living curriculum. Students didn't just read about Islam or Hinduism; they shared firsthand stories of Eid feasts, Diwali lights, and Friday prayers.

The pace was relentless. I would be on a packed bus by 7:15 a.m., standing shoulder-to-shoulder with commuters, the smell of coffee and damp coats in the air. My evenings were often filled with marking exercise books, planning lessons, and calling parents. There were moments of fatigue — dark winter mornings when the sun seemed unwilling to rise, evenings when the rain never stopped, and the homesickness swelled quietly in my chest. But then a student would drop an essay on my desk with a surprising turn of phrase, or a shy Year 9 would volunteer to read aloud for the first time, and I would remember exactly why I was there.

Outside of the classroom, London offered its own education. Weekends were for exploring, strolling along the South Bank and ducking into the British Museum to marvel at ancient scripts, visiting Brixton Market to find yam and plantain that tasted close to home. I discovered a small Jamaican café in Wood Green where the curry goat rivaled any back in Kingston, and the owner, a man named Clive, would slip extra dumplings onto my plate with a wink.

221

Professionally, I began to build a reputation as a teacher who could reach the hard-to-reach students. Word spread among department heads and administrators. I was offered longer-term contracts, eventually securing a permanent post in the same school year. With stability came the chance to innovate—to launch a debating club, to take students on theatre trips to see Macbeth at the Globe, to start a lunchtime "Poetry and Patties" group where students read their own poems over beef patties and ginger beer.

There were challenges, too. London classrooms could be volatile. I broke up fights, mediated disputes between rival friendship groups, and sat in countless meetings about behavior plans. Funding cuts meant fewer teaching assistants, and paperwork sometimes felt endless. But I leaned on the same philosophy that carried me at St. George's—relationships first. I learned my students' stories, met their parents at parents' evenings, and found small ways to affirm them daily.

In 2006, I completed my degree at Middlesex University, and was awarded

Qualified Teacher Status (QTS), a milestone that cemented my academic and professional standing in the UK. Balancing studies, teaching, and family had been no small feat, but it gave me a deeper sense of accomplishment—proof that my move to London had not just been a leap of faith, but a step forward.

By the end of my first decade in London, I had seen cohorts of students graduate and move on. Some wrote back from university. Others dropped by the school years later, wearing work uniforms or carrying their own children, to say thank you. For me, those moments were as valuable as any official recognition. They were proof that teaching was never just about the lesson plan; it was about planting seeds in young lives and trusting they would grow.

London had not been easy. It had demanded resilience, adaptation, and a willingness to start over. But in return, it had given me new ways to teach, a deeper appreciation for cultural diversity, and a richer sense of the global threads that weave through education. In many ways, my classroom in

North London had become a microcosm of the world—a place where accents mixed, faiths intertwined, and literature served as common ground.

I quickly rose in the ranks at St. Thomas More RC School. I became Head of House, overseeing hundreds of students under the banner of Drexel House—a position that was once ceremonial but soon became a platform for change. Drexel House wasn't just a grouping on a spreadsheet or a name attached to colored T-shirts on sports day. Under my leadership, it became a movement. A place of belonging. A banner under which misfits, high-flyers, introverts, and dreamers could all thrive.

I inspired them in morning assemblies—not with tired quotes borrowed from old leadership manuals, but with living stories. Stories of Denham Town, of zinc fences and flickering streetlights. Stories of my own teenage missteps, and of the teachers who still chose to believe in me. "You're not here by accident," I'd say, voice calm but fierce. "And you're not a statistic until you let someone else write your story."

The kids listened. They didn't always obey. But they listened. I made assemblies feel like sermons. I quoted Bob Marley and Maya Angelou. I opened each session with music — sometimes grime, sometimes gospel, sometimes old-school reggae, just enough to get them nodding. Sometimes I'd Walk through the auditorium, high-fiving students as I spoke.

"You—yeah, you in the back—stop hiding. You got something to say."

They loved me for it. Even the teachers who once side-eyed my unorthodox methods couldn't deny the results. Attendance for Drexel House students improved. Behavioral incidents dropped. Grades ticked up. For the first time in a long while, some students felt proud to wear the Drexel badge and to be a part of "Tommy More".

Sports day became a spectacle. I choreographed their chants, recruited a sixth-form student to DJ, and had Drexel House T-shirts redesigned by an aspiring graphic designer in Year 10. When Drexel House won back-to-back first place finishes in the school's annual competitions — athletics, academics, art, and service — it was like a revolution. No house had done it in years. Staff marveled. Other Heads of House tried to copy my methods and even accused of cheating. I am still not sure how that conclusion was arrived at, seeing that I had nothing to do with points tabulation, or recording race placements. My entire day was spent in the area assigned to Drexel House, motivating and high fiving my team. But through it all, I just smiled.

"It's not the methods," I told a colleague. "It's the meaning. They need to feel like it matters. Like they matter."

But my true legacy was not in medals or trophies. It was in my classroom.

Room 3B, down the corridor that always smelled of faint disinfectant and teenage fear, became a sanctuary. Students came in knowing they wouldn't just learn English or Religious Education — they'd be seen. It was a place where no accent was mocked, where slang was welcomed alongside Standard English, where rap lyrics were analyzed like Shakespearean sonnets, and where silence was respected, not punished.

The corridors of the school echoed with the usual chaos—bells ringing, students swarming, fights breaking out near the bike sheds. But Room 3B remained an oasis. Even other staff began to notice.

"I don't know what you're doing in there, Ward," the Head of Year once said, "but whatever it is, it works."

I shrugged. "I just teach them like they matter."

Sometimes I clashed with leadership. I pushed for more culturally responsive texts— beyond the token month of Black history. I questioned why the reading list hadn't changed in twenty years.

"We have to tick boxes, Ward," one senior leader said.

"Then change the boxes," I replied.

I started an after-school program called Voices That Echo — a creative writing group for students whose stories didn't fit into textbooks. They wrote about family, identity, immigration, grief. Some wrote letters to their younger selves. Others wrote spoken-word pieces that were later performed in assemblies.

One boy, Jamal, wrote:

"They told me my accent was too thick

So I thinned my voice until even I couldn't hear myself anymore."

The classroom went quiet. I sat at my desk, heart pounding. These kids — my kids — weren't just passing tests. They were finding their voices.

Being Head of House wasn't just assemblies and sports day speeches. It was hospital visits. Funerals. Bail hearings. House visits where fridges were empty, and heat hadn't been on in weeks. It was finding coats for kids in winter. It was printing off personal statements for students with no home printer. It was buying extra meal tickets when I knew someone was too proud to ask.

It was remembering birthdays and noticing haircuts. It was knowing when to challenge and when to console. And through it all, I stayed steady.

At home, Sharon watched me burn both ends of the candle.

"You can't save them all," she said once, gently.

"I know," I replied. "But I can show them that someone tried."

By my fifth year, Drexel House was no longer just a house. It was a family. Students requested to be moved into it. Parents asked why other houses didn't have mentors like Mr. Ward. Alumni returned during Sixth Form to help younger Drexel students prepare for exams. They wore their old Drexel T-shirts like medals.

At the annual Year 11 Leavers' Assembly, I was given a surprise tribute. One by one, former students appeared on the screen in a video montage.

"Sir, you made me believe I was more than my postcode."

"Thank you for listening when nobody else did."

"You taught me that my story mattered. That I mattered."

I blinked rapidly; heart swollen. One voice came last. It was Aman—the boy who rarely smiled.

"I never told you this, Sir," he said, eyes looking directly at the camera. "But that day you told me my poem sounded like something you'd read in a university anthology—I went home and cried. Not because I was sad. But because nobody had ever said anything like that to me before. You made me want to live louder."

I stood, speechless. The room erupted in applause.

And in that moment, I knew—I wasn't just a teacher. Or a Head of House. I was a mirror, a megaphone, a midwife for identity. I wasn't just helping them pass exams. I was helping them become.

Chapter II: Becoming More

The Woman Who Would Not Bend

During my teaching years at St Thomas More RC School, Sharon enrolled in evening classes. Twice a week, after preparing dinner, checking Jilisha's homework, and sometimes still in her office clothes, she would pack her books and head out into the night. The bus stop became a second kitchen. The upper deck of the 329 became a study hall.

Her courses were brutal — financial accounting, auditing, tax law, business ethics — each one a mountain of new vocabulary, new rules, new frameworks. But Sharon was undeterred. She studied by lamplight, her books and notes spread out across the kitchen table. The fridge hummed behind her, the clock ticked endlessly, and the world outside slipped into darkness. But inside our flat, Sharon's mind was alive.

She translated dense accounting jargon into language she could hold onto, applying lessons to her own household budget. There were nights when exhaustion tugged at her like an anchor and nights when she fell asleep mid-sentence, her head resting on spreadsheets, only to wake and pick up where she left off.

There were setbacks too. A missed deadline here. A failed exam there. Once, she got off at the wrong bus stop in the rain and arrived to class dripping wet, only to be told the session was canceled. There was the redundancy scare at work that made her stomach churn for weeks, the feeling of being invisible in the office because her credentials weren't yet on paper.

But Sharon was made of resolve. She did not complain. She adjusted. She absorbed. She adapted. She advanced. She was a fighter in the truest essence of the word.

Her goal was clear: earn her ACCA qualification—a badge of competence in a world that asked her to prove herself again and again. Not on the first try. Not even on the second. But she got there. Piece by piece. Credit by credit. She turned failure into fuel.

And when she finally passed the final paper — the one that had haunted her through two retakes — she didn't scream or jump or dance. She just sat silently at the kitchen table with the email open on her screen, her fingers trembling slightly.

I saw it first. "You pass?"

She nodded. "Yeh mi pass."

And I exhaled, as if holding that breath for her all those years.

That night, I made her favorite dinner — browned stew chicken with fried dumplings — and poured her a glass of wine. Then, after the kids were asleep, I massaged her feet, gently, reverently.

"You are a warrior," I whispered.

She smiled. "I'm a woman."

But she didn't stop there.

With the ACCA certificate in hand, Sharon pushed further. She enrolled in a bachelor's program in accounting, determined to back up her skills with a formal degree. Three years later, she walked across the graduation stage, modest cap perched on pressed hair, the applause thunderous in my chest.

Still, she wasn't done.

She took on a master's degree in finance, managing group projects and dissertations while still cooking, commuting, and managing Jilisha's teen moods and my many and sometimes thoughtless indiscretions. She could write a 3,000-word paper on corporate risk while timing rice on the stovetop. Sharon redefined multitasking.

I often watched her from the hallway as she typed late into the night—her posture straight, her focus unbreakable. Sometimes I would slip a note into her textbook: "I see you. Proud of you. Always." And she would find it during a break in class, smile quietly, and keep going.

Our love language wasn't grand gestures. It was support. Holding space. Taking turns. Carrying each other without resentment.

When Sharon finally earned her master's degree, the family went all out. Rhys wore my school blazer, wide-eyed. Jilisha clutched a bouquet of pink lilies. I clapped so hard my palms stung.

But more than the ceremony, more than the robe or photos or formalities, it was what Sharon represented that mattered most.

She had rewritten her own narrative. Not as a woman who followed me to a foreign country—but as a woman who built, fought, and triumphed in that country. A woman who juggled baby bottles and bed sheets. A woman who fell behind, got back up, and kept going.

She rose steadily at Haringey Council. First into the finance department, then into compliance and auditing. Her accent no longer dismissed. Her ideas now welcomed. She earned the kind of respect that can't be bought or fast-tracked. It was slow-earned. Fought-for. Deserved.

She mentored younger women in the office, especially the ones from back home, nervous in meetings, unsure of their voices. She told them what no one had told her: "You belong here. Just be excellent and unafraid."

Sharon never shouted. She didn't have to. Her presence did the talking.

And at home, the power of her example seeped into her children.

Jilisha began to speak of herself with authority, debating politics and identity over Sunday dinner, already imagining her own master's and doctorate.

And me? I remained in awe. I always had been. Her strength humbled me. Her steadiness anchored me. If I was the voice in our home, she was the spine.

Together, we built not just a household, but a legacy. A model. A living curriculum for what love, grit, and faith can build over time.

We weren't rich. But we were rooted.
And that, for us, was more than enough.

The Girl Who Would

From the moment she stepped off that
plane in late December 2001, Jilisha Ward had a
light in her eyes that not even the grey skies of
London could dim. She was six years old,
clutching her father's hand at Heathrow
Airport, wearing her blue Vaz Prep School
uniform under a warm cardigan, wide-eyed
and curious about the new world she was
stepping into.

London was colder, faster, louder than
Kingston, but Jilisha adapted quickly. She
brought with her not just a Caribbean accent
and manners learned from her parents, but a
quiet determination, a grace beyond her years.
Her first school in the UK was Grange Park
Preparatory School, nestled in the heart of
Enfield. It was there that the seeds of her
confidence and brilliance were first watered.

Her teachers saw it almost immediately — that rare blend of empathy and intellect. She was never the loudest, but she was always listening. Always thinking. Always writing. She excelled in English and Humanities, drawn instinctively to stories about people, systems, injustices, and survival. At home, she would sit at the kitchen table beside me, reading as I marked papers, occasionally interrupting to ask, "Daddy, what does protagonist mean?" or "Why would someone commit a crime?"

Those questions were never idle. They were the early signals of a mind tuned toward human behavior, ethics, and justice. Even then, she had a way of looking at the world that suggested she wasn't just absorbing it — she was interrogating it. She wanted to understand why people hurt, why they heal, and what makes them choose one path over another.

By age eight, Jilisha was writing short stories in spiral notebooks, often casting herself as the heroine who solved mysteries or stood up to injustice. Her characters were bold, but always kind. They spoke with conviction, but never cruelty. She once wrote a story about a girl who convinced her school principal to change the lunch menu after learning that some students couldn't eat pork for religious reasons. "She didn't shout," Jilisha explained. "She just showed him why it mattered."

Outside of school, she was equally observant. She noticed the way neighbors greeted each other—or didn't. She asked why some children wore secondhand uniforms while others had new ones every term. She was learning, not just from books, but from the streets, the buses, the corner shops, and the quiet exchanges between grown-ups who thought she wasn't listening.

I watched all this with quiet pride. I saw in her the makings of a woman who would not only succeed, but uplift. She had inherited my love of language, my sense of justice, and her mother's poise. But she was becoming something more—a bridge between worlds, fluent in both Caribbean warmth and British resilience.

Years later, when she stood before her classmates to deliver a speech on fairness in education, she began with a memory: "When I first came to London, I didn't know what injustice looked like. But I knew what it felt like." That was Jilisha—always leading with heart, always illuminating the truth.

As she transitioned to St. Anne's High School for Girls, Jilisha found herself surrounded by girls from all backgrounds—Somali, Ghanaian, Jamaican, Pakistani, Polish. It was a vibrant, sometimes chaotic environment, but it became her crucible. The hallways echoed with multiple languages, braided hairstyles, and debates that spilled from classrooms into lunch queues. It was a place where culture clashed and converged, and where identity was both challenged and affirmed.

Jilisha learned to navigate her Jamaican pride with British nuance. She held fast to her roots—still said "*tings*" instead of "things," still preferred plantain chips to banana chips—but she also learned to code-switch, to adapt without erasing herself. Her accent softened, but her sense of self never did. She wore her heritage like a quiet badge, not loud, but unmistakable.

She joined the debate club, where her calm demeanor and razor-sharp logic quickly earned her respect. She didn't shout to be heard—she spoke with clarity and conviction. Her arguments were layered, her rebuttals precise. She once debated the ethics of school

243

uniforms and quoted bell hooks and a Tottenham bus driver in the same breath. Her peers listened. Her teachers leaned in.

Outside of debate, she volunteered with younger students, tutoring them in reading and helping them navigate the social maze of secondary school. She had a gift for making others feel seen. One Year 7 student once wrote in a thank-you card, "Miss Jilisha makes me feel smart." That mattered to her more than any award.

Her essays became legend — thoughtful, layered pieces that often explored the intersection of race, class, and education. She wrote about the hidden curriculum, about how discipline policies disproportionately affected Black girls, about the silence around mental health in immigrant families. Her teachers began suggesting careers in law. "You'd make a brilliant barrister," one said. "You argue with elegance."

But Jilisha had her own ideas.

In Year 10, after watching a documentary on juvenile justice in the UK, she sat quietly for a while, then turned to me and said, "I don't just want to argue cases, Dad. I want to understand why they happen in the first place." Her voice was steady, but her eyes were lit with something deeper, a calling.

I smiled. I knew then: criminology and psychology were in her future. She wasn't chasing prestige—she was chasing understanding. She wanted to know what made people break, what systems failed them, and how healing could be built into justice. She wasn't interested in punishment—she was interested in prevention.

From that moment on, her path sharpened. She began reading case studies, watching courtroom dramas with a critical eye, and asking questions that made me pause. "Do you think trauma can be inherited?" "Why do some people survive abuse and others don't?" These weren't idle musings—they were the early steps of a young woman preparing to walk into the world with both empathy and intellect.

St. Anne's gave her the space to grow. But it was her spirit—resilient, curious, and quietly fierce—that turned that space into a launchpad.

By 2013, armed with strong A-Levels and glowing recommendations, Jilisha left London for Hull University, trading North London bustle for the quieter, coastal rhythm of East Yorkshire. It was her first time truly away from family, and it tested her in new ways. There were moments of homesickness: cold mornings when she longed for dumplings and her mother's arms, group projects with peers who underestimated her. But as always, she rose.

She majored in Criminology and
Psychology, diving headfirst into courses on
criminal profiling, victimology, sociological
theory, and cognitive development. Her
professors described her as "insightful,
methodical, and deeply compassionate." She

didn't just want the grades—she wanted the truth behind the data.

Her final-year dissertation focused on youth recidivism and systemic bias in the UK justice system, earning high praise for both academic rigor and social awareness.

Throughout it all, she never lost touch with home. She'd call me between lectures, sometimes just to discuss a case study or get my thoughts on a political debate. "Dad, the justice system isn't broken," she once said. "It's working exactly the way it was designed—to protect power, not people." I would chuckle at her fire, proud but quietly aware that she was moving into a realm of intellectual leadership I could only admire from the edges.

After earning her bachelor's degree with honors, Jilisha took a short break—working part-time with youth outreach programs in London, helping at-risk teens navigate housing and education. But the academic itch returned quickly.

She soon enrolled in a master's program — focused on Forensic and Investigative Psychology — determined to deepen her understanding of how mental health, trauma, and environment shape behavior. This was not surface-level study. It was case-based, data-driven, and emotionally taxing work. She interviewed offenders, analyzed cognitive distortions, and even completed a research placement with a victim advocacy charity.

During her thesis defense, she was asked what drove her passion for the work. "I come from a place where too many brilliant kids fall through cracks," she said. "I'm trying to help patch the system from both sides."

By the time she walked across the graduation stage to collect her master's degree, her parents were in tears. Her brother Rhys, now a teenager, watched from the audience with wide-eyed admiration. She was no longer just the clever girl with good grades. She was a scholar, a researcher, and — most importantly — a voice for those often unheard.

As of 2025, Jilisha is preparing to begin her PhD journey, exploring a research proposal that combines race, migration, and criminal psychology. She's particularly interested in how identity is shaped by place, policy, and memory — how Caribbean and African diasporas experience criminalization and mental health differently in post-colonial societies like the UK and US.

Her proposal includes ethnographic interviews, comparative policy analysis, and potentially even fieldwork in Jamaica—a full-circle moment she's both excited and nervous about. She often bounces ideas off her father, who remains her greatest sounding board.

"So, you're finally going to be Dr. Ward," I teased one day, stirring tea in the kitchen.

"Maybe," she grinned. "But only if you call me that."

Jilisha's story is not just one of academic achievement—it's a story of legacy.

Of a girl raised on books. Of bedtime stories told in patois. Of two immigrant parents who carved stability out of struggle so she could rise on sturdier shoulders. She is, in every way, her parents' wildest dream come true. A product of faith, focus, and fierce love.

And as she inches toward that doctorate, toward shaping policy and healing systems, she does so not for prestige — but for impact. For every child like her who once asked, "Why is the world like this?" and dared to answer with action.

She carries the cadence of her mother's prayers and the quiet strength of her father's sacrifices. Her brilliance is not loud — it's layered. It shows up in the way she listens, the way she questions, the way she refuses to accept broken systems as permanent fixtures. She has always been the child who noticed too much, who felt too deeply, who asked questions that made adults pause.

I remember her at age seven, standing in front of the television during a news segment about school closures. "Why don't they just fix the schools?" she asked, eyes wide, voice steady. It wasn't naïveté — it was clarity. Even then, she understood that injustice was not inevitable. That someone, somewhere, had the power to change things. And maybe, just maybe, that someone could be her.

Her academic journey has been marked not just by excellence, but by intention. She chose sociology not because it was easy, but because it was necessary. She studied policy not to climb ladders, but to dismantle them. Her research is rooted in lived experience — in the stories of children who fall through cracks, in the voices of families who navigate systems designed without them in mind.

And yet, she remains grounded. She still calls home to ask about seasoning rice properly. She still sends voice notes in patois to her cousins. She still laughs with her whole body, the way she did as a child spinning in the living room to Beres Hammond. Her success has not distanced her — it has deepened her connection to where she came from.

When she speaks at conferences, she wears her locs proudly, her accent intact. She does not code-switch to fit in — she expands the room to make space for herself and others. She is rewriting what it means to be a scholar, a leader, a daughter of immigrants.

And when she prepared to defend her dissertation, she did so with the weight of generations behind her. With the memory of zinc fences and mango trees. With the echo of her grandmother's voice saying, *"Tek yuh education serious."* (Take your education seriously). With the knowledge that her journey is not hers alone — it is a continuation of every step her ancestors took to bring her here.

Jilisha did not just earn two degrees. She built a permanent bridge. And every word she writes, every policy she shapes, every child she lifts — is a stone laid in that sacred crossing.

His Name is Rhys

In February 2007, the Ward family welcomed our second child into the world — a bright-eyed, quietly alert baby boy named Rhys Antonio Ward. Born at North Middlesex Hospital in Edmonton, he was 7 pounds of promise, his tiny fists already curled as if ready to take on the world. I cradled him with reverence, whispering, "My lion cub," while Sharon, exhausted but glowing, reached over to kiss his forehead.

Jilisha, then twelve, immediately stepped into her role as big sister with pride and fierce devotion. From helping change nappies to reading picture books aloud in her soft Jamaican lilt, she became a co-parent in spirit. Rhys was surrounded from birth not only by love but also by stories — stories my grand aunts told in metaphors and sonnets, stories my mother shaped with quiet strength and resilience.

I often sat by the bedroom window at night, holding Rhys close while telling him tales of Denham Town and Kingston's bustling streets, of zinc fences and guinep trees, of domino games played under streetlamps and the unstoppable rhythm of reggae echoing through humid evenings. Even though the baby could not yet understand the words, something in the cadence of my voice seemed to calm him completely. Some nights he would stare up, his dark eyes locked on my face as though searching for the memories buried in the drift of each sentence.

Sharon watched us softly from the doorway, knowing that those moments were laying down the foundation of a bond that nothing could break. She added her own stories too—quiet ones about her mother's gentle discipline, about walking to school in the early morning when the dew still clung to the poinciana leaves, and about the importance of standing tall even when the wind was determined to blow you off your path. Sometimes she would hum church hymns to him while rocking his little cradle, the echoes of her childhood faith drifting through the room like a comforting quilt.

As the weeks stretched into months, the family began to fall into a gentle rhythm. On Sunday mornings, I would brew strong Blue Mountain coffee and play old Barrington Levy or Gregory Isaacs records while Sharon made fried dumplings and ackee and saltfish. Jilisha, hair tied back in a neat bun, would carry Rhys in her arms like a proud little mother, whispering "Morning, little prince" as she kissed the top of his head. Rhys would respond with gummy smiles and little coos, his whole

face lighting up like dawn breaking over a quiet hillside.

When spring arrived and the grey London skies softened, we took Rhys out for walks in Pymmes Park. I would push the buggy slowly along the paved pathway, stopping every now and then to point out ducks gliding over the pond or the cherry blossoms drifting gently to the ground. Jilisha held his tiny hand while Sharon walked beside them, her arm looped through mine, grateful for a moment of stillness in a world that too often demanded our constant motion. Rhys seemed fascinated by everything — the rustle of leaves, the distant bark of a dog, the bright red of a passing double-decker bus. It was as though life itself had opened up a canvas, and he was already quietly sketching his place in it.

At night, the house grew quiet, but the little details of our days lingered like warm embers. Jilisha would kneel beside Rhys' cot and say a short prayer, asking God to watch over her brother while he slept. I often stayed up late, writing journal entries and poems inspired by the feeling of holding my son. Sharon placed her hand on my shoulder as she passed, always pausing to look at the tiny socks drying on the radiator, astonished by how something so small could carry so much meaning.

When Rhys was five months old, I brought home a small Manchester United baby onesie, bright red with the club crest emblazoned on the chest. "He has to start early," I laughed. Sharon shook her head — half amused, half exasperated — but she still took a photo of father and son posing proudly in matching United kits. Jilisha later printed the picture and taped it to her bedroom wall next to her own childhood photos, as though already curating the family's timeline.

Rhys grew quickly, his curiosity outpacing even his physical development. He was the kind of baby who always seemed to be observing the world with intent, as though trying to decode each moment for its deeper message. When I read him Pablo Neruda or Claude McKay at night, Rhys would blink slowly and stretch his little legs, trying to absorb every syllable. When Sharon sang old Jamaican lullabies—"*Brown Girl in the Ring,*" "*Linstead Market*" – he would curl against her chest, as if the songs were made of soft cloth and safety.

By the time his first Christmas came around, the household had completely reorganized itself around him. The living room was decorated with tinsel, handmade ornaments, and a small tree placed just low enough for Rhys to reach out and gently tap the glittery baubles. On Christmas Eve, I played the Nat King Cole Holiday album while Sharon made her famous sorrel and fruitcake. Jilisha wrapped a small stuffed lion for her baby brother—the first gift she ever bought with her own allowance. That evening, Rhys crawled across the rug and reached for it, his fingers brushing the gold ribbon as if he instinctively understood the love it carried.

Sometimes, in the quiet moments after the chaos of the day, I would look at Sharon and whisper, "He's going to change the world, you know." Sharon would smile, not because she thought it was a grand statement, but because she believed it too. There was something in Rhys's presence—quiet, thoughtful, unwavering—that seemed to echo the strength of every ancestor who had carried our family name across oceans and hardships.

As he grew older, Rhys would often sit on my lap and listen to stories from *Storynory*, not as background melodies, but as maps — each one showing him where he came from and hinting at where he might one day go. And even before he could walk, he began to hum when Sharon sang, as if trying to add his own thread to the family tapestry.

By 2018, Rhys was in his final year at Honilands Primary School and preparing for the transition to secondary school. We had set our sights on Goffs Academy, one of the more competitive schools in the area. It was known for its academic rigor and forward-thinking curriculum — particularly in STEM subjects, where Rhys had already begun to show tremendous aptitude.

He sat the entrance exam with quiet confidence, having prepared meticulously. I helped him build his vocabulary through nightly discussions and quiz games. Sharon drilled him on math and reasoning. By the time the results arrived in the post, we were cautiously hopeful — but even we hadn't anticipated what came next.

Rhys had scored a perfect score.

Top percentile. Full marks. The letter from Goffs was glowing: "A truly exceptional student."

I held the page in my hands for several long seconds before even speaking. It wasn't that I was surprised — Rhys had always performed at an advanced level — but seeing it written in formal school stationery, signed by a headteacher who had seen thousands of students over the years, struck me in a deeper way. Sharon read it next, her lips pressed together in quiet pride and then handed it to Rhys who simply nodded and said, "That's good," before asking if he could go outside to practice free kicks in the back garden.

That was Rhys in a sentence — success acknowledged but never celebrated for long. For him, achievement wasn't a destination to linger at. It was a checkpoint. The moment he crossed it, he reset his internal compass and focused on the next stretch of road.

Starting at Goffs Academy marked the beginning of a new chapter. The school was larger and more competitive than Honilands, filled with students from all over the borough, many of whom were bright and ambitious. Some parents worried that their high-achieving children might struggle to adjust or get lost in the crowd. Not us.

On the first day, he took a quiet walk around the campus during lunch, studying the layout like a cartographer drawing a map from memory. By the end of the week, he knew not just his own timetable but the quickest route to every classroom in his year group and the names of all his teachers.

He approached secondary school with the same quiet discipline that had defined his early years. Homework was completed the same night it was assigned. Revision began weeks before tests were announced. When other students groaned about group projects, Rhys simply asked, "Who's in my group, and when do we start?" He wasn't competitive in the obvious sense. He didn't need to outshine anyone. Instead, he had a quiet way of elevating whatever space he entered — lifting the standard just by being there.

By the end of his first term, he had already been placed in the top sets for Mathematics, English, and Science. His

Mathematics teacher, a stern man rarely given to compliments, pulled me aside after one parents' evening and said, "Your son doesn't just understand the material—he sees it."

When I relayed that comment at home, Rhys shrugged and replied, "It's just numbers. You just have to listen to what they're trying to say."

Outside of academics, Rhys joined the school football team—not because I encouraged it (though I did, excitedly), but because he genuinely loved the game. On the pitch, he played with the same precision he brought to his studies. Every pass was calculated, every run intentional. He wasn't flashy. He didn't do step-overs or elaborate tricks. But he read the game like a seasoned veteran, always in the right place at the right time. Teammates soon began calling him "The Architect."

After one match in which he assisted twice and scored the winner, the coach told him, "You could go far in this game if you really wanted to."

Rhys nodded politely and said, "Thank you, sir," but didn't say whether he wanted to or not. In truth, football was a joy—but learning was the heartbeat.

At home, the rhythm remained steady. Dinner together. Stories shared. Lessons embedded in conversations. I would sometimes bring home old philosophical texts—Marcus Aurelius, *Mandela's Long Walk to Freedom*, Baldwin essays—and leave them on the dining table. Rhys always picked them up, reading silently while eating Sharon's stew. Then, without prompting, he would ask questions:

"Why do you think Mandela forgave them after everything they did?"

"Do you think Stoicism still makes sense in modern life?"

What followed were deep, thoughtful discussions that sometimes lasted late into the night and left the room glowing with insight.

Sharon, in her gentle but firm way, ensured that humility remained at the center of his growth. When Rhys came home one day with a certificate for scoring the highest mark in the entire year group, she congratulated him—then handed him a basket of laundry and said, "Well done. Now fold those shirts for me, please."

Rhys smiled and obeyed without protest. It was never about dimming his light; it was about making sure he understood that brilliance is a gift, and gifts are meant to serve, not dominate.

As the years at Goffs went on, the accolades continued. School assemblies came to include his achievements almost as a regular item on the agenda: "Rhys Ward wins the District Mathematics Challenge." "Rhys Ward receives Distinction in National Science Olympiad."

Most students eventually gave up, whispering "Of course it's Rhys" — instead, they started asking him for help. And he gave it — freely, patiently, happily. In fact, many evenings he stayed behind after school unofficially tutoring classmates, explaining concepts in simpler terms, refusing to leave until he saw the moment of understanding light up their faces.

Perhaps the most defining moment came during Year 10 when the school nominated students for the Jack Petchey Achievement

Award—an honor that recognizes outstanding young people across London and Essex. Teachers submit nominations, but the winner at each school is selected by the students themselves.

When Rhys's name was announced, the assembly hall erupted into applause—not obligatory clapping, but genuine, heartfelt cheering. One student later said, "He deserved it. He's the smartest one here, but he's also the kindest."

Sharon and I attended the award ceremony dressed in quiet pride. Rhys accepted the certificate and medal, gave a short, thoughtful speech thanking his teachers and classmates, then walked straight back to sit with us. Sharon squeezed my hand. I whispered, "Well done, Lion." Rhys simply smiled.

Later that night, after the house had settled into sleep, I sat at the dining table, the medal resting in my hands. I thought about Denham Town. I thought about my own education—about the uneven access, the classrooms without enough books, the teachers who tried their best with limited resources. And I said a silent prayer: Thank You for allowing my son to walk roads I could only dream of.

Rhys, meanwhile, slept peacefully, unburdened by the weight of his achievements, already turning unknowingly toward the next morning, the next lesson, the next quiet opportunity to grow.

At Goffs Academy, Rhys continued to excel. By now, his personality had blossomed into something that mirrored both his parents — my introspection and sense of justice, Sharon's precision and quiet ambition. He wasn't interested in popularity. He was interested in understanding how things worked.

In Year 11, when asked during a career workshop what he wanted to become, Rhys replied without hesitation:

"Something to do with hacking. But, you know, the good kind."

That "good kind" would soon find a name: Cybersecurity.

He advanced through his GCSEs with distinction, ultimately progressing into Sixth Form, where he pursued Mathematics, Computer Studies, and Physics—a triad that made his tech ambitions crystal clear.

While many of his peers considered university the natural next step, Rhys took a different path—one that surprised even his teachers. He applied for a highly competitive Amazon Cyber Security Apprenticeship, a four-year program designed to train future experts in digital safety, data protection, and network architecture.

Out of eighty-two thousand applicants across the UK, Rhys was one of twenty seven selected.

"Let me finish what I started," he told me one night over a late dinner of callaloo and dumplings. "I want to build, not just bounce."

I paused, fork halfway to my mouth — not because I doubted my son's decision, but because I recognized the intention behind the words. Rhys didn't want to follow a well-worn path just because it was safe or traditional. He wanted to forge his own. Sharon, who had been listening quietly while pouring tea, simply smiled and said, "Then build wisely."

At home, Rhys never mentioned the praise. What mattered more to him was the work itself and the satisfaction of solving problems that had real-world consequences. One evening, after finishing a particularly difficult assignment involving penetration testing, he sat silently at the dining table, eating reheated steamed fish. I asked if everything was alright.

Rhys nodded and said softly, "Yeah. It's... heavy. But the kind of heavy that makes you stronger."

And I understood completely.

I often looked at Rhys and saw something remarkable — not just talent, but focus. A kind of purposefulness that reminded me of Sharon in her late-night study grinds, and of myself chasing chalk dust and Shakespeare lines across three countries.

I thought of how far Rhys had come — from that tiny baby who I helped to deliver at birth in North Middlesex Hospital, to a young man about to enter the professional world of deciphering encryption algorithms and briefing senior managers.

And above all, I remembered one evening at Honilands Primary, when Rhys, aged nine, had stood on stage at the end-of-year awards ceremony, certificate in hand, and turned to find me clapping in the back row.

He didn't wave. He didn't grin.

He just nodded — quietly, assuredly, as if to say:

"I'm climbing, Dad. Just like you taught me."

Chapter III: Football Family

Rivalry

"Daddy, are you really going to defend Maguire again?"

"No man who turns like a tractor deserves defense," I muttered, but still folded my arms like I was shielding a comrade.

"You always talk about history," Jilisha continued, eyes mischievous. "But we're talking about now. Not when dinosaurs like Roy Keane roamed midfield."

"History matters!" I snapped. "That's why people still study Shakespeare and Haile Selassie!"

"Maybe," she smirked, "but not to pick their fantasy team."

Life has a way of reshaping loyalties, especially when innocence and delight intervene. What began as a simple family shopping trip to Asda in Southgate for her eighth birthday turned into a moment of footballing history within our household — a moment that shifted the balance of allegiance and altered the football map of our family forever.

In her earliest years, Jilisha followed me with wide-eyed admiration, as daughters often do with their fathers. When I sat down on Saturday mornings to catch a Premier League game, she would plop herself beside me on the couch, her small legs tucked beneath her, eyes glued to the screen though she barely understood the offside rule.

She wore the miniature United jersey I had bought her, emblazoned with the name "*Van Nistelrooy*" on the back, and she wore it proudly. The jersey was a size too big, its sleeves nearly swallowing her wrists, but she strutted around the living room like she was walking onto Old Trafford itself. To her, Van Nistelrooy wasn't just a name — he was a superhero stitched in red.

I would point out the players—Rooney with his bulldog determination, Ronaldo with his flair, Scholes with his quiet brilliance—and she would repeat their names like she was learning a new alphabet. "Rooney," she'd say, stretching the vowels. "Ron-al-do," with the hint of a Spanish accent she must have picked up from the commentators. "Scholes," which always came out as "Skulls," making me laugh every time. In those moments, I felt a deep satisfaction. She was becoming part of my tradition, the extension of my footballing heart.

At school, she even bragged to her friends that she was a Manchester United fan. She didn't just support them because I did; she genuinely delighted in their victories and pouted at their defeats. When United beat Liverpool, she ran around the house shouting, "Daddy! We win! We win!" When they lost, she would fold her little arms across her chest, sulking for the rest of the day, refusing even her favorite snack. For a time, I thought she was locked in—a Red Devil for life.

There were rituals we built together, small things that might have seemed ordinary to outsiders but meant the world to me. On game days, she'd help me set out the snacks — plantain chips, patties, or just buttered bread if money was tight. She would hand me the remote with a flourish, like she was bestowing a royal scepter. I, in turn, would pull her close under my arm as the anthem of the Champions League rang out on the TV, those familiar strings sending a chill down both our spines.

When United scored, she didn't cheer like the rest of the fans. She squealed. A high-pitched, unrestrained squeal of delight that filled the room. Then she'd leap up and try to mimic the celebrations — arms out wide like Van Nistelrooy, knees sliding on the carpet like Rooney, or simply jumping up and down, spinning until she was dizzy. I would watch, laughing, thinking to myself: this is how traditions are passed down — not by force, but by joy.

Even her toys weren't spared. She'd line up her dolls in formation, naming one after Van der Sar, another after Ferdinand, and inevitably one after Ronaldo, who always got to take the penalties in her living-room matches. If Barbie missed a shot, she'd scold her the way Sir Alex scolded players from the touchline. "Come on, concentrate!" she'd shout, mimicking his gruffness with uncanny precision.

I remember one Christmas when she was about six, I bought her a small United football, red with the club crest proudly printed across it. She tore the wrapping paper away and gasped as if she'd been given the crown jewels. She refused to put it down, carrying it around the house, bouncing it against the walls, even insisting it sleep at the foot of her bed. That ball saw the beginnings of her dribbles in the hallway, her little feet slapping the tiles as she zig-zagged past invisible defenders.

Trips into town were another story. If she spotted anything red in a shop window — whether it was a water bottle, a pair of trainers, or just a t-shirt with the faintest resemblance to United's kit — she would tug at my sleeve, her eyes wide, asking, "Daddy, is that United?" It didn't matter if it wasn't, in her mind, the world was divided into two categories: things that were United and things that weren't worth noticing.

Saturdays became our sacred father-daughter bonding sessions. While other parents might have taken their children to the park or the cinema, I cherished our mornings on the sofa, wrapped in blankets, United's fortunes dictating our moods for the rest of the weekend. Even Sharon, though not much of a football fan at that point, would shake her head and smile at our antics. "*Unu mad,*" (You're both mad) she'd say in her sing-song Jamaican tone, watching us leap up when United scored. But there was pride in her eyes too—she knew these were the moments that stitched a father and daughter close.

As the years passed, Jilisha's knowledge deepened. She could recognize the players by face, not just by name. She started to pick up on tactics, asking me questions about why Ferguson used certain substitutions, or why Ronaldo always seemed to drift wide before cutting in. Her questions impressed me, but more than that, they warmed me. She wasn't just mimicking me anymore—she was carving her own understanding of the game.

And so, I dared to believe she was destined to be a lifelong Red. We had built too many memories, too much identity, around those red shirts. When I tucked her in at night, she would sometimes whisper, "Daddy, United going win tomorrow, right?"

And I, ever the optimist, would nod firmly. "Of course, baby girl. Always."

But fate, as always, has a sense of humor.

One Cake

It was the week of her eighth birthday when everything shifted. We were living in London by then, adjusting to colder weather, new rhythms, and the sprawling aisles of English supermarkets that seemed to hold everything under one roof. On that particular day, Sharon and I bundled Jilisha into the car and drove to Asda in Southgate to shop for party supplies.

There was excitement in the air. At eight years old, birthdays still carried the magic of endless possibilities. Jilisha skipped along the aisles, her braids bouncing, her eyes darting from balloons to party hats, from colorful cups to cartoon napkins. Sharon and I exchanged amused glances as she filled the trolley with more than we needed — streamers, confetti, plates decorated with cheerful prints. She was in her element, a queen surveying her kingdom, deciding which treasures would make the cut.

We turned into the bakery section, the warm scent of icing and sponge hanging in the air. Rows of cakes lined the glass cases: towering chocolate creations, rainbow-frosted sponges, princess castles frozen in sugar. And then — at the very center — stood the cake that changed everything.

It was an Arsenal cake. Bold red and white icing framed the club's crest, and right in the middle, smiling like some footballing saint, was the unmistakable face of Thierry Henry. To me, it looked less like a cake and more like a trap — a cunning ambush set by North London itself.

Jilisha froze. Her gasp was audible, sharp with delight. "Daddy! Look!" she cried, pressing her palms to the glass as if it were treasure locked away. "That one! Please, Daddy, can I have that one for my birthday?"

My heart sank. This was not part of the plan. A United cake, perhaps. A simple chocolate sponge, fine. But an Arsenal cake with Thierry Henry's grin plastered across it? That was betrayal in buttercream.

I bent down beside her. "That one? The Arsenal cake?'" I asked, hoping she might reconsider. Perhaps she had simply been dazzled by the colors.

"Yes!" Her eyes were wide, her voice certain. "That one with the man on it."

"That man," I said, half-laughing, half-groaning, "is Thierry Henry. He plays for Arsenal. You can't have that. You're a Manchester United fan!"

But she was already lost in the vision of it, entranced by the colors and the smile. Sharon looked at me with a knowing grin, the kind that said, "You're not winning this one." And in that moment, I knew I had lost a battle I never imagined I'd have to fight—not with KC on a school pitch, not with rowdy students in a London classroom, but with a birthday cake in the bakery section of Asda Supermarket.

I pleaded my case. "Sweetheart, you can't just change teams because of a cake. Football is loyalty, it's tradition, it's family." She tilted her head, unbothered, and said with all the innocence in the world, "But Daddy... it's my birthday."

And that was it. The case was closed. Sharon burst out laughing, right there by the glass case, while I stood in silent defeat, wondering if Sir Alex Ferguson had ever lost a match this badly. Jilisha got her Arsenal cake, and I walked out of Asda carrying it like contraband, half-expecting United fans to jump out from behind the tills and strip me of my loyalty.

That cake, bright and defiant, marked the beginning of a shift I could not undo. Thierry Henry, smiling in sugar and food dye, had stolen my daughter's heart — and I, a lifelong Red Devil, had been powerless to stop it.

That cake became the centerpiece of her eighth birthday celebration. As friends gathered, as balloons floated and music played, there it was on the table: Thierry Henry smiling up at us all, presiding over the day like a royal guest.

When the time came to cut the cake, Jilisha insisted on slicing straight through Henry's grin, laughing as if she had discovered a secret power. I watched from the sidelines, still shaking my head, but I couldn't help but smile too. It was a moment of pure innocence, but also of declaration. She was choosing her own path, carving it out with a plastic knife and icing-stained fingers.

From that day forward, her allegiance shifted. She was no longer a United girl. She was an Arsenal fan through and through. She asked for Arsenal shirts, wanted to watch Arsenal games, and even practiced shouting "Come on you Gunners!" with a passion that startled me.

At first, I dismissed it as novelty. Children are drawn to the brightest colors, the biggest personalities, the loudest celebrations. But weeks turned into months, and her devotion did not waver. She pestered Sharon to take her to the sports shop in Wood Green so she could pick out Arsenal pencils and stickers. At school, her friends knew her as the girl who "liked Henry more than anyone else." She drew the Arsenal cannon in her notebooks, tracing it over and over until it became second nature.

Our home slowly shifted colors. Where once a red United scarf hung on the coat rack, an Arsenal one appeared beside it. Her bedroom wall, once dotted with posters of Ronaldo and Van Nistelrooy, became a shrine to Henry, Pires, and Bergkamp. Sharon played along, perhaps enjoying the mischievous satisfaction of seeing me outnumbered in my own house. On cold mornings, she'd wrap Jilisha in an Arsenal beanie before school, grinning at me as if to say, "Your reign is over."

Match days took on a new energy. No longer was it just me and my daughter united — literally and figuratively — under one banner. Now the living room became a battleground. If United and Arsenal played on the same day, the remote control was contested territory. If the two giants faced each other, the house turned into a stadium of its own. I in my United jersey, Jilisha in her Arsenal kit, Sharon egging her on with sly comments like, "Henry's class, you know. United can't touch him."

I found myself strangely conflicted. Part of me mourned the loss of our shared allegiance, the simplicity of those early years when she echoed my chants and celebrated my team's goals. Yet another part swelled with pride at her independence, her refusal to simply inherit my loyalties without question. In her devotion to Arsenal, I recognized a spark of something greater: her own identity beginning to take shape.

She wasn't content to be a spectator either. In the backyard, she practiced Henry's runs, darting down the patch of grass with her ponytail flying behind her, arms out wide as though thousands were cheering. She perfected the calm, statuesque pose Henry struck after scoring, hands on hips, chin tilted upward. Whenever she scored a goal past the makeshift net—two flower pots with a stick laid across— she would shout, "That's for Arsenal!" The neighbors chuckled at the sight, but I saw destiny in those childish games.

What cemented it further was the camaraderie she found with Sharon. Together, they became a team of two, mother and daughter bound not just by blood but by footballing defiance. They teased me when Arsenal won, leaving the living room decorated with makeshift banners of red and white construction paper. Even when Arsenal lost, they found comfort in each other's sighs, united in their disappointment. I was the outsider now, the lone Red Devil in a household that had turned Gunner.

Still, there was joy in the rivalry. Football has a way of weaving laughter into competition, of creating stories that linger long after the final whistle. Every chant, every debate, every playful jab added texture to our lives. That cake, with Henry's face grinning from beneath layers of sugar, had not just marked a birthday — it had marked the birth of a new chapter in our family's story.

And though I sometimes shook my head at the thought of raising an Arsenal fan, deep down I knew I wouldn't trade it for anything. She had found her voice, her team, her passion. All it took was one cake to turn the tide.

Sharon Joins

What stung even more was Sharon's decision to join her. She confessed later that she never really cared too deeply about football — at least not enough to pick a side. But once she saw the joy in Jilisha's eyes, she made her choice.

"I'm an Arsenal fan too," she declared one evening, smiling at me across the dinner table. "It'll be fun to nag you a bit."

And so, it was settled. From then on, I was surrounded. My daughter and my partner became lifelong Gunners, while I remained loyal to United. Match days turned into playful battlegrounds. If Arsenal won, they teased me mercilessly. If United triumphed, I gloated with all the pride I could muster.

At first, I protested, hoping Sharon was only joking. But she doubled down, learning Arsenal chants and songs so she could belt them out with Jilisha from the living room. They clapped in rhythm, their voices rising in unison, while I sat in my corner, arms folded,

293

pretending not to be annoyed. Yet, even through my mock frowns, I felt a warmth in seeing them so united, mother and daughter bound not just by blood but also by footballing loyalty.

Our home began to feel like two stadiums compressed under one roof. One corner of the living room flew United red; the other turned Arsenal white and red. Scarves were draped on chairs, mugs appeared on the kitchen counter emblazoned with the Arsenal crest, and Sharon went as far as buying Jilisha Arsenal-themed bedsheets. "She needs to sleep under the cannon," she said with a wink, as if it were a sacred rite of passage.

On weekends, the television became a contested prize. If Arsenal and United played at the same time, we negotiated like diplomats, sometimes resorting to recording one match so we could watch the other live. When Arsenal faced United head-to-head, the tension filled the room. I'd wear my United jersey proudly, while Sharon and Jilisha sat shoulder to shoulder in theirs, whispering strategies and predicting goals as though they were part of Wenger's coaching staff.

When United scored, I would leap up with a roar, my celebration deliberately exaggerated just to needle them. I'd pace the room, pointing at the television as though my presence alone had influenced the outcome. When Arsenal scored, the two of them would shriek with delight, jumping up and down in mock triumph, circling me like hunters taunting their prey. It became a dance, a ritual of give-and-take that made every match memorable, no matter the result.

What surprised me most was how the rivalry never soured. It wasn't bitter — it was joyful, mischievous, a constant reminder of that one birthday shopping trip that had shifted the balance of our footballing loyalties. Arguments about offsides or penalty calls always ended with laughter. Even when voices rose, it was all in jest, followed by hugs, shared meals, and the unspoken understanding that football was only part of the bigger picture: love, family, and togetherness.

Over time, I realized Sharon's choice wasn't just about football — it was about solidarity with her daughter. She may not have cared deeply for the game, but she cared for the sparkle in Jilisha's eyes, for the confidence she found in declaring her loyalty to Arsenal. By joining her, Sharon was affirming that bond, strengthening it through chants, scarves, and inside jokes that would last a lifetime.

In the end, I was glad they had each other. Even as I remained the lone Red Devil in the house, I took pride in knowing our little family had found joy in something as simple — and as complicated — as football. The rivalry became our inside story, our shared laughter, the thread woven through birthdays, weeknights, and lazy weekends. And though I often claimed to be "outnumbered," deep inside I knew I was the luckiest of the three.

Rhys' Choice

But when Rhys came along, balance was restored. From the moment I brought home his first Manchester United onesie, bright red with the club crest on the chest, his destiny seemed written. He didn't know it yet, of course, but I did.

As he grew older, he gravitated naturally to my side of the rivalry. While Jilisha and Sharon waved Arsenal scarves, Rhys sat beside me, eyes glued to Old Trafford on the TV, absorbing the rhythm of the game. When I explained why Cantona was king, why Ferguson's hairdryer treatment built dynasties, or why Rooney's overhead kick against City was immortal, Rhys nodded like a young disciple.

By the time he was seven, he was debating Jilisha at the dinner table.

"Arsenal play nice football," she would tease, "but United play dinosaur football. Caveman football."

Rhys would fold his arms, forehead creased. "At least our dinosaurs have trophies. When last Arsenal win di league?"

The table would erupt in laughter — Sharon and Jilisha groaning dramatically, me grinning like a proud coach.

Our living room became a divided stadium. On one side, Sharon and Jilisha in red-and-white jerseys, chanting "Ar-se-nal! Ar-se-nal!" On the other, Rhys and I draped in the deeper red of United, fists pumping as we sang "Glory, glory Man United!"

When the two teams faced each other, the atmosphere was electric. Sharon prepared snacks, pretending not to care, though she always leaned forward when the match grew tense. Jilisha shouted at the screen like a pundit, sharp and animated, while Rhys sat taut, reading every movement. I paced like a manager on the touchline, muttering tactical notes under my breath.

One unforgettable Saturday, United stole a late winner at the Emirates. Rhys leapt onto the sofa, fists in the air, screaming, "YESSS! Daddy, we beat dem!" I hugged him tightly, both of us chanting. Across the room, Sharon and Jilisha glared with mock fury. A cushion flew my way. Sharon crossed her arms. But even in defeat, there was laughter.

The rivalry was never just about football. It became a language of love in our home — a way of sparring without bitterness, of teaching loyalty, resilience, and the beauty of sticking with something even when it disappoints you.

For me and Rhys, United was heritage: a bridge to my grandfather's love of the game, to my own days on the pitch in Denham Town, to the brotherhood of Scots Kirk. For Sharon and Jilisha, Arsenal was rebellion and joy — an embrace of flair and fire, born from one unforgettable birthday cake with Thierry Henry's smile iced across it.

Our divided loyalties became our unity. Rivalry didn't fracture us — it enriched us, adding color and story to the legacy we were building.

On big match days, our household transformed into a stadium. Sharon popped popcorn or baked jerk chicken wings, always serving the Arsenal fans first with a wink. Rhys wore his classic '99 Beckham kit; I kept to my 2008 Ronaldo jersey. Sharon sported her scarf, while Jilisha, ever the Arsenal queen, donned her old-school Henry shirt.

I stalked the room like a Premier League manager, fuming at poor pressing and barking tactical instructions no one could hear. "Close him down, Rhys! Look how deep Casemiro dropping!"

Sharon was the calm assassin—sipping tea, dropping sly barbs without looking up. "I thought Varane was supposed to be world-class."

Rhys erupted at every chance—fist pumps, Fortnite dances, even running into the kitchen yelling, "GGMU!"

Jilisha, meanwhile, was surgical. She didn't shout; she waited, then delivered verdicts like exam scores: "Oh dear. De Gea slipped again?"

Some nights were glorious, others cruel, but all stitched into the fabric of our family. One of my favorites was United's 8–2 demolition of Arsenal at Old Trafford in 2011. Rooney's hat-trick, Young's screamers, the scoreboard lighting up like a pinball machine—it was footballing carnage. I can still see Sharon and Jilisha's stunned faces. "Eight–two," I said that night, grinning. "Never forget." To this day, it remains my trump card.

But Arsenal had their nights, too. January 2023: Arsenal 3, United 2. Rhys celebrated Rashford's opener with a moonwalk across the tiles. Sharon rolled her eyes; Jilisha fumed. Yet by the 90th minute, Nketiah's late winner had Sharon and Jilisha swaying, singing North London Forever while Rhys stared in disbelief. I put an arm around him. "Good game. It's a long season."

He wasn't consoled, and Jilisha twisted the knife: "You said that last season."

Still, win or lose, the laughter always returned. After the teasing, after the goals, after the heartbreak—we ate dinner together. Football never soured into resentment. It became our ritual, our banter, our bond. Years later, I asked Jilisha why she really chose Arsenal.

She thought for a moment. "Because it felt like mine. You already loved United. You taught me to love football, but when I saw that cake, when I saw Henry's smile—I wasn't copying you. I was choosing for myself."

I nodded slowly. She nudged me, grinning. "But you made me love football first. So really, you only have yourself to blame."

We laughed. And I realized that was the heart of it: our rivalry wasn't division. It was inheritance and rebellion, heritage and choice, all blending into a story that still binds us.

As Rhys grew older, the banter evolved. He started to develop his own takes on players, tactics, and team selection. He challenged me more often.

"Dad, we need a new keeper. De Gea's done."

"But he's loyal!"

"This isn't a marriage. It's football!"

Sometimes, I would just nod, watching my son grow into a passionate young man—opinionated, smart, assertive. I saw myself in Rhys. The way he'd stay up late watching highlight reels, or the way he argued passionately over a missed offside.

But what I cherished most was that football became a language of love in our home.

When life got heavy—bills, school stress, work politics—football was a release valve. When Jilisha left for university and homesickness crept in, she'd send voice notes during games.

"Tell Daddy Arsenal's top of the table again."

That night, I didn't say much. I simply sat next to Rhys, passed him the remote, and said, "Pick the highlights. Let's figure out where the defending went wrong."

Rhys chuckled, eyes puffy, and replied, "You mean in life or in football?"

"Both," I said, smiling.

Football in our household wasn't just about rivalry. It was about rhythm. About connection. About joy.

On Christmas mornings, there were always football-related gifts. New jerseys. A framed print of the 1999 treble-winning team. Once, Sharon gifted me a mug that read: Sir Alex > Wenger. It's not personal. Just facts.

I didn't drink from it. But I kept it on the mantle out of respect.

In return, I gave Sharon a throw pillow that said: Arsenal plays beautiful football.

Unfortunately, the league isn't a beauty pageant.

She used it proudly.

And even when Sharon and I had our moments of tension — over me wasting money, responsibilities, or parenting — football became the neutral ground. It was the place where we could meet as equals. As fans. As people who understood the value of passion, loyalty, and heartbreak.

Over the years, our living room became a museum of memories. Scarves draped across curtain rods. Posters of players past and present. Rhys added a signed Bruno Fernandes photo. Jilisha brought home a print of Thierry Henry's famous knee-slide against Spurs.

Every piece told a story.

Every match added another chapter.

When Manchester United lifted the Carabao Cup in 2023, Rhys and I celebrated like it was the Champions League. I danced around the kitchen, holding a wooden spoon like a trophy.

Sharon, sipping wine, said dryly, "Let me know when you win a real one."

And when Arsenal came heartbreakingly close to winning the league that same year, I placed a tiny second-place rosette on Sharon's pillow.

She retaliated by changing the Wi-Fi password to *GunnersRule2023*.

But through it all—every cheer, every tear—there was only love.

Football was the soundtrack to our lives. Not always in harmony. Sometimes dissonant. But always powerful.

And I wouldn't have had it any other way.

Simply U

At the same time, I kept my heart tethered to community and culture. One of my favorite haunts in North London was Burger's Barbershop—known affectionately to regulars as Simply U. More than just a place to get a shape-up or a fade, Simply U was a cultural institution, a modern-day village square. Jamaican and African men of all ages gathered there to debate football, politics, music, and women. It was where you learned the latest gossip, heard conspiracy theories about the Queen, and argued passionately about whether Pelé or Maradona was the true G.O.A.T.

I wasn't just a customer—I was part of the furniture. Sometimes I'd stop by not for a cut from my favorite barbers Patrick and Snoopy, but just for the vibes—debating Burger about Man Utd vs Arsenal and StGC vs KC, after taking a seat under the hum of fluorescent lights and watching clippers dance over scalps as stories spilled like Red Stripe from a cold bottle. Sometimes, minor tutoring sessions would happen right there—young boys struggling with GCSE English sitting in the corner while I explained poetry or essay structure in between banter and laughter.

"Alright, young blood," I would say to one of the boys, waving a copy of *Of Mice and Men*. "Lennie never meant harm, but the world don't rate Black men or simple men. That's why George shoot him — not because he hate him, but because he love him. See?"

The boy would nod, eyes wide, understanding literature through the lens of struggle and tenderness.

But Simply U wasn't just for the men. On the opposite side, separated by just a space on the floor, with a steady hum of hair dryers, Karen and Rhona ran their own kingdom — a small but mighty salon space where women came to be transformed. Karen, with her quick wit and precision hands, specialized in silk presses and protective styles. Rhona, quieter but no less skilled, had a gift for braiding — her fingers moved like they were dancing, weaving stories into cornrows and box braids.

Sharon would go there every other Saturday, her hair wrapped in a scarf, her spirit ready for renewal. She'd sit in Rhona's chair, sipping sorrel and catching up on the latest family news. Jilisha, still young but already full of grace, would sit beside her, flipping through magazines and occasionally glancing at her reflection with quiet pride. Karen would tease her gently, "Yuh know yuh hair growing like wild bush, right? Mi haffi tame it today." (You know your hair is growing like wild bush, right? I have to tame it today.") And Jilisha would laugh, that soft, melodic laugh that made the whole room feel lighter.

The salon side of Simply U had its own rhythm—gospel music on Sunday mornings, Dancehall on Friday nights, and a steady stream of affirmations. Women shared recipes, parenting tips, and prayers. They talked about fibroids and finances, about raising sons in a world that didn't always see them. And when the men got too loud in the front, Karen would shout, "*Burger, turn down di foolishness! Mi trying to do edges back here!*" ("Burger turn down the foolishness! I am trying to do edges back here!")

310

There were days when the whole shop was alive with booming laughter, dominoes clicking in the back, and the sizzling aroma of jerk chicken cooking in foil trays. Other times, it held a more reflective mood — men with tired eyes and heavy silences, women with weary shoulders and quiet strength. Still, they gathered.

There was an unspoken rule in Simply U — you could be vulnerable there, but only in the coded language of survival. You could talk about your child support woes, your immigration hearing, your loneliness. But it would come cloaked in humor or storytelling.

"*Mi son nuh want nuttin to do wid mi now,*" (My son does not want anything to do with me now) a man named Trevor once confessed, rubbing his jaw. "*Mi miss di days when him did think mi a superhero. Now, mi is just a man who late on school fees.*" (I miss the days when he thought I was a superhero. Now I am just a man who is late on school fees).

Snoopy, without looking up, said, "Still be the superhero. Even Batman have bad PR sometimes."

I, hearing that, went quiet. I thought about Rhys. About the years I spent commuting to and from school, chasing promotions, missing bedtime stories. I made a mental note to call home early that evening.

Simply U was more than nostalgia. It was resistance.

Jilisha giving me a fade

In a city that often-rendered Black men invisible, that barbershop made us central. And in a world that often-dismissed Black women's beauty as burden, Karen and Rhona made it sacred. Here, we weren't suspects or statistics — we were scholars, comedians, prophets, and fools. We discussed Pan-Africanism with the same intensity as the latest Dancehall clash. And I, with my teacherly bent, often brought in books to leave on the counter.

I donated worn copies of *The Souls of Black Folk, Small Island, The Fire Next Time,* and *A Brief History of Seven Killings*. Occasionally, I'd find them being flipped through between trims.

"You read that one, Burger?"

Burger, the owner of the barbershop, who attended my rival school Kingston College in Jamaica, would shrug.

"*Mi start it. Heavy ting, yuh know. But good. Mi cyaan lie.*" (I started it. It's a heavy thing you know. But good. I cannot lie).

And that was all I needed. A spark.

Soon, informal "*Read & Reason*" sessions started in the back of the barbershop. Once a month, I would bring five or six young men — most of them students or ex-students — into the shop after hours. Burger would pull down the shutters. Patrick would order food. Karen and

Rhona would sometimes stay late, chiming in from the salon side. And I would guide discussions about identity, migration, masculinity, and memory.

They read *Akala*. They read *Stuart Hall*. They read poems by Linton Kwesi Johnson and verses by Tupac. They talked about fatherhood, fear, and future.

One evening, while discussing the poem *Colonization in Reverse* by Louise Bennett, a boy named Kezzie—barely sixteen—stood up and said:

"I feel like we colonizing them back with our presence. But they still don't know what to do with us."

I blinked. That line stayed with me for weeks.

I wrote it in my journal:

They still don't know what to do with us.

And I thought about that every time I was called *"articulate"* in staff meetings, every time I was passed over for promotion, every time someone looked surprised when I mentioned I held two degrees and was working on a third.

Still, Simply U was where I could exhale. It was where I could talk patois without translation, and where I could confess that I was tired, without being told to "take a mental health day" as if healing was a 9-to-5 benefit.

And whether it was a boy learning to write from his chest, a woman reclaiming her crown in Karen's chair, or a father finding his voice again—Simply U was where we remembered who we were.

The Call

By 2013, I found myself staring at the same horizon I had faced back in Kingston nearly fifteen years earlier.

The questions returned:

- "What else is out there?"

316

- "Can I grow here anymore?"

It wasn't dissatisfaction, not entirely. My job at the school in was stable, my students respected me, and my colleagues often turned to me for guidance. Sharon had carved out a network of friends. The kids were thriving — Jilisha, graceful and articulate, was preparing for university; Rhys was a curious sponge soaking up the world around him.

No, it wasn't dissatisfaction. It was restlessness. The kind that sits just beneath the skin, subtle but persistent, that tugs at the soul during quiet train rides, that lingers during Sunday afternoons when everyone else is napping and you're staring out the window wondering — What next?

London had been good to me. In some ways, it had made me a man. It had tested me, stretched me, taught me how to stand firm under pressure, how to teach through red tape, how to connect with students who came from war-torn regions, language barriers, broken homes. It had given me experience, resilience, and a beautiful multicultural household. But I felt something slipping. A kind of possibility, perhaps. A sense that I was no longer becoming, but simply existing. And for someone like me — who believed in perpetual growth, in the audacity of movement — that was a slow kind of death.

One evening in early spring, I sat at the kitchen table long after Sharon and the kids had gone to bed. A cup of lukewarm Milo in one hand and my laptop open in front of me, I scrolled through job listings — not just in London, but in New York, Atlanta, Toronto... and then, Florida.

There was something about Florida.

Maybe it was the way the name rolled off the tongue — soft and sunlit. Maybe it was the images in my mind: palm trees swaying over quiet cul-de-sacs, children riding bikes past lakes, Caribbean accents in the supermarkets. Maybe it was the promise of another fresh start. I clicked on a listing:

"English Teachers Wanted – Lee County Public Schools."

318

I read it three times.

The pay wasn't extraordinary. It was, in fact, lower than what I was earning in London. But the opportunity to teach in a system that was actively recruiting international talent piqued my curiosity. There was a sense of invitation in the posting. A signal that someone, somewhere, was opening a door.

Over the next few weeks, I became obsessed.

I devoured research on U.S. teacher certification requirements, state-specific licensure pathways, the cost of living in Fort Myers, and visa sponsorship routes for teachers. I also joined forums filled with educators from Ghana, Jamaica, and the Philippines who had made the move and were sharing their journeys — some full of triumph, others cautionary tales.

I reached out to Jamaicans in Miami. Found a group of British expats in Orlando. I even cold-emailed two principals in Lee County

319

with a short message, attaching my résumé and a paragraph that began:

"My name is Horatio Ward. I am a Jamaican-born, British-trained educator with over 15 years of experience…"

I didn't expect a reply. But one did come — brief, professional, but encouraging:

"Your profile is impressive. If you're serious about relocating, I'd be happy to speak with you about our openings. Let me know."

That was all I needed. Permission to dream again.

Sharon, ever the realist, was cautious. Understandably so. We had just begun to feel settled in Enfield. Our house had become a home. The children had a rhythm. Rhys had friends. Jilisha was preparing her personal statement for UCAS. It wasn't the best time.

But she saw the fire return to my eyes when I spoke about it — the way my voice lifted at the end of sentences, the way I jotted down to-do lists on scraps of paper, the way I walked around with a different kind of energy. She knew that version of me. It was the me who left Jamaica in search of something more. The me who fought past setbacks with defiance. The me who did not sit still when my soul started to stir.

And she knew better than anyone: when I felt called, I followed.

We made a pact. "We'll just look into it," Sharon said, her tone gentle but protective. "We're not packing bags yet."

But I was already mentally mapping schools, neighborhoods, the proximity to the beaches.

In July 2014, after months of phone interviews, paperwork, and prayers, I received an offer from a middle school in Lehigh Acres, Florida. The principal sounded warm. The HR coordinator promised visa sponsorship. The move was real.

And now came the hard part: letting go.

The farewell tour was emotional. My students wrote letters. My colleagues surprised me with a send-off lunch, complete with a signed copy of *Of Mice and Men* — my favorite classroom text — annotated with personal messages in the margins. My best friend, Colin, didn't try to convince me to stay. He just said, *"Do yuh thing, Rambo. As long as it no dull yuh shine"* (Do your thing Rambo. As long as it doesn't dull your shine).

The family planned for Sharon and the kids to remain in London a bit longer. I would go first, find my footing, and send for them once things were stable.

And so, in November 2014, with two suitcases, a folder of documents, and a heart full of trepidation and anticipation, I stepped onto a plane once more — bound not for vacation, but for reinvention.

Act III

Chapter I: The Harvest

I Am Here

I landed in Florida in the fall of 2014 with two suitcases, a heart full of hope, and no clear road map beyond the job contract in my hand. The heat was a different kind of brutal — thick, slow, unforgiving. It clung to me like doubt. Fort Myers was a city I had never set foot in, yet somehow it felt like a place I'd always been moving toward. Wide roads unrolled beneath open skies; palms swayed as if they had stories to tell; and an unfamiliar quiet unnerved me after years of London's constant hum.

The teaching job that had drawn me to the U.S. fell through within weeks due to administrative delays with the visa conversion process. It was a bureaucratic mess. Papers misplaced. Emails unanswered. Positions filled. I found myself stranded in a country that promised opportunity but quickly showed me its cold shoulder. I remember sitting on the edge of the motel bed, staring at the ceiling fan spinning like a slow accusation. I had crossed an ocean for a future that now felt like vapor.

Fortunately, I had family.

My Aunty Bar took me in. Aunty Bar, my mom's sister, was a no-nonsense Jamaican woman with a booming voice and a heart like breadfruit—tough on the outside, soft on the inside. She lived on the east side of Lauderdale Lakes, in a modest home filled with lace curtains, portraits of grandchildren, and the perpetual smell of fried plantains and bay rum.

Her house was a living archive of migration and memory. Plastic-covered sofas. A Bible open on the coffee table. A calendar from a Caribbean church pinned to the fridge.

"Mi tell yuh seh America nuh easy," (I told you that America is not easy) she said on my first night, handing me a cup of ginger tea,*"But yuh come yah wid faith, and dat will carry yuh."* (But you came here with faith and that will carry you through.)

Her words settled into me like balm. I didn't know what the next day would bring, but I knew I wasn't alone.

The weeks that followed tested me in ways I hadn't expected. Each morning I woke to the sound of Caribbean radio drifting through the thin walls of Aunty Bar's house, announcers mixing patois with the Queen's English, a rhythm of home transplanted to foreign soil. The announcer's voice would crackle through the kitchen as I ate fried dumplings and eggs, and for a brief moment I could pretend I was back in Kingston. But then I'd step outside and the scale of Florida would overwhelm me—

lanes upon lanes of traffic, houses stretched far apart, everything wide and sun-drenched, as though space itself had no end.

I sent out résumés daily, chasing down any lead — public schools, charter schools, tutoring agencies. Some interviews came through, but my visa status seemed to hang over every conversation like an unspoken warning. "We'll be in touch," they'd say, shaking my hand with polite smiles that masked rejection.

Money dwindled quickly. The small savings I'd carried from London seemed to evaporate in this land of bills and hidden costs. Insurance here, application fee there, gas money gone after a few drives to Miami and back. I found myself counting dollar bills like a child counts marbles, each one more precious than the last.

Through it all, Aunty Bar was steady. She never made me feel like a burden. She had been in America long enough to know that struggle was the first language of migration. She told me stories of her early days cleaning houses in

Miami—of aching backs and swollen feet, of employers who barely looked at her as she scrubbed their floors. "*But mi never shame*," she said, sipping her sorrel one evening. "*Because mi know mi story never end deh so. Mi jus' start.*" (I was never ashamed, because I know my story didn't end there—I was just getting started.)

Her resilience was contagious. I started helping around the house, fixing computers and running errands. It wasn't work in the formal sense, but it gave me a rhythm, a purpose while I waited.

By December, I began to carve out a fragile routine. On some days, I would take long walks through the neighborhood, sweating under the Florida sun but refusing to stay locked inside. On other days, I rode the bus into Miami, sitting among strangers who spoke Spanish, Creole, and English in equal measure. The bus became its own classroom— immigrants clutching grocery bags, teenagers glued to their phones, old men nodding off after night shifts. Everyone seemed to be moving toward something, though what that something was, remained unclear.

Christmas that year was bittersweet. Back in London, the cold would have been biting, the streets decorated with glowing lights, and my friends gathering for drinks. In Jamaica, it would have been music, food, and the familiar laughter of family. Here in Florida, it was quieter. We cooked a modest meal — curried goat, rice and peas, sorrel — and we gathered around the small dining table in Aunty Bar's house. I called Mama back home. Her voice cracked on the phone, filled with both pride and worry. *"Mi son, mi know yuh strong. Dis a just one season. Better a go come."* (My son I know you are strong. This is just one season. Better will come.)

Those words became my compass.

In January, the tide began to shift. A charter school in Miami Gardens reached out. The principal, a Haitian-American woman with sharp eyes and a firm handshake, listened as I explained my situation. She looked at me for a long moment before saying, "You sound like a teacher who belongs in a classroom. We'll see what we can do." For the first time in months, hope felt tangible.

329

While the paperwork dragged on, I took on odd tutoring jobs through church contacts and community centers. The children reminded me why I had come in the first place. Their curiosity was raw, unpolished, and uncontainable. When one boy solved a math problem he had been struggling with for days, his face lit up, and in that glow, I rediscovered my calling. Teaching wasn't just a job — it was the thread that tied my past, present, and future together.

Looking back now, I realize that those early months in Florida were less about failure and more about foundation. Struggle, after all, is not the opposite of success — it is the soil in which success grows. I learned patience in those long afternoons of waiting. I learned humility in accepting help. And I learned resilience by refusing to board the next flight back to London when despair whispered its invitation.

Over time, Florida's heat no longer felt like doubt clinging to me. It became endurance, pressing against me but teaching me to breathe through it. The wide roads no longer felt empty — they became paths of possibility. And the palms, swaying in the breeze, no longer whispered stories of strangers. They whispered my own, reminding me that migration is never just about geography. It is about becoming.

And through it all, Aunty Bar remained the quiet hero of that chapter. Her voice, her home, her ginger tea — each was a reminder that roots stretch across oceans. In Lauderdale Lakes, in that house of lace curtains and plastic-covered sofas, I found my first American anchor.

Teaching Through Sales

By early 2015, I found myself walking into strip malls and church halls with a leather satchel, a clipboard, and a stack of brochures — not lesson plans. I had traded the whiteboard for policy documents, the classroom bell for cold calls. It was a strange pivot; one I hadn't rehearsed for. But life, I was learning, doesn't always wait for rehearsals.

Selling life insurance wasn't part of any grand plan. It began with a chance meeting at a networking event—a fellow Jamaican man, sharp-dressed and silver-tongued, told me about "the opportunity of a lifetime." The pitch was simple: low overhead, flexible hours, uncapped commission. He spoke with the kind of confidence that made you believe the American dream was still alive and well, tucked inside a laminated brochure and a well-rehearsed script.

I was skeptical. But times were lean. The school job market had cooled. Bills hadn't. So, I leapt.

My first stop was American Income Life Insurance Company. The onboarding was fast-paced and intense—script memorization, role-playing, and a crash course in selling protection to families who often had little to spare. The company had a union-based model, which meant we were often welcomed into homes with a sense of trust already built in. But trust didn't guarantee a sale. I had to learn how to listen differently—not for literary themes or student struggles, but for financial fears, generational gaps, and the quiet desperation of parents trying to secure something for their children beyond the present.

The early weeks were brutal. Rejection stung sharper than a red pen slash on a poorly written essay. People hung up mid-sentence. Others made appointments and never showed. The competition was ruthless—some agents whispered misinformation, undercutting prices, promising miracles. But I wasn't built for gimmicks. What I did have was authenticity. Presence. Clarity.

I spoke to people like they mattered and explained terms like whole life and term coverage with the same rhythm and storytelling I once used to break down Maya Angelou and Langston Hughes. My voice didn't sell fear. It sold peace of mind. I'd walk into a barbershop in Fort Lauderdale, introduce myself respectfully, and end up staying for an hour— talking football, fatherhood, and final expenses. I made eye contact. I listened. And in a market oversaturated with hustlers, that made all the difference.

I mapped routes with military precision. I was in Hollywood on Monday, in Miami on Tuesday, Miramar on Wednesday and Lauderdale Lakes on Thursday. Friday was catch-up. Saturday, if I was lucky, a rest day — or another pitch. Some days, I burned through a tank of gas and made nothing. Other days, one deal would flip my entire week. It was feast or famine. I kept an emergency pack of peanut butter crackers and bottled water in my glovebox. I learned to smile through rejection, to shake it off and knock on the next door.

By June 2015, the commission checks started coming in with more consistency. One month, I made more than I had in three months as a teacher. I paid off old bills, sent a tidy sum back to London for Rhys's school trip, and tucked some into savings. I bought a new suit. Not flashy — just tailored, dignified. I believed that even if I was knocking on doors in the blistering Florida heat, I should look like someone worth trusting.

I remember my first sale vividly; a retired couple in Miami. The husband had worked construction for thirty years; the wife had raised four children and now babysat her grandkids. They didn't have much, but they wanted to leave something behind. I walked them through the policy with care, answered every question, and when they signed, the wife looked at me and said, "You explained it like a teacher. I understood everything." That moment reminded me: I hadn't left teaching. I had just changed classrooms.

Eventually, I transitioned to National Agents Alliance (NAA), but this model was different—more entrepreneurial, and more aggressive in its recruitment and expansion. It was a culture of hustle, of motivational calls and leaderboard rankings. I was introduced to the world of multi-level marketing, where mentorship was currency and success was measured in downlines and override commissions. It wasn't always my style, but I adapted. I found my rhythm.

At NAA, I began mentoring new agents, helping them navigate the emotional terrain of rejection and resilience. I created training materials, led small group sessions, and reminded folks that selling insurance wasn't just about policies — it was about people. I saw young agents blossom under guidance, and I saw others burn out. The turnover was high, but the lessons were lasting.

One of the most powerful moments came during a church hall presentation in Miramar. I was speaking to a group of migrant workers, many of whom had never considered life insurance. I broke down the policy in plain language, shared stories of families who had benefited, and answered questions with patience. At the end, a woman approached me with tears in her eyes. "I didn't think people like us could afford this," she said. "But you made me feel like we mattered." That stayed with me.

Eventually, I moved on to Americo Insurance. The transition was strategic — Americo offered more flexible products, better underwriting options, and a digital platform that made applications smoother. It felt like a step forward, a chance to refine my craft with tools that matched my evolving approach. By then, I wasn't just selling I was building. I had a small team, a growing client base, and a reputation for integrity.

Americo gave me room to breathe. I could tailor policies to fit families instead of forcing families to fit policies. I began focusing on underserved communities — immigrants, single parents, retirees living on fixed incomes. I saw insurance not as a transaction, but as a form of dignity. A way to say, "Your life matters. Your legacy matters." I also began reconnecting with my roots as an educator. I hosted financial literacy workshops, partnered with local churches and community centers, and created handouts that explained insurance in culturally responsive ways. I used metaphors from gardening, storytelling, and migration — ways of speaking that resonated with the people I served. I wasn't just selling anymore. I was teaching again.

Looking back, that season of my life was a crucible. I had arrived in Florida with two suitcases and a teaching contract that dissolved like mist. I had slept on a small bed in Aunty Bar's garage turned bedroom, ridden city buses to interviews, and swallowed pride more times than I could count. But I had also built something — slowly, deliberately, with grit and grace.

Teaching and mentoring new agents at NAA, 2015

Insurance taught me how to listen differently. How to speak with empathy. How to meet people where they were, not where I wished they'd be. It taught me that legacy isn't just about what we leave behind – it's about how we show up in the lives of others, even when we're uncertain, even when we're rebuilding.

Rookie of the Year 2015 National
Agents Alliance

By the end of 2015, I had carved out a new kind of classroom. One without desks or bells, but full of stories, questions, and quiet transformations. I had become a steward of futures, a guide through uncertainty, and a witness to resilience. In January 2016, I won the Rookie of the Year award at National Agents Alliance, after joining the company in May 2015, a full five months after many other agents. I amassed over $255,000 of new business in seven months, which placed me number one as a rookie for 2015 and in the top five of all agents for that year.

And through it all, I never stopped being a teacher. I just changed the subject.

The CBD Shop

In 2019, with Florida's medical marijuana industry booming and public attitudes shifting toward holistic wellness, I made a move that shocked many: I opened a CBD shop.

I called it **Relax & Relief CBD.**

Located in a small flea market in Bonita Springs, the shop was clean, bright, and welcoming. Shelves were lined with oils, balms, tinctures, teas, and gummies. Brochures explained the benefits of cannabidiol for anxiety, pain, sleep, and inflammation. I learned the science. I knew the legal fine print. I took online certifications and trained myself with the same rigor I once applied to preparing for lesson observations.

But more than that, I made it culturally accessible. I played soft reggae in the background. Displayed local art. Hosted "Wellness Wednesdays," where customers could come in for consultations and free herbal tea. Retirees, veterans, single moms, athletes — they all came. Some skeptical. Some desperate. Many returned.

It was a space of healing. A space of community. But it was also exhausting.

I ran the shop during weekends, often worked late into the night restocking inventory, balancing the books, and managing the shop's growing online orders. I wore too many hats — owner, marketer, counselor, janitor.

A defining moment in my CBD shop-ownership journey came in 2020, when I was invited to speak at the CBD Industry Association Mastermind Summit—February 7-8, at Coconut Pointe Resort in Bonita Springs, Florida. It was the first time I'd be stepping onto a stage not just as a retailer, but as a voice for the way I believed this industry should work: transparent, responsible, and relentlessly focused on the people we serve.

In the weeks leading up to the event, I turned my daily routines into talking points. I laid out our intake forms, our training sheets, and the battered binder of standard operating procedures we'd built by trial and error. I wrote "What do we do differently?" at the top of a legal pad and filled the page: third-party lab tests for every batch; QR codes linking to Certificates of Analysis; clear hemp-derived labeling and <0.3% Δ-9 THC compliance; no medical claims—ever; and an education-first approach that teaches customers about the endocannabinoid system, "start low, go slow," and drug-interaction cautions. The more I prepared, the more I realized the talk wasn't about product—it was about trust.

343

The resort ballroom buzzed like a beehive—manufacturers, formulators, shop owners, attorneys, and a few skeptics who had come to see whether the industry was maturing beyond hype. I was on a panel called "Retail that Lasts," sandwiched between a national brand rep and a compliance consultant. When my turn came, I told the room that our most powerful marketing "campaign" was a laminated chart on our counter explaining how to read a COA. People laughed, then started taking pictures of the slide. I could feel the temperature of the conversation change.

Questions came fast: How do you handle banking? What do you do when a popular brand won't share test results? How do you navigate social-media ad bans? I answered with the same honesty I give customers across the counter. We diversified payment processing and kept cash controls tight. We dropped brands that refused transparency—no matter how pretty the label. We focused on content and community over ads: workshops for seniors, Q&A nights for veterans, and partnerships with wellness providers who cared more about outcomes than affiliate links. "If you want staying power," I said, "build a store that could pass a surprise audit and a grandmother's sniff test on the same day."

Midway through, a young owner stood up and asked the question that has shaped me ever since: "How do you earn trust in a market where people have been burned?" I took a breath. "By practicing radical clarity," I said. "Price fairly. Post the COA. Admit what CBD can't do. Track lots and batches like you're running a pharmacy. And when you make a mistake, fix it publicly. Trust isn't a line in your bio; it's a habit your customers can witness."

After the session, we clustered in the hallway and swapped business cards until my pocket felt like a filing cabinet. A chemist offered to help refine our terpene reporting; a lawyer reminded me to update our return policy language; three owners asked for our staff-training outline. Back home, I implemented everything we'd promised on stage. We rebuilt our batch-tracking spreadsheet, added scannable stickers to every jar, and created a "Know Your COA" brochure that customers still tuck into their wallets. Revenue lifted, yes—but more important, complaints dropped, and referrals rose. The shop felt calmer, smarter, sturdier.

On the last evening, I stepped outside and listened to the Gulf wind move through the palms. The industry still had headwinds— regulatory uncertainty, sloppy actors, and plenty of noise—but I felt steadier than I had in years. Speaking at the summit didn't make us the biggest store in Florida. It did something better: it clarified our standard. From that weekend on, every decision ran through the same filter—Does this deepen trust?—and if the answer was no, we didn't do it. That was the moment my business stopped chasing the market and started leading the people who mattered most: the customers who put their health, their money, and their hope in our hands.

Though I was now teaching full time again, I continued to run Relax & Relief CBD in the background. Sales dipped slightly in early 2021, but loyal customers kept coming back. My small online store picked up traffic from out-of-state clients, especially those looking for natural remedies during the pandemic anxiety.

Eventually, I partnered with Kassy, who created beautifully scented candles and soaps — and who brought both charm and structure to the operation. Kassy greeted every customer as though she had known them for years and often shared stories, connecting the calming properties of CBD to the need for mental resilience. Within weeks, several regulars began coming in not just for products, but for conversation.

I still made weekly check-ins, restocked inventory, and continued to promote wellness events via social media. On Saturday mornings, I would drive over before the store opened, sweeping the floor and straightening displays with meditative precision before heading to school to grade papers. It became part of my rhythm—the classroom feeding my heart, the shop tending to my spirit.

On one particularly quiet afternoon, I sat behind the counter scrolling through online orders when a woman walked in with her teenage daughter. She hesitated at the door until Kassy greeted her warmly and guided her to the display of herbal teas. After a few minutes, I joined them. The woman explained that her daughter had been struggling with crippling anxiety since the start of the pandemic and nothing seemed to help. I listened gently, then offered a small sampler pack—free of charge—with instructions on how to brew the tea in the evenings.

"Tea isn't just something you drink," I said softly. "It's a moment you give yourself."

Two weeks later, she returned. Her daughter waited in the car, smiling through the window. The woman pressed my hand and said, "Thank you. She's sleeping again."

It was then I realized that the shop wasn't a side business. It was a testament to survival, entrepreneurship, and healing.

Every jar of balm, every bottle of tincture, held a story—of someone trying to reclaim calm, restore balance, find a way forward. And in that sense, it wasn't so different from the classroom. Both spaces required patience. Both required faith. Both asked me to believe—again and again—that healing is possible.

So, I kept going.

Teaching by day.

Serving by evening.

Rooted in two worlds that, in truth, were never separate at all.

Chapter II: Foundations of a Teacher's Journey

The Classroom

By 2019, I was living in Cape Coral having moved there in the fall of 2017. Cape Coral was a quiet avenue of hope tucked beneath the surface — one that hadn't yet found its voice. The transition was practical: a new job in insurance, a new city, a new rhythm for our family. I learned the language of policies and premiums, sharpened my communication, and built trust with clients navigating uncertainty. It was meaningful work, and it sustained us.

But by the fall of 2019, the ache of the classroom had become too loud to ignore.

Insurance had taught me resilience, yes. It had refined my listening and deepened my empathy. But it hadn't fed my soul. I didn't just want to provide for my family — I wanted to pour into people again. I missed the spark in a student's eyes when a metaphor landed. I missed the hush that followed a powerful

351

poem. I missed the sacred tension of a classroom where transformation was always possible.

So, I began the process — paperwork, exams, re-certifications. The Florida Department of Education required transcripts, verification of foreign qualifications, and a maze of forms that seemed designed to frustrate. I spent evenings combing through requirements, tracking down documents from London and Kingston, and praying for clarity in the chaos. But I pressed on, determined to return to the space where I belonged.

When the acceptance email finally arrived in February 2020 — offering me a position at Mid Cape Global Academy in Cape Coral — I stared at the screen for a long time. Relief washed over me, followed by anticipation, and then something else: reverence.

Teaching wasn't just a job. It was a sacred calling I had stepped away from and was now being invited back into.

The timing was uncanny. COVID was just beginning to cast its shadow across the world, and schools were bracing for disruption. But I knew, even then, that I was stepping into something deeper than curriculum or classroom management. I was returning to the work that had always felt like home.

And Cape Coral, once just a place to land, had become the soil where I would plant new seeds.

First Days

Mid Cape Global Academy was unlike anything I had known in Jamaica or London. The corridors smelled faintly of disinfectant and cafeteria pizza, with hand sanitizer stations posted like sentries at every turn. Posters of college logos and motivational slogans lined the walls: "Be Respectful. Be Responsible. Be Remarkable." But the energy was quieter now, muted by masks, staggered schedules, and the weight of uncertainty.

The student body was a tapestry of cultures — Latino, African American, Haitian, Jamaican, Cape Verdean, and white working-class kids. English, Spanish, and Creole mixed in the hallways like overlapping soundtracks. Some students carried the heaviness of broken homes and economic struggle. Others floated with the lightness of teenage bravado, even behind face coverings.

On my very first morning, a boy slouched in the back of the hybrid classroom — half in-person, half virtual — muttered, "Man, we got a sub already?"

I smiled, leaned against the desk, and replied, "No, bredrin. I'm here for the long haul. Better get used to me."

The class laughed. A few eyebrows rose above masks. A connection sparked.

Florida classrooms ran on a different rhythm. Standardized testing loomed like a shadow, pacing guides were rigid, and the pressure to "teach to the test" weighed heavy — even in the middle of a pandemic. But I refused to let the soul of education be stripped away. I wove stories into lessons, connected Shakespeare to hip-hop, and made space for students to share their voices — whether through a screen or six feet apart.

I launched a virtual debate club and introduced "Poetry Fridays," where students could write in patois, Spanish, Creole, or English and share their truth without fear. At first, my accent threw some of them off.

"Where you from, Sir?" a girl asked during a Zoom breakout session.

"Kingston, Jamaica," I replied.

"Say something Jamaican!"

So I grinned and said, *"Yuh see me? Mi deh yah fi teach, but mi also deh yah fi listen."* (Do you see me? I am here to teach, but I am also here to listen.)

The chat lit up with emojis. From that day forward, they trusted me more — not just as a teacher, but as someone real.

Legacy

As months turned into masked semesters, I grew into my role—not just as a teacher, but as a builder. I mentored younger staff, encouraged colleagues to embrace culturally responsive teaching, and took students on virtual field trips that showed them a bigger world beyond Cape Coral.

I became known as the teacher who expected excellence — but gave grace. Students who were written off elsewhere often found refuge in my classroom. One boy, Jamari, told me after class, "Sir, this is the only room where I feel smart."

That was worth more than any paycheck.

I knew then that returning to teaching wasn't just about reclaiming my profession. It was about planting new seeds in new soil, ensuring that my children — and every child I taught — understood that education is a bridge, not a burden.

Late at night, when the house was still and the day's numbers tallied, I'd catch myself reminiscing. Not about money — but about minds.

The spreadsheets and policy applications from my insurance days faded into the background, and what lingered was the echo of a student's breakthrough, the spark in their eyes when a metaphor landed, the hush that fell over the room when a poem demanded reverence. I missed that. I missed the challenge of reluctant students — the ones who crossed their arms and dared you to make learning matter. I missed crafting essay prompts that pushed them beyond the surface, that asked not just what but why.

Insurance had taught me discipline, resilience, and the art of listening. It had sharpened my communication and deepened my empathy. But it hadn't fed my soul.

I realized then that the job — lucrative as it might become — was only a means, not an end. My purpose had always been clearer than my circumstances. I wasn't meant to sell policies. I was meant to ignite people.

Because deep down, I knew: the classroom wasn't just calling. It was waiting.

It waited in the silence between verses of a Langston Hughes poem. It waited in the margins of a student's journal, where truth often hides. It waited in the AVID Club flyers I still kept tucked in a drawer, reminders of the spaces I once helped shape.

The classroom was more than a place — it was a promise. A sanctuary. A stage for transformation.

I was proud of what I had built in the insurance world. I had weathered setbacks, learned the language of contracts and commissions, and helped families secure peace of mind. But something still tugged at me. That old familiar restlessness.

A whisper.

It came in quiet moments — while folding laundry, while driving past a school bus, while hearing a child recite something with conviction. It was the whisper that said, "You were made for more than transactions. You were made for transformation."

So, I listened. I didn't announce it. I didn't rush it. I simply began. One step at a time. One document at a time. One prayer at a time.

Returning to the classroom wasn't just about employment. It was about alignment — about coming home to work that had always felt sacred, about choosing purpose over comfort and legacy over convenience.

And I was ready.

Chapter III: Growth Takes Hold

Home

In December 2020, after six years of shared living, rented rooms, borrowed couches, and endless compromises, I made a decision: I was going to use the money I had saved up from life insurance and CBD to buy a home. Not just a place to stay — but a space to exhale. To build. To reclaim a sense of permanence that had long felt out of reach.

Since leaving London and starting over in Florida, I had lived in basement apartments, a garage, and makeshift accommodations cobbled together by friends or kind landlords. It was survival — but it wasn't stability. And I had come too far, worked too hard, sacrificed too much, to remain in transit forever.

So, I began the search.

The housing market in Southwest Florida was unpredictable. Prices rose and dipped like the tides. The pandemic had warped everything — real estate, credit access, job security. Friends warned me against it. "Now's not the time," they said. "Wait until the market cools down."

But I had waited my whole life. Waited on immigration papers. Waited on job confirmations. Waited for my children to join me. Waited for paychecks to stretch far enough. Waited on the system. On the stars. On myself.

Now, I was done waiting.

Each weekend, I scoured listings. I walked through houses with a notepad and a vision. I wasn't looking for granite countertops or double garages. I was looking for sunlight. For possibility. For peace.

And, after months of searching and second-guessing, I found it: a modest two-bedroom home tucked in a quiet cul-de-sac in Lehigh Acres, a slowly blossoming suburb just east of Fort Myers. The neighborhood had young families and retirees, pickup trucks and basketball hoops. Mango trees and mailboxes adorned with wind chimes. It was humble. But it was honest.

The house had good bones — a solid roof, new plumbing, and wooden floors that clicked like dominoes when walked on barefooted. It gave a sort of holiday home, log cabin in the woods type vibe, which I instantly fell in love with.

In the first hour of walking through it, I noticed how the light behaved like a respectful guest — never harsh, always finding the edges of doorframes and the grain of the wood. The porch faced just enough east to catch the soft sun, and when the morning breeze came off the trees it carried a smell of clean timber and something green. The rooms weren't big, but they were honest. Doorways aligned the way old houses sometimes do, creating a clear sightline from the front step to the kitchen window, as if the place wanted to breathe straight through.

There were quirks, of course. A stubborn latch in the guest room, cabinet hinges that sighed, a hairline crack above the fireplace like a smile held too long. None of it felt like trouble — only a conversation the house wanted to have with its next owner. I imagined rugs that would muffle the evening, a reading chair by the window, a kettle on just before dusk. The first rain on that roof would sound like permission. With a little paint, a few tightened screws, and regular sweeping of the porch, the house would do its part. All I had to do was show up, listen to its habits, and let its good bones teach me how to live there.

The backyard stretched wide enough to fit three more houses. It held my jerk chicken grill and the long-held dreams of a Caribbean man who once stared at zinc rooftops in Denham Town and wondered what life might be like "over there." Now "over there" looks like fresh-cut grass underfoot, a sturdy fence, and a patch of sky that belongs to no one and everyone at once. Today, the grill stands like a small altar—with jerk chicken hissing in the evenings, plantains caramelizing at the edges, smoke lifting a scent that makes neighbors drift toward the gate with plates in hand. Folding chairs circle up, a speaker hums a quiet riddim, (rhythm) and someone marks off wickets with chalk so the children can bowl and bat until the porch light comes on.

I planted garden beds along the back, the kind that teach patience: callaloo, thyme, Scotch bonnet, a brave tomato vine that leans into the fence for support. On Sundays, the hose arcs like a silver rope, and the youngest children run through it squealing while the old heads argue the rules of dominoes. In the quiet after the last plate is washed, I sit and listen to the yard breathe. The boy who once watched planes

365

climb out of Kingston Harbor has landed. "Over there" has turned into "right here" — not a fantasy, but a place where I can invite others in, lay out food, pass on stories, and let the night close softly around us like a promise kept.

I signed the papers with trembling hands.

The moment the keys dropped into my palm; I felt it: arrival. I didn't hire a contractor. I became one. Not out of frugality, but out of something deeper — something ancestral. The act of building with my own hands felt sacred.

Each weekend and every quiet evening after school, I traded my lesson plans for paint trays, my red pen for a hammer, my teacher's voice for the silence of focus.

I painted the walls myself — earthy tans in the living room, deep blue in the office, a splash of turmeric in the kitchen that reminded me of curry bubbling on Sunday afternoons. These weren't catalog colors. They were Caribbean hues — colors with memory. Colors that spoke in patois and gospel. Colors that reminded me of Mama's kitchen, Sharon's laughter, and the sea in Negril at dusk.

I unrolled the batik tapestry Sharon had brought back from Jamaica years ago. It depicted a market scene—women balancing baskets on their heads, children chasing goats, elders sitting in the shade of ackee trees. I hung it in the hallway, where the light hit it just right in the afternoon. It was more than decoration. It was a portal.

By the front door, I nailed a photo of Mama—her hands on her hips, her eyes full of knowing. She stood in her garden in Kingston, wearing a faded apron and a look that said, I've seen storms, and I've survived them all. That photo became my compass. Every time I left the house, I touched the frame and whispered, "Guide me."

In the backyard, I planted a mango tree with soil from Home Depot and prayers from home. I pressed my fingers into the dirt like it was ritual, whispered names of ancestors, some whom I had never met but somehow still carried — Aunty Clemmie, Sister Lurline, Beckwith, Uncle Boyie, Aunt Bee, Aunt Amanda, Claudette, Oswald, Bernice. The tree was young, but it stood upright. Rooted. Just like me.

I hosted my first Christmas there just weeks after closing. The paint was still fresh on the baseboards. Boxes weren't all unpacked, but the house already felt lived in — because it was loved in.

Sharon flew in with pepper shrimp in foil containers, wrapped tight like sacred offerings. She arrived with her usual grace, her laughter filling the hallway before she even stepped through the door. She brought more than food — she brought memory.

Rhys, tall and confident now, helped string lights on the porch. His shoulders had broadened, his voice deeper, but he still asked me which bulbs should go where.

Jilisha, in her no-nonsense tone, made a shopping list and insisted on real sorrel — not the store-bought kind. She took charge of the kitchen like a general on a mission.

We played Beres Hammond and Luther Vandross. The speakers pulsed with soul and longing. Sharon swayed to Rock Away, eyes closed, hips moving like memory. Rhys tried to remix Never Too Much with trap beats — Jilisha rolled her eyes and told him to stop disrespecting legends. We laughed until the walls shook.

The dining table was mismatched — borrowed chairs, plates from three different sets. But it held abundance. Curry goat, rice and peas, callaloo, macaroni pie, plantains, and of course, the pepper shrimp. We said grace, not just for the food, but for the journey. For the years that tested us. For the home that now held our laughter like a sacred hymn.

That night, after everyone fell asleep, I stood alone in the backyard under the Florida stars. The mango tree was still young, barely taller than my shoulder. But it was alive. Growing. Becoming.

I raised a glass of red wine and whispered:

"This is for every version of me that didn't give up."

The house wasn't perfect. The AC groaned on hot days, the faucet in the guest bathroom dripped, but it was mine. More than that—it was ours. It was proof that resilience could be brick and mortar, that legacy could be painted on walls and planted in soil.

I had crossed oceans, changed countries, weathered storms—and here I stood, not just surviving, but rooted.

The mango tree would rise.

And so, would I.

Back to the Building

When schools reopened their doors in 2021, the return wasn't a triumphant march — it was a stagger. Students shuffled back in with masks, half-hidden faces, and the weight of months spent in bedrooms and living rooms. The building felt both familiar and foreign, a place where laughter returned in bursts but silence lingered in corners.

I knew the hardest work wasn't catching up on grades. It was rebuilding trust. Restoring rhythm. Re-learning how to be together.

On the first day back, I didn't open with grammar drills or reading comprehension sheets. I opened with one question written in bold across the board:

"What did the pandemic teach you?"

Some stared at it blankly. Some shrugged. But slowly, hands rose.

"Patience."

"How to cook."

"That my grandmother is stronger than anyone I know."

"That Wi-Fi can break your heart."

The room shifted. Shoulders relaxed. Laughter bubbled. Some eyes watered. We were learning already learning each other again.

I reintroduced rituals. Journals every Monday. Read-alouds every Wednesday. Friday reflections. I blended old with new—*Ahead of the Class* still lived online for students who preferred digital learning, but now I projected videos in class, pausing for live discussions. Students who had once hidden behind black Zoom screens now debated themes out loud, their voices cracking but steadying with every sentence.

AVID

That year, I was asked to step deeper into AVID. The principal pulled me aside after a staff meeting.

"Horatio, you have a way of making kids believe in themselves. We need that energy in AVID."

I accepted.

AVID (Advancement Via Individual Determination) wasn't new to me—but in Florida, it became a lifeline. Many of my students were first-generation college hopefuls. They didn't have uncles or aunts who had gone before them, no family blueprint for FAFSA forms or personal statements. They had grit, but they needed guidance.

So, I set up AVID binders with care and taught Cornell notes like it was an art form. I modeled inquiry with passion—turning every dull worksheet into a chance to ask, "Why does this matter?" We held Socratic seminars that sometimes turned into therapy sessions, where students argued passionately about justice, belonging, or whether pineapple belonged on pizza.

I pushed them to see themselves beyond the moment.

"Your story doesn't end here," I'd say. "This classroom is just the preface. Write the rest bold."

They believed me because I believed it first.

By spring 2022, the halls sounded alive again. Pep rallies returned. Sports matches drew crowds. My students began dressing up for spirit week as if reclaiming a stolen rite.

In my classroom, poetry was once again king. We studied Jason Reynolds beside Shakespeare, Amanda Gorman beside Maya Angelou. I invited students to perform spoken word pieces at assemblies, and when one shy Haitian girl performed her poem "I Am Not Invisible" to a standing ovation, I felt the room bend with possibility.

Parents called. Not to complain, but to say thank you.

"My son actually likes English this year."

"My daughter talks about college now."

And every evening, when Sharon asked how my day went, I no longer just smiled. I told stories. Stories of students who found their voices again. Stories of breakthroughs that happened not on tests, but in moments of courage.

Looking back, I realize 2021-2022 wasn't about "catching up." It was about re-rooting. About reminding students—and myself—that education isn't just about standards and benchmarks. It's about survival, about imagination, about building bridges strong enough to carry us from one uncertain shore to the next.

By the time summer came, I wasn't just a teacher again. I was whole again because the classroom wasn't simply where I worked. It was where I became.

Chapter IV: New Ground

LAMS

By August 2022, I had transferred to Lehigh Acres Middle School, and I walked into the new school year with a steadier step. The storms of the pandemic years had passed, but their echoes lingered. Students carried scars that weren't always visible—missed milestones, fractured friendships, quiet anxieties. My task was clear: to remind them, again and again, that they were capable of more than survival. They were built for thriving.

I leaned heavily into AVID at Lehigh Acres Middle. It became more than a program—it became a philosophy. Organization, inquiry, collaboration, reading, and writing weren't just strategies; they were lifelines. I trained my classes to use Cornell notes not just for English but for science, history, even their personal reflections.

When students grumbled, I told them, "Discipline is the bridge between dream and destiny." And slowly, their binders began to mirror their lives—ordered, intentional, forward-facing.

Tutorial sessions grew into something powerful. I watched students guide each other through difficult math problems, science labs, and essay outlines. Some of the best moments weren't when I explained, but when I stepped back and heard one student say to another, "Wait, let me show you how I figured it out." That was AVID at its core—students teaching students, confidence passed like a torch.

379

I started by rebuilding the room itself. On the first teacher workday, I dragged the desks into a loose horseshoe so no one could disappear in the back row. I taped college pennants along the whiteboard — FGCU, Florida A\&M, UCF, a handful of out-of-state schools I'd visited — and added a blank banner that read, "Add yours here." I posted sentence stems at eye level for inquiry ("I notice...," "I wonder...," "What evidence supports...?") and set a small table near the door for supplies students could take without asking: pencils, sticky notes, highlighters, compassion. The room needed to say, "You belong. You are safe. We're going somewhere."

The first weeks were triage and trust. Kids arrived with the timing of alarms — some too early, many late, a few convinced the bell didn't apply to them. More than once, a student froze at the threshold like it was a border crossing. So, we built routines that could catch a heart before it fell: warm-ups on the board, a daily quote, a two-minute write. When the quote was "We are what we repeatedly do," hands shot up.

"Even when what we repeatedly do is stay up past midnight?" someone asked.

I grinned: "Especially then — habits are honest." There were chuckles, and the shoulders in the back row dropped a notch.

AVID binder checks became a Friday ritual. Not a gotcha, but a mirror. I'd clap and call, "Tabs up!" and a field of color would ripple across the room — dividers labeled Math, Science, Language Arts, History, "Life." We graded with a rubric: dated notes, completed summaries, questions in the margins. When binders were thin, I sat with the student and rebuilt the system from scratch, hole-punching handouts like we were stitching a wound. J., who used to stuff everything into his hoodie pocket, eventually slapped his binder on the desk like a passport. "Stamped and ready," he'd say. It wasn't about paper. It was about narrative control.

Cornell notes surprised them. At first, they copied headlines like stenographers, writing to survive the next quiz. Then we practiced the left column: questions only. I modeled out loud how to interrogate a text: "If the author claims X, what would disprove it? What's the missing voice?" We practiced summaries that weren't just endings, but new beginnings. When a student wrote, "This section is about photosynthesis," I wrote back: "Yes, and why does the plant's hunger matter to us?" The next week she wrote, "Plants feed on light; we feed on the plants; the sun feeds everything." That line glowed in the margin like a small sunrise.

Tutorials were the heartbeat. Twice a week, groups formed around student questions, not teacher assignments. They brought points of confusion written clearly on TRFs (Tutorial Request Forms): "How do you find the slope if the line is vertical?" "Why did the author break the paragraph right there?" At first, they wanted answers like vending machines. I taught them to price the question higher than the answer. The presenter would explain; the group would ask probing questions; the presenter would revise. When someone blurred into silence, a peer would slide a whiteboard closer: "Draw it." Those were sacred minutes —

eyes up, pens moving, the quiet electricity of kids constructing their own clarity.

Socratic seminars in English grew from cautious circles to true conversations. We started with low-risk texts: poetry with wide margins, editorials with obvious claims. Students learned to cite and build: "I want to extend what L. said with a different example," "I'm respectfully disagreeing because the data on line 17..." I enforced two simple rules: speak once before you speak twice; bring someone in. The first time S., who had barely spoken since August, said, "I want to hear from M.," the room shifted. It was the sound of belonging arranged by peers, not by me. We ended seminars with kudos—one sentence of gratitude or specific praise—and I watched faces open like windows.

Discipline changed, too. We tried to make accountability the same shape as community. When conflict flared—snapping words, slammed binders—I thought of the pandemic's residue: the loneliness that calcified into defensiveness.

We used restorative questions: "Who was affected?" "What do you need to make it right?"

I learned to listen without forming my closing argument.

Once, after a blowup, a boy muttered, "You teachers always think..."

Then he stopped. "Always think what?" I asked.

He swallowed. "That I'm the problem."

We sat in the hallway, two chairs against a cinderblock wall, and mapped out a plan: a signal when he felt the wave coming, a break pass, a spot to cool down. He returned to class fifteen minutes later, and when he met my eyes, I nodded like a third base coach waving him home.

We made space for joy. On "College Mondays" we wore university shirts and played "major match," guessing majors based on course lists. On "Future Fridays" we wrote letters to ourselves three years ahead: "Dear Me, stop apologizing for being excellent." We hosted a parent night with student tour guides who explained Cornell notes to families in two languages, flipping their binders like proud sales reps. A mom hugged me near the door and whispered, "I didn't know how to help before. Now I do." No data point in the district dashboard measured that, but it measured me.

Reading was stubborn for some, so we made it social and visible. The classroom library grew — paperbacks arranged face-out, a "Book I Finished" wall where students signed their names under covers. When the reluctant readers rolled their eyes, I matched them to books with short chapters and quick stakes. "Two pages at a time," I said. "Small wins compound." During sustained silent reading, I walked slowly, listening to the room breathe. I learned who pretended to read (pages never turned) and who disappeared into stories like they found oxygen there.

Writing bled into everything. We kept one-pagers — visual, written responses with quotes, questions, and images. We wrote exit tickets that asked, "What confused you today?" and "Where did you surprise yourself?" We revised with "glow/grow" feedback — one luminous strength, one concrete improvement. I taught them that revision wasn't a punishment but an artist's privilege. When R. added three sentences to clarify her claim and breathed, "Oh, that's what I meant," I realized I was watching a child catch up to her own mind.

There were setbacks: the post-holiday dips in motivation; a hallway fight that left two students suspended and five more shaken; a week when attendance cratered, and I taught to a half-empty horseshoe; and a quiz on which nearly everyone missed the inference question—proof that my instruction had been muddy.

We reteach. We repair. We try again. I kept a sticky note on my laptop: "Slow is smooth. Smooth is fast." Another: "Assume good intent. Train better habits." On tough days, I clung to both like railings.

We also chased evidence. Not to worship numbers, but to respect them. Students set quarterly goals—GPA targets, attendance streaks, behavior points—and tracked progress on simple dashboards. We celebrated growth not just in big jumps but in persistence: the student who went from zero to three assignments submitted on time, then five, then ten. I used common assessments as a map, not a verdict. When the data showed weak analysis in paragraph twos across the board, I built a mini-lesson and retooled sentence stems. Feedback loops got shorter. Victories got louder.

What I loved most were the small stories that made a school year: the morning K. left a note on my desk— "I used the question column to study for science and got my first B."

The day F. asked for extra Cornell paper for her little brother.

The way the back-row trio, once allergic to participation, fought to be the group presenter in tutorials because "we got the process now."

The afternoon a guidance counselor poked her head in and asked, "What are you doing in here? It smells like effort."

I laughed, but I knew what she meant. Culture has a scent when it's working: a mix of Expo marker, warm laptops, and earned pride.

We ended the year with a gallery walk — one-pagers, best paragraphs, Cornell notes that showed growth from September to May. Students walked around with sticky notes, leaving comments for each other: "Your question made me think," "I liked how you backed up your claim," "This drawing helped me understand the text." When they came back to their own work and read the notes, the room filled with that particular hush: the sound of being seen. Then we took one last set of notes together, not on a text but on the year. In the summary section, I asked them to write one sentence that began with "Because of this class, I..." The answers made me swallow hard. "...plan my week." "...ask questions even when I'm scared." "...believe that I'm college material." "...know how to study without staying up all night." I tucked those papers into a folder labeled "Why."

By August 2023, when I set up the room again, I kept the horseshoe. I refreshed the pennants and left the blank banner. I refilled the supply table. But I added one new sign above the door, right where students could see it as they left: "Take what you learned and teach someone else." That was the quiet promise of AVID, of the year, of my work at Lehigh Acres: that skills become habits, habits become character, and character turns knowledge outward. The storms had passed; their echoes would fade. In that hallway light, with backpacks slung and voices rising, the future didn't feel fragile. It felt like something we were already building — one binder ring, one good question, one shared victory at a time.

Beyond the Classroom

In 2023, I began saying "yes" more often to roles outside my classroom. What started as small steps — sharing a strategy here, offering a reflection there — soon grew into regular presentations at faculty meetings, where I spoke about the power of WICOR strategies. Some afternoons, exhausted though I was, I found myself sitting with colleagues from other departments, coaching them through AVID practices.

"It's not just English," I told the science team one day. "It's learning how to learn." And I meant it. Watching a biology teacher use Socratic Seminars to help students untangle cell structure or seeing a math teacher invite reflection journals after algebra lessons, gave me fresh energy. Those moments reminded me that the real work of teaching was never confined to one classroom or one subject. It was in the ripple effects — the way an idea traveled, adapted, and bloomed in places I hadn't expected.

On the first afternoon I presented, I brought artifacts instead of slides: student one-pagers with fluorescent highlights, worn Cornell pages with questions blooming down the margins, and a stack of exit tickets bound with a paperclip. I laid them out on a table like proof. "This is what it looks like when thinking leaves a trail," I said.

A veteran teacher in the third row crossed her arms. "Our kids won't do this," she said, not unkindly, just tired.

I nodded. "Some won't. At first." I told her what I tell students: "we don't start with belief; we start with habits. Belief shows up later, sneaking in behind practice."

Mentoring new teachers changed my pace. Instead of sprinting bell to bell, I learned to walk slowly in the moments that mattered. We met on Tuesdays, a rotating group of rookies who still called the copier "the machine." We planned the first six weeks like an architect plans load-bearing walls: how to greet at the door, how to use a seating chart without turning kids into coordinates, how to teach procedures as lessons instead of lectures. We practiced a three-beat routine I live by: "bellwork, binders, brain" — five minutes to settle, two minutes to check materials, then we launch. I told them to narrate the positive and redirect with dignity.

When one of them asked, "What if I'm not a natural disciplinarian?"

I said, "Good. Be a natural relationship builder. You can learn the rest."

Cross-department coaching made school feel like a single organism. In science, we used Question and Response stems to push lab groups beyond "It changed" to "The mass decreased by 0.4 grams; I wonder if evaporation played a role." In math, reflection journals turned speed into sense. Students wrote: "Today I kept rewriting 3/4 as 0.34; next time I will…" and then filled in strategies they learned from peers. History teachers adapted Cornell notes for DBQs, labeling sources by reliability and bias. In art, the teacher borrowed our "glow/grow" feedback and taped it above the critique wall: "Glow: What's working? Grow: What could be sharpened?"

Even the band director showed up to a meeting and said, half-joking, "Can AVID fix our measure counts?"

We laughed and built a rehearsal reflection that asked, "Where did your section carry the melody? What did you listen for?"

We tried something ambitious in October: an AVID "learning walk." Five teachers volunteered to turn their rooms into fishbowls, inviting colleagues to watch for ten minutes during tutorials or Socratic circles. We made a tiny script for observers so no one would default to judgment: "What student moves do you notice? Where do you see inquiry? What could be transferable to your content?" After the walks, we met in the library and debriefed over store-bought cookies.

A PE teacher said, "I never thought to use Cornell in health—now I'm seeing how my kids could study stress management like a system."

A chemistry teacher admitted she'd been skeptical, then added, "I watched a kid take the marker from another student and say, 'Explain your step, I'll write it.' I want that energy in my lab groups."

Family engagement became a second classroom. On a chilly January evening, we hosted "Binder Bootcamp + College Night." Students led the tours, which felt right; they were the experts. In the media center, I watched a ninth grader explain the question column to her aunt in Spanish, then handled her a highlighter like a baton. At the financial aid table, our counselor demystified FAFSA while a toddler tried to climb into a bin of crayons.

A grandmother came to me near the door and said, "I didn't finish high school. I want different for him." She pointed to her grandson, who stood tall like the compliment was a coat on his shoulders.

I told her, "We're building the road together. He's not walking it alone."

Saying yes had costs. My inbox learned to reproduce overnight. I missed a dinner or two I shouldn't have. Once, I fell asleep grading and woke with a binder tab imprint on my cheek. I started running again, slow loops around the neighborhood, to reset the noise in my head. I set a boundary I'd never set, after 7 p.m., emails could wait.

When a colleague teased me, "Mr. AVID finally says no!" —I smiled. If I was going to model balance for my students and my mentees, I had to practice it. On Saturday mornings, I took my notebook to Starbucks and wrote for me, not the job: small scenes, scraps of gratitude, a list titled "Proof of Good Work" where I captured moments I'd otherwise forget.

Data didn't scare me anymore; indifference did. In staff meetings we built a simple assessment calendar that respected teacher bandwidth. We picked three standards per quarter for common checks and wrote rubrics we could actually use. When we met, we asked two questions: "What helped your students learn this? What did we assume they'd know that they didn't?" In one meeting, the algebra team showed how a quick number talk before notes raised accuracy by ten points. In another, the ELA team discovered that starting essays with quotes from the text turned thesis statements into patchwork; we began with claims instead, then folded in textual evidence. The change felt small; the student writing didn't.

Equity was the throughline. We disaggregated data without weaponizing it. We tracked who raised hands in seminars and who never spoke. We noticed who needed more wait time, who benefited from sentence starters, who showed up to tutorials with perfect TRFs but stayed quiet when the whiteboard came out. We built supports that didn't shout "accommodation," just good teaching dressed in respect: visuals embedded in notes, translated agendas, flexible due dates paired with check-ins. I kept an extra set of colored pens in every room I coached because I'd seen how color-coding steps made processes feel less like a maze.

There were moments that felt like the job was working on me while I worked on the job. After a PD, a colleague pulled me aside. "I'm not good at this AVID stuff," she said, gesturing at the binder in her arms. "But I'm good at caring." I told her that that was the center, and strategies were just a way to aim care.

Another day, a first-year teacher slid into a chair in my room and said, "My lesson bombed." I poured water into a paper cup and pushed it across the desk.

"Tell me the story," I said. She did: the pacing, the stuck place, the boy who rolled his eyes so hard it felt like a door slam. When she was done, I asked, "What would you keep if you taught it again tomorrow?"

She blinked. "The opening. It was strong."

"Good," I said. "Start there. Build outward."

She texted me later that week: "It worked."

One of my favorite yeses came in spring when we took a small group to a local university. The bus was loud with the kind of excitement that says scared and thrilled are cousins. On the tour, students asked practical questions: "Do freshmen have to live on campus?" "How much does a meal plan cost?" In the library, they looked up at floors of books and whispered like they were in a cathedral.

At lunch, one student stared at a bulletin board for a long time and said, "There are so many clubs. You can just…join?"

On the ride back, I overheard a conversation about majors between two boys who usually only talked sports.

"I might do engineering," one said. "I like building."

The other nodded. "I like arguing. Maybe law."

I smiled out the window and thought, the future just got names.

By May, the leadership muscle I'd been exercising felt less like strain and more like posture. At our final faculty meeting, we did a gallery walk of teacher practices — three-minute lightning shares taped to the walls: "How I use exit tickets to reteach," "Binder check hacks," "Sentence stems that get quiet kids talking." We closed with a prompt I stole from my students: "Because of this year, I…" The sticky notes that bloomed on the chart paper were ordinary and dazzling: "…call parents faster," "…stopped grading everything," "…gave kids more chances to fix it," "…joined a colleague's class to learn." I tucked a few of those notes into my folder, next to the student "Whys."

On the last day with my mentees, we didn't talk about strategies. We talked about stamina. About how to stay soft without getting swallowed, firm without getting brittle. I told them the truth: some days you'll feel like a lighthouse; other days you'll feel like a flickering bulb in a hallway that needs repainting. On both kinds of days, do the small right things. Greet them. Ask a better question. Close the loop on feedback. Protect five minutes of joy.

One of them laughed and said, "Is that the AVID way?"

I said, "It's the human way, disguised as AVID."

I ended the year the way I began: by rearranging desks. I left the pennants up and added two more from schools our graduates planned to attend. I restocked the supply table. On the board, I wrote the same words that hung above my door: "Take what you learned and teach someone else." Because that's what saying yes to leadership really did—it multiplied my classroom until it didn't fit inside four walls anymore. It turned strategies into culture, culture into a shared language. It reminded me, when the work was heavy, that a single, well-placed yes can ripple through a building like a bell.

The Faculty Class

Standing in front of my colleagues during professional development was its own kind of classroom. The desks were replaced by long tables, the students by adults with weary eyes and full coffee mugs, but the goal was the same: engage, connect, and inspire.

I remember one session in particular. I had been asked to present on WICOR strategies. Many of my colleagues were curious but cautious, worried that the phrase meant "one more initiative" piled on top of their already full plates. I started not with theory, but with stories. I told them about my student who had shut down every time she was asked to write about "family traditions" — until I invited her to write about the way her grandmother told stories on their porch in Creole. Suddenly, her pen moved with confidence.

I watched the room change as teachers realized that incorporating WICOR strategies into their lessons wasn't an "extra," it was a lens. It wasn't about adding more work; it was about making the work matter to the students sitting in front of us. That day, several teachers stopped me afterward to say, "I never thought about it like that before." Moments like those reminded me that teaching the teachers could be just as powerful as teaching the students.

But presenting to colleagues required a different kind of courage than teaching adolescents. Teenagers will test your patience, yes, but adults will test your credibility. In the faculty room, people listened with arms folded, measuring every word, deciding whether to buy in or dismiss. I had to learn quickly that colleagues, just like students, wanted to see authenticity before they gave their trust. If they sensed performance without substance, they tuned out. If they felt you respected their experience, they leaned in.

Over time, I began structuring professional development sessions the same way I built lessons for my students: begin with a hook, invite participation, allow space for reflection, and close with something practical they could use the very next day. A lesson for a room full of eighth graders and a session for a room full of teachers both hinged on the same principle — people need to feel that their time is valued.

One of the most memorable moments came during a workshop on building community in classrooms. I introduced an activity where teachers paired up and shared stories of a student who had surprised them — either through resilience, humor, or a hidden strength. At first, the room was quiet, hesitant. Then laughter broke out at one table, tears at another. Soon, the energy shifted. Teachers realized that before we could build community with students, we had to nurture community among ourselves. Later, a veteran teacher pulled me aside and said, "I didn't expect to feel something in a PD today. Thank you for reminding me why I started."

Another time, during a training on using inquiry strategies across disciplines, a math teacher raised his hand and admitted, "I don't know how to make this work with quadratic equations." Instead of giving him an answer, I turned the question back to the group. Within minutes, other teachers offered suggestions: framing word problems around real-life contexts, using student-generated questions as entry points, and creating collaborative problem-solving challenges. By the end, he was jotting notes furiously, inspired not by me, but by the collective wisdom of his peers. That, I realized, was the real magic of the faculty room as a classroom — it wasn't about one voice but about sparking dialogue that multiplied ideas.

Still, not every session was smooth. There were times I stumbled, moments when I saw eyes glaze over or heard the shuffle of restless bodies. Those instances humbled me, reminding me that just as I ask my students to adjust and persevere, I had to model the same resilience with adults. Failure in front of peers was uncomfortable, but it was also instructive. It taught me that leadership is less about flawless delivery and more about the willingness to risk vulnerability for the sake of growth.

The more I facilitated, the more I came to perceive my own professional development not as a burden, but as a privilege. Standing in that space meant I could influence more than my own roster of students — I could indirectly reach hundreds of lives through the teachers I supported. Every idea that resonated, every practice that was adopted, had the potential to ripple outward into classrooms I might never step into.

In the end, the faculty room became my second classroom, a place where the students had degrees and the textbooks had been replaced with lesson plans, but the learning was no less urgent. And just like with my students, the measure of success was not in applause or compliance, but in the quiet moments afterward — when a colleague lingered to ask a question, or later shared a story of how an idea had changed the way they taught. Those were the moments that reminded me: whether in front of children or adults, teaching is still about sparking light where there was once hesitation and reminding people of the purpose that brought them into the room in the first place.

AVID Beyond English

Of all the roles I embraced, working with colleagues on AVID strategies was the most energizing. English may have been my home base, but AVID reminded me that the skills of inquiry, organization, and reflection were not bound by subject matter. At its core, AVID was never about teaching what to learn — it was about showing students how to learn. Once teachers in other departments began to see that, their classrooms were transformed in ways even they hadn't expected.

One of my earliest breakthroughs came with the science department. A biology teacher approached me after a PD session, skeptical but curious. "I just don't see how Socratic Seminars fit into cell structure," she said. I smiled, because I had heard that line before. We decided to try it anyway. The next week, her students sat in a circle debating: "If mitochondria are the powerhouse of the cell, what happens to the 'city' of life when its power grid fails?" The conversation that followed was electric, students compared cells to neighborhoods, cities, even families. They challenged each other, questioned analogies, and laughed while still learning. That teacher pulled me aside later and admitted, "I've never seen them this engaged with science vocabulary."

Math presented another challenge. Many teachers felt that AVID belonged to the "word-heavy" subjects. But I showed them how reflection journals could fit naturally into algebra and geometry. Instead of simply solving problems, students were asked to write about their process: "Where did I get stuck? How did I overcome the mistake? What strategy might I try differently next time?" At first, some students groaned at the extra writing, but soon they began to recognize patterns in their thinking. "I keep rushing through step two," one wrote, "and it always throws off my answer." That kind of metacognition — stepping back to observe themselves as learners—was exactly the point. And when the math teachers saw test scores rising, their skepticism turned to enthusiasm.

Even electives found their place in the AVID ecosystem. In physical education, a coach introduced peer tutorials after practice. Students broke into small groups to reflect on teamwork strategies during games, discussing what worked, what didn't, and how to adjust. It was AVID in motion—collaboration, communication, critical thinking—applied to the basketball court. Meanwhile, in art class, the teacher used AVID's focused notes to help students record techniques during demonstrations. Instead of passive watching, students created step-by-step guides they could revisit later, building independence in their craft.

What amazed me most was not the adoption of AVID strategies, but the creativity with which teachers reshaped them. I didn't hand out scripts; I offered tools. Each teacher adapted those tools in ways that fit their discipline and personality. Seeing that affirmed my belief that AVID wasn't a program to be forced, but a philosophy to be lived.

And the ripple effects were undeniable. Students began to recognize the consistency across classrooms: Cornell notes in science, collaborative study groups in math, reflective writing in art. They no longer saw learning as a patchwork of isolated subjects, but as a unified skill set they could carry into any domain. More than once, a student told me, "It feels like all my teachers are on the same team now." That, to me, was the real victory.

For me personally, working with AVID beyond English was both humbling and invigorating. It reminded me that the best ideas are not monopolized by one department. When a science teacher or coach showed me a new twist on an AVID strategy, I found myself jotting notes like a student. Personal learning in those moments meant stepping back, celebrating innovation, and realizing that influence is a two-way street. I gave ideas, yes, but I received just as many in return.

Service

Perhaps the greatest shift in my understanding of teaching was realizing it was never meant to be about me. Early on, I thought teaching meant carrying the torch at the front, being visible, being the one others looked to. But over time, I learned that the truest form of teaching is fundamentally based on learning and is often invisible — it is service. It is less about recognition and more about quietly creating conditions where others can thrive.

I began to notice that some of the most powerful leaders in our school were not the ones making speeches at assemblies or sending out polished memos. They were the ones who stocked the copier with paper before anyone else arrived, who stayed after hours helping a colleague figure out a new grading system, who knew which student needed a sandwich more than a lecture. These were acts of service without fanfare, yet they shaped the heartbeat of our school far more than anything printed on an agenda.

Service, I discovered, required humility. It meant being willing to do the unglamorous work, the kind that never shows up in evaluations. It meant letting go of ego — allowing others to shine, even if you had planted the seeds of their success. I remember meeting with a teacher who later became known as one of the most innovative voices in the building. She was often invited to present ideas that, in truth, had begun in quiet conversations between us. But instead of feeling overshadowed, I felt proud. Her success was my success, even if my name was never mentioned.

The paradox of service is that it multiplies influence. By investing in others, by lifting them up, you extend your reach far beyond what you could accomplish alone. A single idea shared with a colleague could ripple into dozens of classrooms. A small act of encouragement could spark the confidence that changes a career. The impact is exponential, even if it is rarely credited to you.

I came to see service not as a spotlight but as a lantern. A spotlight blinds and isolates, drawing attention to one person. A lantern, on the other hand, casts light outward, illuminating the path for others to walk alongside you. When teaching becomes service, the focus shifts from self to community, from control to empowerment, from achievement to growth.

And perhaps the deepest truth of all was this: when you serve, you are changed too. Service softens pride, sharpens empathy, and reminds you daily that education is not about climbing ladders but about lifting lives. In the end, teaching as service, became less a role I held and more a posture of the heart—a quiet decision, renewed each day, to put others first.

Looking back, I have come to see that the true measure of service is not in titles held or applause received, but in the unseen ripples we leave behind. A stone dropped into water disappears quickly, but the waves it creates travel far beyond the point of impact. Teaching—and leading teachers—has taught me that our influence works the same way. We may never see the full reach of our actions, but they travel outward, nonetheless.

There are students whose names I may never remember, but who carry with them a habit, a phrase, or a spark of encouragement that shifts the trajectory of their lives. There are teachers I mentored who may one day guide others with the same patience I once showed them. And there are colleagues who adopted strategies that became second nature, embedding themselves into the culture of a school long after my own footsteps have faded from its hallways. These are the ripples, and they matter.

What humbles me most is knowing that some of the strongest waves will never return to me. A student I once pushed to speak up in class may years later may soon lead a boardroom discussion with confidence. A teacher who once doubted her worth may one day mentor a new generation, offering reassurance born out of her own transformation. I may never know these stories, but that is the beauty of legacy — it does not need to be seen to be real.

And I learned that ripples do not stop at the walls of a school. Students carry them into their families, their communities, and their futures. Teachers carry them into new positions, new schools, and sometimes into entirely new careers, bringing with them the lessons and encouragement they once received. A word spoken in one moment can echo across decades. That realization reshaped the way I thought about my role. I was not just teaching for today; I was planting seeds for a harvest I might never see.

What gives me peace now is knowing that service, at its core, is not about permanence but about continuation. We are all links in a chain, inheritors of wisdom from those who came before us and custodians of knowledge for those who will follow. My hope is not to be remembered as the loudest voice in the room, but as someone who kept the lantern lit long enough for others to carry it forward.

If I have left anything behind, let it be this: the belief that consistency is more powerful than charisma, that relationships matter more than rules, and that service is the highest form of leadership. Those truths, passed from one teacher to another, from one student to another, are the ripples that endure. And though I may never trace where they lead, I trust they are still moving, still spreading, still lighting paths I will never walk myself.

As the school year closed, I looked at my AVID students — many of them the first in their families to even imagine college — and I thought about my own journey. The restless boy in Kingston. The young teacher in London. The immigrant hustling in Florida. The father who found poetry in football rivalries.

And now, the teacher again — older, weathered, but still burning with the same fire: to make words matter, to make lives matter. I could see pieces of myself in their laughter, their stubbornness, even in their complaints about Cornell notes and tutorials. They were echoes of my own restless spirit, sitting where I once sat, daring to dream beyond what the world told them was possible.

I told my students on the last day:

"This isn't the end of a school year. It's just an intermission. Life will keep handing you acts. Some will break you. Some will build you.

But all of them — every single one — are yours to claim."

Some clapped, some smiled, some rolled their eyes in that way teenagers do when they don't want to admit they're moved. But I knew the words had landed somewhere. I could see it in the way a few lingered after class, asking small questions — about college applications, about writing, about life itself. I could see it in the quiet nod of the shy girl in the back who had finally found her voice during a Socratic seminar. I could see it in the boy who once swore he'd never make it past 7th grade but now talked about trade school with a seriousness that was new, and real.

Because teaching, writing, living — it was all the same work. The work of becoming.

Becoming isn't a straight line. It's a crooked, winding journey through alleyways of doubt and open roads of possibility. I thought back to Kingston, to the boy who ran barefooted after a football in Denham Town, who danced with his friends in the hot nights, who scribbled dreams in a school notebook without knowing those scribbles were poems. I thought about London, where I carried Expo markers and lesson plans into classrooms full of immigrant children whose parents, like me, had crossed oceans chasing hope. I thought about Florida, where I carried boxes, debts, and determination, working jobs that had nothing to do with the classroom until the classroom called me back.

Each of those acts had broken me, built me, and pushed me into becoming. And now, in this room of AVID students, I was passing the same truth on. That education was not just about GPAs and college acceptance letters. It was about courage. It was about the audacity to say, "I am more than where I started."

As the bell rang and the room emptied, I sat for a moment in the silence. Posters curling on the walls, desks scuffed from restless hands and sneakers, sunlight slanting across stacks of unclaimed papers. A school year gone. A new one already whispering on the horizon.

I gathered my things slowly, smiling at the thought that when these students looked back years from now, they might not remember the lessons on rhetorical devices or the long tutorials on focused notes. But maybe they would remember the feeling — that their lives were acts worth performing, worth claiming. And maybe that would be enough.

For me, it always was.

Chapter V: A Rising Voice

Onwards

Outside of the classroom, I took on voluntary mentorship roles with younger teachers — who were still shockingly underrepresented in the system. It wasn't a formal program. No district initiative. No budget. Just a calling. A quiet conviction that if we didn't build the village ourselves, it might never be built.

We started small. A few one-on-one conversations after staff meetings. A couple of check-ins during lunch duty. Then I created an informal WhatsApp group called **The Educated Ones** — a name that felt both aspirational and ancestral. It was a digital barbershop, a sacred circle, a place where we could be brilliant and vulnerable at the same time.

We exchanged lesson plans, vented about admin policies, and hyped each other up on rough days. One teacher would drop a link to a culturally responsive unit on *The Hate U Give*. Another would share a voice note about surviving parent-teacher conferences with grace. We celebrated small wins—like getting a student to finally turn in an assignment—and held space for the hard losses, like losing a kid to the streets or watching a colleague burn out.

We organized meetups at Starbucks and the Mexican restaurant in Lehigh Acres, where we'd trade classroom hacks over jerk tacos and cold ginger beer. Sometimes we'd gather in our classrooms, surrounded by shelves of Baldwin, hooks, and Achebe. The conversations flowed like rhythm and blues—equal parts pedagogy and poetry.

I listened more than I talked. And when I did speak, I offered truth wrapped in humility.

"Remember," I told one overwhelmed first-year teacher, "you don't have to be perfect. Just be present. Show up for them. Every day. That's where the power is."

She nodded, eyes glassy, shoulders unclenching for the first time in weeks.

I became known as the one you went to before quitting. The one who'd talk you off the ledge. The one who'd help you rediscover your "why." Not with platitudes, but with presence. With stories. With reminders that teaching is not just a job—it's a ministry. A form of resistance. A daily act of love.

One teacher, Ms. Jefferson, said at a staff meeting:

"Mr. Ward saved my career before it even started."

She wasn't exaggerating.

She had walked into her first year full of fire, but quickly found herself drowning in paperwork, classroom management struggles, and the quiet isolation that comes when you're the only Black woman on staff. I invited her to one of our meetups. She showed up late, sat quietly, and cried into her ginger beer. We didn't rush her. We didn't fix her. We just held her.

Later that night, she texted me: "I didn't know I needed a community until I found one."

That became our unofficial motto.

We didn't just mentor — we mirrored. We reminded each other that our presence in the classroom was revolutionary. That our very existence disrupted narratives. That our students needed to see us whole, not just competent.

"I am enough."

"My classroom is a sanctuary."

"I teach with love, not fear."

That's the thing about legacy—it multiplies.

The Educated Ones grew. We added another teacher from Jamaica.

But it wasn't about numbers. It was about impact.

It was about the teacher who said, "I stopped code-switching in my classroom because of you."

The one who said, "I finally brought my students' home languages into our poetry unit."
The one who said, "I teach differently now—because I teach with my whole self."

And it was about the students, too. Because when teachers feel seen, they teach in ways that help students feel seen. When teachers are affirmed, they create classrooms that affirm. When teachers are mentored, they become mentors. I saw it happen again and again. A ripple effect. A quiet revolution. A legacy unfolding in real time.

And through it all, I remained grounded. Not in ego, but in purpose. In the belief that mentorship is not about hierarchy—it's about humanity. About walking alongside someone and saying, "You're not alone. You're never alone."

That's what The Educated Ones became. Not just a WhatsApp group. Not just a support circle. But a movement. A movement rooted in radical love, cultural affirmation, and the sacred power of showing up. And I kept showing up. Because that's where the power is.

The Rise of Ahead of the Class

Later that spring, I resurrected my old teaching website, Ahead of the Class—and transformed it into a full online hub for literacy, motivation, and mentorship. What began as a pandemic lifeline had now become a digital sanctuary. It wasn't flashy. I didn't have fancy equipment or studio lighting, just a laptop, a stack of books, and the same fire I carried into every classroom from Kingston to Cape Coral. The same urgency to reach students where they were—emotionally, academically, spiritually— now pulsed through every upload, every caption, every comment thread.

I added downloadable handouts, curated book recommendations, and writing prompts that invited students to explore their roots, their dreams, and their voices. I created a "Mentor's Corner" for new teachers navigating the emotional terrain of the profession, and a "Legacy Lab" where students could submit poems, essays, and reflections that would be featured on the site. It became a space where pedagogy met purpose, where rigor was braided with radical love.

The homepage carried a simple message: "This is a place for those who teach, those who learn, and those who refuse to give up on either." And that message echoed through every resource I posted. Whether it was a video on figurative language or a reflection on grief in the classroom, I made sure the tone was always affirming, always real.

Even now, aheadoftheclass.godaddysites.com continues to evolve. It's not just mine anymore — it belongs to every student who's ever felt unseen, every teacher who's ever questioned their impact, and every community that believes education should heal, not harm. It's a testament to what happens when we teach from the heart, when we mentor with memory, and when we build spaces that honor both struggle and triumph.

I didn't set out to build a movement. I just wanted to keep teaching. But sometimes, the most powerful classrooms aren't bound by walls — they're built from stories, stitched together by hope, and powered by the quiet determination to keep showing up.

The content took off. Not viral, but impactful. I got emails from teachers in Georgia who said, "I used your website in my PD session. It changed the way my staff sees student voice."

Comments from students in Jamaica who wrote, *"Mi neva know seh poetry could sound like mi."* (I never knew that poetry could sound like me.)

Messages from young Black boys who said, "I never saw a teacher who looked like me and talked like me until now."

And so, I kept going.

And through it all, I kept my life grounded in its original mission: to be a place where words could heal, ignite, and transform.

Honors and Grief

In October, I was nominated for Lee County's Golden Apple Teacher Award. Though I didn't win, the nomination itself sparked celebration in my classroom. It was as if the entire class had been waiting for a reason to erupt in joy—not just for me, but for what I represented. But that same month, I got word from my aunt: my beloved Uncle Desmond, my

427

mom's brother had passed away. The news came in a phone call. Her voice was steady, but I could hear the tremble beneath it.

"He went peacefully," she said. "He was listening to the radio, humming along to Toots and the Maytals."

I thanked her, hung up, and sat in silence. Uncle Desmond was the one who told me, "Words can be yuh weapon and yuh wings my yute." (Words can be your weapon and your wings my youth).

He was a man of street wisdom, a nursing aide by trade, a griot by instinct. Uncle Desmond was a sanctuary for stories. He had a way of listening that made you feel like your words mattered. Like your life was worth narrating.

In the weeks that followed, I found myself thinking about the strange symmetry of that month. Public honor and private grief. Celebration and mourning. The applause of colleagues and the silence of loss. It reminded me that life rarely offers clean lines. That joy and sorrow often arrive hand in hand, asking us to hold both without dropping either.

I began to see Desmond's influence everywhere.

In the way I paused before giving feedback, choosing words that uplifted rather than corrected.

In the way I encouraged students to write in patois, in Spanglish, in the dialects of their homes.

In the way I reminded them that their stories didn't need permission to be powerful.

I started keeping a journal again—not for grading, not for publication, just for reflection. I wrote about the banner in the hallway. About the candle on my windowsill. About the way grief had softened me, not broken me. I wrote about legacy, and how it's not always loud. Sometimes it's a whisper passed down in a tailor's shop. Sometimes it's a line in a book. Sometimes it's a teacher standing in front of a class, saying, "Let's begin."

430

I also called Aunty Bar again. We talked about Desmond's funeral, about the hymns to sing, about the coconut tree he brought to my house, and she planted in the front yard.

Back at school, the Golden Apple nomination faded from the bulletin board, replaced by winter concert flyers and semester reminders. But the impact lingered. Students still called me "Forever Teacher." Parents still waved at me in the pickup line. And in my heart, Desmond's voice remained.

"Words can be yuh weapon and yuh wings."

I began ending each class with a quote — sometimes from Achebe, sometimes from Desmond, sometimes from the students themselves. I called it **The Last Word.** It became a ritual. A way to honor the day, the lesson, the lives in the room.

One day, a student named Elijah asked, "Can we write our own Last Words?" And what followed was a flood of wisdom:

431

"I am not what they expect — I am more."

"My story starts here, but it doesn't end here."

"Grief is love with nowhere to go."

I collected them. I posted them on the classroom wall. I read them when the days felt heavy.

And I realized something: the award, the banner, the letters — they were beautiful. But the real honor was this.

The trust.

The transformation.

The torch passed from one generation to the next.

Now I help others find theirs.

Every voice I uplift.

Every quiet moment when a student dares to believe in themselves.

That, too, is worth climbing for.

The Quiet Legend

It wasn't just one uncle I carried in memory, though. Not long after Uncle Desmond passed, I received word: my Uncle Neily had passed. Neily was my cousin Oneil's father, a man whose presence was felt in that unspoken, steady way that fathers often carry. He wasn't the loudest voice in the room, nor the kind of uncle who filled every silence with talk. He was quieter, but his life was stitched into the fabric of our family in ways you only notice when the fabric begins to tear.

He was the one who first introduced me to the game of football, and as a young, starry-eyed boy growing up in Denham Town, I was mesmerized by his skills when he played with his friends on Wellington Street. His movement was smooth, effortless, like the ball was an extension of his foot. To me, he was a kind of local hero. The respect was so real that someone even painted his likeness on the side of a house on Wellington Street, immortalizing him in a mural that proclaimed his greatness to everyone who walked by. For a boy like me, who worshipped the rhythm of football, that mural was as holy as any cathedral window.

On Sundays, I would make the walk that felt like a pilgrimage. I would sneak out of 17 Tulip Lane, trace the edge of the gully, and head down toward Regent Street. From there, I'd cut across North Street, walk over the small bridge by the gully, with the corners alive with chatter, domino games, and the smell of frying fish, until finally, I turned onto Wellington Street. The closer I got, the more the noise swelled — shouts, laughter, the thud of a ball kicked hard against concrete. By the time I reached the playing area, my uncle was already there, weaving through defenders, pulling tricks that left them stranded, his skill drawing cheers from the crowd that gathered like churchgoers around a sermon.

I can still hear the voices that rose above the rest. His brother's booming call would echo across the street, a mixture of pride and playful taunting whenever Neily slipped past an opponent. And then there was his best friend, Nyamwell. If Neily was the quiet flame, Nyamwell was the firecracker. He had a booming laugh; the kind that rolled through the street and made strangers smile even if they didn't know the joke. His shouts were legendary: *"Gwaan, Neily! Show dem how fi dweet!"* (Go on Neily! Show them how to do it!). He would clap his hands so hard it was as if the rhythm alone could push the ball forward. When Neily scored, Nyamwell was often the first to rush into the street, throwing his arms around his friend in celebration, as if the victory belonged to them both.

Their friendship was one of those neighborhood bonds that became part of the landscape. You couldn't think of Neily without thinking of Nyamwell. They had grown up side by side, played barefoot ball on cracked concrete, weathered hardships together, and now, in adulthood, their camaraderie still shone bright. If Neily's calm presence drew respect, Nyamwell's larger-than-life energy amplified it. He was Neily's cheerleader, confidant, and partner in every Sunday spectacle. For the rest of us—wide-eyed boys pressed against zinc fences, desperate to imitate the legends before us—it was proof that football was not just about the game. It was about community, about friendship, about the joy of having someone who knew your story so deeply that they could celebrate your victories as if they were their own.

Those walks, that ritual of streets and sounds, stitched themselves into my boyhood, binding family, football, and faith in the community together. Neily wasn't just playing for himself; he was playing for us—for the brothers who cheered, the friends who believed, the nephew who watched wide-eyed at the sidelines, and the neighborhood that carried his legend like gospel.

Distance always makes grief complicated. I was thousands of miles away, teaching, parenting, trying to balance a life built on responsibility, and yet part of me felt nine years old again—standing on the sidelines, watching my uncle dazzle with his football skills, or sneaking his bicycle for joyrides down Tulip Lane when he visited Aunty Bar. I remember the giddy speed of those rides, the air rushing against my face, until my recklessness betrayed me and I went crashing into the wall of the gully beside Mother Mack's shop. I would limp back, knees scraped and elbows stinging, expecting a scolding. But Neily, instead of anger, would shake his head with that quiet smile that carried more understanding than words ever could, and he would comically proclaim, *'Lance, one day yuh wi learn fi ride bicycle.'* (Lance, one day you will learn how to ride a bicycle). He wasn't quick to lecture; his lessons were often in what he didn't say, in the patience he extended.

Neily belonged to that generation of men who bore their burdens in silence. He worked, provided, carried himself with dignity, and let others do the boasting on his behalf. If my father was the voice that pushed me toward discipline and my mother was the heart that softened those edges, Neily was the steady reminder of humility. He was proof that greatness doesn't always arrive with noise. Sometimes it is the quiet consistency of showing up — for your children, your community, your game — that leaves the deepest mark.

Grieving from afar is a peculiar thing. There's no funeral procession to walk behind, no grave to lean over, no chorus of hymns to carry your sorrow into the air. Instead, grief lingers like a delayed echo, sneaking into the quiet moments of your own life. For me, it came in the classroom when I saw a boy with restless energy remind me of my own youthful recklessness. It came on the football pitch when I watched my son Rhys run with the same abandon I once felt, and I thought of the bicycle, the gully wall, and the man who forgave me without a word. It came late at night when the weight of responsibility felt heavy, and I would remember that Uncle Neily carried his own without complaint, always steady, always there.

Uncle Desmond and Uncle Neily's passing both reminded me of the fragility of time, of how quickly the men we look up to become the ancestors we honor. It also reminded me of the importance of telling these stories — because murals fade, bicycles rust, and football pitches change, but words can preserve what time tries to erase. Uncle Neily was not just a football legend of Wellington Street. He was a father, an uncle, a man of quiet strength whose life rippled far beyond his own. In me, in Aunty Bar, in Oneil, in Nyamwell's laughter, and in all of us who ever watched him command a ball or ride that bicycle down the lane, his spirit continues to run free.

Grief has a way of layering itself, one sorrow pressing on top of another. I still carried the ache of my earlier uncle's passing, his charge to me ringing like a psalm: weapon and wings. He had believed that education could be both a defense and a launching pad, both a shield and a means of flight. That mantra had become my north star in the classroom. Now, Neily's death folded itself into that grief, and I found myself holding two uncles at once—one who had spoken directly into my calling, and another whose absence reminded me of the fragility of fathers, of men who give what they can before time calls them home.

I began to look at my students differently. When I saw a boy struggling to stay awake in the back row, I wondered about the father who might not be there to wake him, to guide him, to tell him he was more than his postcode. When a girl snapped at me with all the fire of teenage rebellion, I thought of how grief twists inside the young, shaping anger into armor. Each lesson, each conversation, carried with it a weight: I was not just teaching Shakespeare or grammar — I was filling gaps left by absences, trying in my imperfect way to stand where others had been pulled away too soon.

And so, as the months rolled on, I carried my uncles with me. One gave me a mantra, the other a reminder. Together, their legacies pressed me forward. In every staff meeting, in every student's question, in every after-school moment when a child lingered because home felt too empty, I heard them both. Weapon and wings. Presence and absence. Lesson and legacy.

I stood taller, not because the grief was gone, but because I had learned how to wear it.

The school year pressed forward. Pandemic fatigue lingered, but so did resilience. Students shuffled in with hoodies pulled over tired eyes, earbuds hidden beneath masks.

441

Some carried stories of loss—grandmothers buried, fathers gone too soon, siblings hospitalized. Others carried burdens invisible to the eye but heavy to the spirit.

And I listened.

Every morning, I greeted them at the door as though it were ritual. "Morning, King." "Good to see you, Queen." "Glad you made it, champ." I refused to let them slip into invisibility.

Chapter VI: Breakthroughs

Beginnings

As the months arrived and passed, I felt a shift—not only in my classroom, but in my spirit. The seeds I had been planting for years were beginning to bear fruit.

The school year opened with energy. Students filled the halls with laughter, gossip, and the unmistakable swagger of youth. I greeted them each morning like they were stepping into sacred ground: "Morning, King. Glad you're here." "Morning, Queen. You look ready for the world today." For some, it was the only affirmation they would hear all week.

And throughout all, those affirmations mattered more than ever.

Something was different in the air. Perhaps it was the collective resilience of a generation that had weathered the disruptions of the pandemic, or perhaps it was the quiet determination inside me that said, "This is the year things turn." Whatever it was, I could feel it the moment I stepped into my classroom. The atmosphere buzzed with possibility, as if both students and teachers were ready for more than just survival — they were hungry for growth.

I began the year with a new ritual: starting every class with a reflection question. At first, it was simple — "What's one word that describes how you feel today?" The responses were brief, sometimes silly. But as weeks passed, students grew more open. They wrote words like "determined," "anxious," "hopeful," and occasionally, "lost." Those slips of paper became tiny windows into their inner lives, reminders that behind each set of eyes was a story far more complex than their grades or behavior.

My classroom walls themselves became a canvas of breakthroughs. Anchor charts of AVID strategies hung next to student artwork and motivational quotes, forming a collage of learning and identity. I wanted the room to whisper to every student who walked in: "You belong here. Your voice matters." And slowly, they began to believe it. Students who once hid in the back began raising their hands. The quiet ones started sharing their writing aloud. The skeptics began to lean into discussions with curiosity instead of cynicism.

One of the most powerful moments came early in the semester when I introduced a unit on resilience in literature. We read excerpts that mirrored the struggles my students faced characters battling poverty, identity crises, and fractured families. I asked them to connect the text to their own lives, and what unfolded stunned me. Students who rarely spoke in class poured their stories onto paper: the fear of losing housing, the responsibility of caring for siblings, the ache of absent fathers. Their vulnerability filled the room with a kind of raw holiness. I realized then that 2023 wasn't just about academic progress—it was about breakthroughs of the heart.

But it wasn't only the students who were breaking through. I felt a deepening in my own voice as an educator. Years of trial and error, of adjusting lesson plans and refining strategies, had given me a confidence that no longer wavered with every setback. I trusted my instincts more. I embraced creativity without fear of failure. Most importantly, I stopped trying to be the perfect teacher and leaned instead into being a present one.

By mid-year, I saw the fruits of this shift everywhere. Classroom discussions became richer. Students began using academic vocabulary unprompted, not because they were told to, but because they owned it. Colleagues began seeking me out, not just for strategies, but for encouragement. And for the first time in years, I felt that elusive alignment — the sense that I was exactly where I was meant to be, doing the work I was born to do.

The school year was however not free of challenges. There were still days when exhaustion pressed heavy, when lessons flopped, when the weight of systemic pressures threatened to crush morale. But the difference was this: I no longer saw those moments as failures. They were part of the process, evidence that growth was happening. Each difficulty became another chance to model resilience for my students, to show them that setbacks are stepping-stones, not dead ends.

It was in 2023 that I fully embraced a truth I had been circling for years: breakthroughs rarely arrive as fireworks. More often, they come as small, steady shifts — like students choosing to believe in themselves, or a teacher finally realizing that presence matters more than perfection. And when those small shifts accumulate, they create a tide strong enough to carry an entire community forward.

The Movement

By year's end, I reflected on the symmetry of my journey — public recognition and private grief, classroom breakthroughs and personal sacrifice. It was a year when triumph and loss walked hand in hand, each shaping the other. The applause from colleagues, the gratitude of students, the visible fruit of years of labor — these were moments that lifted me. But beneath them, there were nights when I sat in silence, carrying the weight of absence, missing the voices that once anchored me. Leadership had brought me into new light, but grief kept me grounded in the shadows.

Yet through it all, one truth shone clear: I wasn't just teaching English. I was building a movement. Every time a student believed in their own voice, every time a new teacher stood stronger because of guidance, every time AVID strategies rippled beyond my classroom, I felt the momentum of something larger than myself. Education was no longer just my profession — it had become my ministry, my offering to the world, a way of keeping alive the dreams of those who came before me.

On New Year's Eve, I stood by the mango tree. Its branches stretched wider now, reaching into the night as if they too were hungry for the sky. I touched its trunk, the bark rough beneath my palm, and whispered the names of those I loved and lost. The names of ancestors whose struggles carved the path beneath my feet. Each syllable was a prayer, a vow that their stories would not fade into silence.

The wind rustled through the leaves, and for a moment, it felt as though they answered back. I thought of how that tree had witnessed seasons of drought and storm, and yet it kept growing, stretching outward, bearing fruit. In its resilience, I saw a reflection of my own journey. Like the tree, I had weathered seasons of loss, yet I stood rooted, determined to rise again.

"We are still rising," I said quietly, almost a whisper, yet it carried the force of a declaration. Rising through the setbacks, rising

449

through the exhaustion, rising through the grief that sometimes threatened to swallow me whole. Rising because to remain grounded in despair would dishonor the sacrifices of those who made my path possible.

That night, fireworks crackled in the distance, painting streaks of light across the sky. I thought of my students, stepping into a new year with untapped potential. I thought of my colleagues, carrying the torch of education in ways that often went unseen. And I thought of myself, not as an individual standing alone beneath a tree, but as part of a much larger story — a story of survival, resilience, and hope.

2023 was not simply a year of breakthroughs; it was a year of beginnings. Beginnings of deeper clarity about my purpose. Beginnings of new connections with students and colleagues. Beginnings of a vision that stretched beyond my classroom into something generational, something enduring. The mango tree reminded me: we rise not only for ourselves, but for those who came before, and for those who will come after.

As the clock struck midnight and the new year began, I felt the quiet resolve of someone who knows the road ahead will not be easy, but who has chosen to walk it anyway. For in the rising, there is healing. In the rising, there is legacy. And in the rising, there is always hope.

2024 –Facing Change

The year 2024 opened not with fireworks, but with quiet resolve. I had stopped making resolutions. Instead, I made commitments—steady promises to myself, my family, and my students.

The mango tree in the backyard had grown sturdier, its leaves spreading like open palms. Each morning before school, I touched its trunk and whispered: "Another year. Another chance." It grounded me before stepping into the whirl of teaching, mentoring, and life. The year 2024 opened not with fireworks, but with quiet resolve. I had stopped making resolutions. Instead, I made commitments — steady promises to myself, my family, and my students.

My commitments were simple enough to fit on a sticky note. "Teach with clarity. Protect my energy. Tell the truth kindly. Call home more. Eat fruit that didn't come in a plastic cup." It looked ordinary on paper, but I knew the difference between a wish and a plan was practice. So, I built rituals around the commitments until they clicked like seatbelts — morning prep while the house was still quiet, a midday walk around the courtyard to reset my breathing, a hard stop on emails when the sky started to fade.

At school, I rearranged the horseshoe yet again, tugging desks forward by an inch as if proximity itself could help a student risk a better question. I swapped two posters: the one about deadlines made room for a new one about process — drafts, feedback, revision, repeat. I stood at the door and greeted kids by name, even the ones who tried to slide by with hoodies up like they were in witness protection. "Morning, T," I said to a boy who had skipped the first week back. "Glad you're here." He kept walking, but the stiffness left his shoulders before he reached his seat.

January's lessons were modest on purpose. We wrote short paragraphs that had to earn their commas. We read op-eds and charted the skeletons under their skin — claim, evidence, counterclaim, call to action. I taught them to annotate with restraint: one highlight for a main idea, one for a question, one for a connection. "Don't color every sentence," I said. "Not every firefly needs a jar." They smiled at that, and the margins stopped screaming. In tutorials, I kept repeating the AVID mantra: Questions first. The answers will come.

Saying yes to leadership didn't mean saying yes to everything. I learned to weigh invitations the way you weigh luggage — what's essential, what's extra, what will break your back if you insist on hauling it all. I still presented at PDs, still mentored, still coached lesson design after school, but I scheduled recovery into the calendar like it was a class I couldn't skip. On Thursdays I left by 4:15, no exceptions.

A colleague teased me— "You turning soft?" —and I laughed.

"No," I said. "I'm turning sustainable."

One afternoon the power flickered during seventh period and the room plunged into a low, humming dark. Groans rose like a chorus. I slid the blinds open and said, "We can still do this." We pushed desks to the window light and ran a Socratic seminar on paper, passing a single clipboard around like a talking stick. The quiet students wrote first, then handed the words forward; the talkers had to respond in writing. When the power snapped back on, no one moved. "Keep going," someone said. So, we did, and I thought: "this is what I want to multiply—resilience that doesn't wait for perfect conditions."

Family took a different shape in 2024, softer and closer. I cooked more on Sundays, the kind of meals that leave leftovers and make the house smell like a memory: curry chicken, rice and peas, roasted sweet plantains that never lasted long. We ate at the table with our phones face down, which felt like both victory and rebellion. I called my mother on Wednesdays on the drive home, just to hear her laugh shake loose the day's dust. When I forgot, she texted three mango emojis and I knew to call back.

The mango tree itself became a classroom. In late February a storm tore through, and I found a heavy branch snapped and leaning like a tired arm. I cut it clean, sealed the wound with paste, and whispered a promise I wasn't sure trees needed to hear: "I'll take care of you as you've taken care of me." New shoots appeared a month later, small and eager, and I brought a photo to school. "Growth isn't always up," I told my students, holding the picture. "Sometimes it's repair." They nodded the way kids do when they understand something they can't quite name.

Midyear data meetings arrived like they always do—with charts, percentiles, and the quiet dread that we might be reducing children to decimals. I brought student work instead. "Let's read what they wrote," I said. "Let's look at how they revised." The algebra lead slid a paper across the table: a reflection from a student who admitted she'd memorized steps without understanding and then explained, clearly, where she finally felt the concept click. We changed our plan on the spot. Fewer timed quizzes, more conferences. Less guessing what they didn't know, more asking and listening.

The hardest commitment, surprisingly, was rest. I could schedule a rubric but not always a nap. So, I made rest measurable: feet on grass for five minutes after work, no phone; one chapter of a novel before bed; a Saturday morning with no school emails. It felt odd to treat peace like an assignment, but the effect was real. I came to school less brittle, more human. Students noticed. "You seem lighter," one said in March.

I said, "I'm learning to carry only my share."

There were days that buckled anyway. A student I'd been calling home for all year withdrew without warning, and the empty chair grated every time I looked over. Another student's grandmother passed, and his jokes turned sharp for a while, like he wanted to be sent out so he wouldn't break in the room. We made space. He stapled a black ribbon to the corner of his notebook and wrote a letter he never planned to send. I told him grief is a teacher with terrible bedside manner but excellent lessons. He nodded, eyes on the desk, and breathed like someone coming up from deep water.

Spring brought field trips and fire drills in equal measure. We visited a community college across town and stood in the advising center while students learned how to read degree audits. One asked the counselor, "What if you change your mind?"

The counselor grinned. "You will," she said. "The trick is to change it with information." On the bus ride back, heads leaned against windows and the noise softened into that half-sleep hum. I looked at their faces and thought about the promises we'd made to each other — show up, try again, extend grace — and felt the mango tree in my chest.

I kept writing with them. Every other Friday, we set a timer for ten minutes and wrote without stopping. The rules were simple: don't judge, don't fix, don't erase until the bell. We wrote about first jobs and last arguments; about the music you blast when you're angry and the quiet that follows when the anger leaves. I shared my pages sometimes, the messy ones with arrows and scratched-out lines, so they could see process, not just product. "Teachers don't get graded," a student teased.

I replied, "Yes we do, every day, by thirty pairs of eyes each class period."

In April we built a mini unit around the idea of thresholds—moments of crossing. We read short memoirs and noticed the doors they walked through: the first day in a new language, the last day in an old house, the hour you realize you are the adult in the room. Students mapped their own thresholds on index cards and taped them to the wall. The display looked like a city at night, lit by small squares. During passing period, other students slowed at the doorway to read. A boy pointed at one card that said, "I forgave my father," and whispered, "That's heavy," like he was lifting it with both hands.

Outside of school, I tried to be braver with time. I visited an old coach who'd been sick, and we sat on his porch and watched the sky change temperatures. He asked about my students the way some people ask about stock prices — curious, hopeful, invested. "Still teaching them to argue with evidence?" he said.

"Always," I replied.

He laughed and coughed and said, "Good. The world needs fewer opinions and more informed ones."

When I left, he handed me a mango from his yard, still warm from the sun. "Medicine," he said. I didn't argue.

Testing season arrived with its usual edge, but we tried to meet it with systems, not stress. We practiced stamina like runners: short bursts, rest, longer bursts. We learned how to mark a hard question and move, then return. On the morning of the first exam, I put a bowl of cut mango on the back table next to sharpened pencils and a stack of fresh sticky notes. "Fuel," I said.

A student took a piece, paused, and said, "It tastes like a promise."

I replied, "Keep one to yourself and one to the test."

By May the mango tree was full of small green fists—little futures waiting to soften. The backyard smelled like rain even when it didn't fall. I started waking earlier, just to stand there with my coffee and listen to the street birds brag about the day. I thought about all the ways classrooms are gardens: you plant, you prune, you pull weeds, you wait. Sometimes a storm snaps a branch, and you learn to cut clean and seal the wound. Sometimes a seed you forgot you planted surprises you with leaves.

We closed the year with a portfolio defense. Students chose three pieces—one they were proud of, one that showed growth, one that still frustrated them—and presented to a small panel of peers. They named strategies, mistakes, revisions. They practiced saying, "I'm still working on…" without flinching. When a quiet student finished, the panel applauded, and he stood there blinking like applause was a language he hadn't heard in a while.

He said, "I didn't know I could talk about my thinking like that."

I replied, "You can. And you will."

At the final faculty meeting, we tried something new. Instead of celebrating perfect scores, we celebrated perfect repairs. Teachers shared stories of lessons that bombed and how they rebuilt them. The science department talked about switching lab partners mid-unit to break up unhelpful patterns. The math team showed how they used error analysis as a weekly ritual. We wrote our own commitments on index cards and tucked them into our badges where we'd see them every time we scanned into the building. Mine said, simply: Teach with clarity. Protect your energy. Tell the truth kindly.

On the last day, after the bus loop quieted and the hallways went reflective with summer light, I walked the perimeter of my room like a guard making a final round. I stacked the dictionaries, capped the markers, erased the board in slow strokes. I took the blank banner down and wrote four new words in the corner of it before I rolled it up: "Another year. Another chance." Then I carried my bag out to the car and drove home, where the mango tree waited, wide-handed and unhurried.

That evening, I stood under the tree and felt the year settle. I thought about resolutions — the way they flare and fade—and how commitments are different. They are quieter. They return you to yourself when the noise of the world turns your head. I pressed my palm against the bark and named them again, not like a checklist but like a prayer: clarity, care, courage, rest. The wind lifted through the leaves like pages turning. Somewhere in the neighborhood a child laughed, and a dog barked back, and a door closed gently. The ordinary music of a life. I went inside to call my mother.

The Classroom as Sanctuary

At Lehigh Acres Middle School, my classroom had become more than a room — it was a sanctuary. Students knew they could exhale there, that their voices would not just be tolerated, but celebrated. Some arrived each morning with heavy burdens — parents working multiple jobs, uncertainty about housing, fears they could not name aloud. In my classroom, I wanted them to feel the opposite of invisible. Here, they were seen. Here, they were safe.

I deepened the practice of "The Last Word." What had begun as a way to close lessons had become a ritual, something students looked forward to with almost sacred reverence. By spring, it wasn't just me or my students choosing the final thought of each lesson — sometimes parents contributed, sometimes visiting teachers, sometimes former students who sent in words via email or voice notes. The circle widened, and with it, the sense of community.

We ended class with truths like:

"Silence is not the absence of voice — it's the waiting of it."

"Hope is a kind of homework we all must do."

"Don't just write the essay — write yourself free."

The students carried these lines like armor, like lanterns in a world that was still uncertain. I noticed them scribbling favorite ones in the margins of their notebooks, decorating binders with quotes, or whispering them to each other before big tests. The words were not just closing lines — they had become living mantras.

One afternoon, a student who rarely spoke raised his hand during "The Last Word." He had lost his father only months before, and grief weighed heavily on his young shoulders. When I nodded to him, he cleared his throat and said quietly, "Even broken crayons can still color." The room fell silent. Some students wiped away tears. In that moment, it was clear: the sanctuary wasn't mine alone — it belonged to all of us.

What I hadn't expected was how far the ripple extended. Parents would stop me in the car line to say, "My daughter came home quoting you again." A mother once emailed: "Thank you for teaching my son words he can lean on when mine fail him." The classroom had become more than a space for lessons; it was a workshop for resilience, a training ground for courage.

And I knew — this was bigger than me. It wasn't about branding or followers. It was about giving teachers and students a reminder that they were part of something holy, something worth fighting for. Education wasn't just a career. It was a calling.

BSI – Lemuel Teal

In September 2024, the Bureau of School Improvement (BSI) came calling. At first, the district's message seemed routine—another email about vacancies, transfers, and "strategic placements." But as I read further, I realized it wasn't a general notice. It was directed at me. The district had chosen to reassign me from Lehigh Acres Middle School, the place where I had poured years of effort into building both classrooms and culture, to Lemuel Teal Middle School—one of Lee County's most fragile campuses.

The reasoning was clear: Lemuel Teal needed proven teachers, leaders who could bring stability and urgency to a building on the brink. The school carried the weight of a "D" grade, just one stumble away from an "F." Staff morale was low, discipline referrals were high, and trust in leadership was frayed. On paper, the assignment was daunting. In my spirit, it felt like both a burden and a calling.

Leaving Lehigh Acres wasn't easy. I hugged my department, shook hands with colleagues who had become brothers and sisters, and promised my students I'd still be cheering for them. But deep down, I understood the moment. My career had always led me into hard spaces—Denham Town, London classrooms scarred by inequity, Florida campuses struggling under testing mandates. This was another crucible.

When I walked into Lemuel Teal that September morning, it all told a story. The grade of "D" wasn't just a letter on a state report; it was a weight pressing on the entire community. Students internalized it, teachers felt shackled by it, and parents questioned whether their children's futures were in jeopardy.

But as I surveyed the campus, I knew one truth: no letter could measure a child's potential. Behind every data point was brilliance waiting to be called forth. And I wasn't alone in that belief.

Standing alongside me was Onika Vassell, a stalwart in every sense of the word. Onika had the kind of presence that steadied a room—calm, firm, unwavering. Where I brought energy, storytelling, and vision, she brought precision, structure, and relentless follow-through. We quickly realized that our partnership would be essential. If Lemuel Teal was going to rise, it wouldn't be because of one person's fire. It would be because of a team effort—our gifts braided together into something stronger.

Those first weeks were about listening and observing. Onika and I sat together in classrooms, not as evaluators but as allies. We watched the way students shifted in their seats, the way teachers struggled to balance pacing with discipline, the way hope flickered but hadn't yet caught flame. In afternoon meetings, we compared notes.

"Discipline is choking instruction," she said one day.

"And instruction is losing kids because the texts don't reflect their lives," I replied.

So, we strategized. I pushed for culturally responsive lessons — stories that made students lean in instead of tuning out. She designed systems that supported teachers, creating clarity around expectations and consequences so instruction could breathe. Together, we anchored Professional Learning Communities (PLCs), breaking down data into human stories.

We told our colleagues often: "This isn't about surviving until June. It's about building something sustainable." Slowly, trust grew — not just between us, but across the building. Teachers began to stay after meetings, lingering to brainstorm rather than rushing out. Students began to test us less and trust us more.

By November, signs of change emerged. Onika's discipline structures created consistency students could rely on. My AVID based initiatives infused classrooms with fresh energy — quick writes, poetry journals, and text-to-self reflections. Together, we convinced reluctant students to attend after-school tutoring, often by making personal phone calls to parents and guardians.

470

The tutoring sessions became a lifeline. One evening, as we supervised a crowded room of seventh graders working on reading comprehension, Onika whispered, "This... this is what turnaround looks like. Not fireworks. Just steady work."

She was right. Progress came in inches, not miles. But every inch mattered.

Of course, setbacks tested us. December brought fatigue — teachers weary from constant pressure, students restless before winter break. Discipline referrals spiked, and some staff questioned whether the climb was possible. But Onika's steadiness balanced my fire. When I wanted to storm ahead, she reminded me of pacing. When she felt drained by endless paperwork, I reminded her of purpose. We held each other accountable.

By spring 2025, momentum had taken hold. Benchmark assessments showed growth in both reading and math. Students who once shrugged at assignments were now staying after school to revise essays. Teachers began experimenting again—trying new strategies instead of clinging to survival.

Onika and I doubled down. She led discipline data dives and teacher coaching cycles. I organized student showcases—poetry slams, debate sessions, and essay galleries. We created a visible culture of achievement.

The students felt it. "Sir, it feels different this year," one seventh grader told me in April. "Like people actually believe in us now."

When the state results came in June, the building erupted. Lemuel Teal Middle School had climbed from a "D" to a "C." For many, it was just one letter. For us, it was revolution.

Teachers wept in the lounge. Students cheered in the hallways. Parents called the office just to say thank you. And in that joy, Onika and I exchanged a quiet glance that said it all: we had done it—together.

The Return

The Bureau of School Improvement operates on cycles. Once a school stabilizes, teachers are reassigned to new sites in need. And so, in August 2025, I made my way back to Lehigh Acres Middle School as head of English and the return felt like a homecoming. Colleagues embraced me, students shouted my name, and the building itself seemed brighter. But I was not the same teacher who had left a year before. I carried with me the lessons of Lemuel Teal: the importance of structure and fire working together, the knowledge that true change is collective, and the memory of what teamwork with a stalwart like Onika could accomplish.

On my first day back, I stood at my door as students streamed in. "Morning, King. Morning, Queen." But this time, my voice carried something extra — a conviction shaped by the climb at Teal. I knew, beyond doubt, that no school is beyond redemption when belief takes root and teamwork carries the weight.

Looking back, the BSI transfer was more than a detour. It was a crucible. Lemuel Teal's rise to a "C" wasn't my victory or Onika's alone—it was ours, and it belonged to every teacher, student, and parent who dared to believe again.

The experience reminded me that education is not a solo act. It is chorus and collaboration, structure and spirit, strategy and soul. And in that blend, I found not just professional growth, but confirmation of something I had always believed: when educators work together with conviction, schools rise.

Now, head of English department at Lehigh Acres Middle, I carry both memory and mandate. The mango tree in my backyard continues to grow taller, its roots firm, its branches wide. Each morning, I whisper the same prayer: Let my work bear fruit—not just for me, but for every child, every colleague, every school that dares to climb.

Because the Bureau of School Improvement didn't just move me. It expanded me. And it reminded me that legacy is built not in isolation, but in partnership—shoulder to shoulder, voice to voice, with stalwarts like Onika Vassell.

Now, in 2025, back at Lehigh Acres Middle School, with decades of experience behind me and still more ahead, I've become more than a teacher. I'm a mentor, a leader, a cultural bridge.

At school, colleagues call on me for advice on WICOR strategies, for insight into reaching reluctant readers, for help crafting culturally responsive lessons. I lead professional development workshops with the same passion I once gave to morning assemblies at Drexel House—where I learned that a microphone and a story could shift the energy of an entire building.

And yet—my favorite place remains the classroom.

The whiteboard.

The journal prompt.

The moment when a child, once quiet and hidden, finally raises their hand and says:

"I think I get it now."

That moment—that flicker of self-belief—is still worth climbing for.

I've taught in rooms with peeling paint and broken blinds. I've taught in state-of-the-art buildings with smartboards and ergonomic chairs. But the magic has never come from the walls—it's always come from the people inside them. From the way a student's eyes shift when they realize they've written something beautiful. From the way a classroom hums when a story hits close to home.

My pedagogy has evolved, but the heart of it remains the same: relationship first. I don't teach content — I teach connection. I teach courage. I teach the art of becoming.

Each year, I begin with a ritual. I write three words on the board: **Voice. Story. Power.** Then I ask my students to tell me what they think they mean. Some shrug. Some guess. Some stay silent. But by June, those words are no longer abstract — they're lived. They're written into poems, essays, speeches, and quiet acts of resistance.

I've had students write about deportation, about losing siblings to gun violence, about growing up in motels and shelters. I've had students write about joy too — about dancing in kitchens, about grandmothers who smell like cinnamon, about the first time they felt seen. And I've learned to hold space for all of it. To honor the full spectrum of their humanity.

I've watched a student named Amira, once terrified to speak in front of the class, deliver a spoken word piece about colorism that left the room in stunned silence. I've watched a boy named Tyrese, who used to skip school twice a week, show up early just to finish a poem he started the day before. I've watched students argue passionately about Baldwin and Bennett, about Kendrick and Keats, about whether a metaphor can carry grief or if it simply disguises it.

These are not just academic moments. They are spiritual ones. They are the reason I still rise before dawn, still laminate handouts, still write personalized feedback in the margins of every draft. Because I know that somewhere in that scribble is a seed — and my job is to water it.

Outside the classroom, my role has expanded. I mentor new teachers, especially those who feel overwhelmed by the system's demands. I tell them, "You don't have to be perfect. You just have to be present." I remind them that the best lessons often come from the moments we didn't plan—the spontaneous discussion, the unexpected question, the story that derails the syllabus but heals the room.

I've also become a bridge between generations. Parents who once sat in my classroom now send their children to me. They stop me in the parking lot, in the grocery store, at church, and say, "You taught me how to write my story. Now teach my daughter." And I do. With reverence. With gratitude. With the quiet understanding that legacy is not built in grand gestures—it's built in consistency.

There are days when the work feels heavy. When the system feels too rigid, too political, too indifferent to the soul of teaching. But then a student leaves a sticky note on my desk that says, "Thank you for seeing me." And I remember why I'm here.

I remember the boy from Tulip Lane.

The one who read by kerosene lamp.

The one who taught himself to dream in a world that didn't always make room for dreamers.

I remember the teacher who told me, "You have something to say."

And I remember the first time I believed her.

Now, I try to be that voice for someone else.

I've also begun working on a second book—a companion to A Journey in Three Acts—this one focused on pedagogy, on the philosophy of teaching as healing. It's part memoir, part manual, part manifesto. I write it in the evenings, after the house has settled, with a cup of coffee and the unwavering silence of my backyard echoing in the dark.

Because even now, with all I've done, I still believe I'm becoming.

I still believe that every classroom is a sanctuary.

That every child is a story waiting to be honored.

That every teacher is a torchbearer in a world that desperately needs light.

And so, I keep showing up.

For the students who haven't spoken all year.

For the ones who write poems in the margins of math worksheets.

For the ones who think they're invisible.

For the ones who know they're brilliant but need someone to say it out loud.

I keep showing up.

Because that flicker of self-belief—that moment when a child says, "I think I get it now"—is not just a milestone.

It's a miracle.

And it's still worth climbing for.

481

Chapter VII: 2025

The Mango Tree Years

By 2025, the mango tree in my backyard had grown tall enough to cast shade over half the lawn. Its branches stretched wide, sturdy and unapologetic. Each morning, as I sipped coffee on the porch, I watched it sway in the Florida breeze and thought: this tree is my mirror. Rooted in soil that wasn't its birthplace, yet thriving. Carrying history in its trunk yet reaching for the sky.

When I planted it, the sapling stood awkward and thin, as if embarrassed to be seen. I remember tamping the soil with my shoe and wondering if it would survive the first summer. Florida sun can be generous, but it can also be merciless. Storms come with little warning; winds speak in a language of uprooting. I watered anyway. I staked it against the gusts. On certain mornings, I spoke to it like a friend who needed reminding: you belong here; hold fast.

The tree listened in the way trees do — saying nothing and answering everything. Each new leaf was a small affirmation. Each season of growth announced itself not with fanfare but with quiet insistence. It was not the tallest tree in the neighborhood, but it carried itself with a certain resolve, a kind of immigrant pride: I did not choose this soil, but I will honor it with my reach.

I came to expect its company the way one expects sunrise. The sound of leaves rubbing together became my morning hymn. Birds nested in its upper branches as if they, too, trusted its hold. And I, standing beneath it, felt my own spine lengthen. We were, the tree and I, two arrivals who had decided that flourishing would be our answer to distance.

The mango tree taught me definitions I had been slow to claim. Strength is not loud, it is patient. Belonging is not given, it is grown. Hope is not a mood; it is a practice. I traced those truths along the bark with my fingertips, then carried them into the day like tools.

I used to think roots were about origin stories — where you are born, which flag claims you, the street names of your childhood. But by 2025, I understood roots differently. Roots are decisions repeated. Roots are the unshiny, daily agreements you make with a place and its people.

Florida was never in my early plans. It arrived like a plot twist that refused to be rewritten. For a long time, I spoke about it as if I were passing through: a way station, a chapter break, an address on borrowed time. But students refused to let me remain temporary. They tethered me — first with their questions, then with their trust. Colleagues handed me pieces of their hard days and asked me to help carry them. Neighbors waved from driveways and brought over plates at odd hours. The place kept insisting I was already home.

The tree helped me finish the conversation I was avoiding. It did not ask the soil to be Jamaica. It did not compare the taste of rain or the shine of the sun. It simply reached. It learned the minerals under it, the winds around it, the rhythm of birds that used it as a rest stop. Watching it, I understood you can honor the land that raised you and still give yourself fully to the land that holds you now. Love is not a subtraction.

My roots deepened through habit as much as through revelation. Morning greetings at school that turned into ritual. After-school conversations that became mentorship. Weekend planning that felt less like work and more like stewardship. Each repeated act was another filament burrowing down, finding purchase.

I stopped waiting for the feeling of arrival and began practicing it. I joined hands

485

with the work already happening around me. I learned which grocery store carried sorrel in December, who sold the best patties at the corner market, which mechanic understood my car's stubborn rattle without the upsell. I discovered the Florida constellations that guided us home from late games. I learned the way the air changes thirty minutes before a storm. This is how place becomes part of you: not by proclamation, but by familiarity. Not by documents, but by memory.

At school, I found myself measuring the year against the tree. Early spring: first buds, first drafts. Late spring: the canopy thickens, discussions deepen. Mid-summer: fruit hangs heavy, students shoulder the weight of final projects and the sweetness of earned confidence. The tree became a calendar even when I wasn't looking at it.

I styled my classroom after the yard — light where I could get it, shade where students needed it, open pathways between desks like foot tracks in grass. I wanted the room to breathe. I wanted students to feel the permission to stretch, to angle themselves toward what nourished them. On the whiteboard, next to the day's objectives, I kept a simple sentence in small letters: Grow here. Sometimes a child would trace the words with their eyes before they found their seat; sometimes I caught them mouthing it under their breath before a test. I never pointed it out. It was a quiet signpost, like the way the tree's shadow points to noon.

The rituals that anchored us in 2024 deepened in 2025. "The Last Word" no longer belonged to me. Students nominated each other or reached into a shared jar of cards collected from parents, alumni, visiting teachers. Some days the last word was a line of poetry, other days a sentence a child wrote that morning, trembling but brave. I watched those words leave the room like birds lifting off the branch, carrying pieces of us into other periods, other homes.

There was a boy who could not sit still unless he was drawing. His notebooks were a forest of sketches—margins crowded with faces, sneakers, city skylines. One afternoon, I asked him to design a cover for our class anthology, and the way his shoulders rose told me I had named something in him that wanted naming. When the printed copies arrived, the class chanted his name. He held the book the way you hold a newborn—carefully, astonished. Some fruits are paper and staples, but they are fruit all the same.

A girl who rarely spoke began leaving me notes on scraps of paper. They were not essays. They were fragments, weather reports of the heart: Cloudy at home. Sunny at school. Thank you for shade. I kept them tucked inside my lesson planner like pressed leaves. On days when I wondered whether any of this was working, I would read one and remember: shade is not a solution, but it is a beginning.

Florida Does Florida

Florida has a way of reminding you that everything you love is provisional. Storm season teaches the body a choreography of readiness: move the furniture, charge the devices, fill the bathtubs, stock the candles, park the car nose-out. Each weather update becomes a sentence whose ending you cannot read. You learn to prepare without catastrophizing, to respect the ocean's memory.

That year a storm spun itself into a name people repeated with a hush. It flirted with the Gulf, eyeing coastlines like a shopper running fingers over fabric. We watched the cone maps and, like every family in reach of the spiral, made choices. I wrapped the mango tree's young branches in soft ties. I cleared the yard of loose things that could become weapons in a hard wind. We prayed without bargaining.

When the storm finally came, it was both less and more than promised. The house held, the tree bent and straightened, the yard filled with a confetto of leaves. We were lucky. Others were not. The morning after, we checked on neighbors, shared extension cords, delivered coffee in paper cups to those without power. The street bloomed with the small mercies of a block that remembers it is a village when sirens quiet.

Under the mango tree, I untied the supports and ran my hand along the bark. The trunk felt steadier than the year before. The storm had not made it stronger; its own growth had. That realization settled in me like a lesson I should have learned earlier: strength is built before the crisis. What holds you in the gale is the work no one claps for—the early bed, the daily walk, the apology offered before it calcifies, the poem written when no one is looking, the syllabus revised at midnight because the kids deserve better by morning.

We had learned that lesson the hard way when the maps stopped teasing Tampa Bay and the spiral tightened over our coast. The National

Hurricane Center would later write that the storm made landfall near Cayo Costa in Lee County, a Category Four with winds you could not negotiate with. At the time, what I knew was the sound of everything we owned humming in unison — the fridge, the phones, the portable chargers — like a choir singing toward a silence we hoped would not come.

I am not someone who takes pictures during a storm, but I will never forget the angles — the palm fronds bent flat like hair, the air salted and electric, the rain falling sideways and then, somehow, upward. Reports would later describe storm surge like a slow-tsunami, ten to fifteen feet above ground in places not far from us, a wall of water that does not look like a wall until it lifts your living room from its studs. We did not see it break our street, but friends in Fort Myers Beach called with voices thin as strings. "It's in the ceiling," one said. "How can water be in the ceiling?"

Neighbors compared plans over the hum. One family drove inland to stay with cousins; another moved two streets over to a house on a slight rise; an older couple refused to leave, taping their windows with the same careful attention they once used for wrapping gifts at Christmas. I carried sandbags like they were stubborn children. In the kitchen, I filled jugs and labeled them with black marker. The radio sprinkled advisories between songs, some voices steady, some tight with the effort of sounding steady.

When the worst passed, the quiet was louder than the wind. We stepped outside and counted roof shingles like playing cards. The mango tree still standing, scuffed but upright, leaves torn and shining. I breathed a thank-you I did not know who to address. Then the block did the math of mercy: Who has power? Whose freezer can be a communal ark? Which outlets,

492

which extension cords, which generators can be shared until the grid remembers us? We became a village in the time it takes to ask, "You good?" and mean it.

In the days that followed, news leaked back into our lives in pixelated streams. The causeway to Sanibel was in pieces, blue water cutting the road like missing pages. I stared at the images because I needed not to look away. So many of us have loved that stretch of road — the slow, bright crossing, the birds peering down like patient ushers.

Now it was a necklace with a broken clasp, our neighbors stranded on an island famous for shells and quiet mornings. The camera panned and I thought of the people whose rituals were snapped mid-motion: the barista who could not open the shop, the teacher whose classroom was mud, the family whose photo albums had become pulp.

At school, we rewrote the week in dry-erase marker. The library became a cooling center. Teachers with power at home laundered clothes for colleagues who didn't. Students arrived with stories like weather maps: patches of calm, sudden squalls, spirals of fear. We gave them paper and the chance to make a record. "Write what you saw," I said, "and what you wish you hadn't." A boy described furniture walking through his living room toward the back door as if it suddenly remembered the Gulf. A girl wrote about her grandma's hand shaking so hard she couldn't dial the phone. We read aloud only if we wanted to. We cried if we needed to.

I kept thinking about preparation as a kind of love. Not the dramatic kind that throws itself between you and danger, but the patient kind that buys batteries in June, that labels cords, that knows where the passports live. In my classroom, we talked about the storm like we talk about literature: foreshadowing, tone, theme. The theme, I told them, is not disaster; it is design. Storm surge is physics and geography meeting human choices — where we build, how we evacuate, what we ignore when the sky is blue. This was not to blame but to locate agency, because recovery deserves authorship too.

On a Saturday, our AVID kids organized a supply drive in the parking lot. Families pulled in, trunks popped, and the asphalt turned into a river of bleach, tarps, diapers, pet food, extension cords, and sturdy gloves. A crew from the football team hauled pallets like they were pushing a sled. The band director showed up with a battery-powered speaker and soft music that somehow made everyone move a little longer. A grandmother arrived with a bag of soap and a plate of pastelitos. She pressed the plate into my hands like medicine. "Sugar keeps courage standing," she said.

The stories accumulated: a nurse who worked a double shift without power at home; a lineman who slept in his truck between poles; a teacher who taught by the light of a borrowed generator, her students' faces glowing like pages. And the sorrow, too: families sifting through what water turns into the same color of ruin — photographs, couches, the soft animals of childhood, the months of rent saved in an envelope. I learned that disaster compresses time; a day lasts a year, and a year folds back into a single, shimmering hour when the light hits a scar at the right angle.

When school resumed in something like a pattern, I assigned an essay called *"What Holds."* It wasn't about the storm, not exactly. It was about the structures—visible and invisible—that keep a person together when the wind decides to test its strength against yours. Students wrote about aunties and coaches, about prayers and playlists, about the perfection of a neighbor's generator at the right moment. One wrote about the Sanibel bridge, not as a ruin but as a promise. "If people can build it once," she said, "people can build it again." She was right. The first temporary repairs arrived far quicker than anyone expected, and the island found its way back to mainland errands and mainland medicine.

At home, the mango tree taught revision. Salt had crisped the leaf edges like a cook with a heavy hand. I pruned what was beyond saving and left what still had a chance. Weeks later, new growth arrived in shy bursts, bright enough to embarrass the damage. I showed the kids a photo sequence—storm, prune, sprout— and asked what the sequence meant. "That patience looks like nothing until it doesn't,"

497

someone said. I wrote that on the board and underlined it twice.

The deeper lesson landed slowly: most of the people who survived the surge did so because of choices made before the first band of rain. Warnings were heeded and evacuations taken seriously. Community networks activated. The National Hurricane Center's report would later confirm what our grief already knew — that storm surge claimed more lives than wind or rain, and that so many of those losses happened here, where the Gulf lifts its hand, and the land is low and full of stories. We told the truth to each other in hallways and over fences: next time, leave sooner; next time, pack the photos in plastic; next time, collaborate with your neighbors before the sky turns.

And because schools are where next times start; we built them into our curriculum. Science classes analyzed coastal geography and urban planning. Math used real surge data to practice interpreting graphs with consequence. English collected oral histories and honored them with careful punctuation and kinder drafts. Our AVID tutorials included disaster-prep scenarios because inquiry is not only academic; it's a life skill: Who do you call? Where do you meet if the cell towers fail? What does a go-bag hold besides batteries and snacks?

By the following spring, the neighborhood had an extra softness to it, like a muscle after it has healed but still remembers the stretch. Blue tarps grew scarce, but not all at once. New roofs flashed under sun that had returned to its regular job. The mango tree flowered, tentative and then generous. I started taking my coffee outside again, the way I had before the storm taught us to measure mornings differently. From the porch I watched a utility truck roll past, crew laughing, windows down, music lifting. The street looked ordinary from there—trash bins lined like chess pieces, kids biking without hands, a dog named Coco who always forgets he is small—and ordinary felt like luxury.

When the next summer came, we replaced resolutions with a family drill that took twelve minutes and ended with cold mango slices. We checked the go-bags, updated numbers, walked the route to a friend's taller house. Then we put everything back and went about our day. Preparation had become a ritual not of fear but of respect. Respect for water and wind. Respect for the people who rebuild bridges, reconnect wires, restock shelves, reopen schools. Respect for a county that knows both the cost of vulnerability and the dividend of community.

I still touch the mango tree most mornings. The bark has thickened where my hand tends to land, a little oval the size of belief. Some days I pray; some days I promise. Always I listen. The leaves talk in a language of friction and light. The sky above them is the exact blue that fools you into thinking nothing bad could ever happen here. But we have learned better. We have learned to love without pretending permanence. We have learned to build strength on ordinary days, to tighten the hinge before the storm rattles it, to call the neighbor before we need the neighbor, to anchor the boat even when the water looks like glass.

Florida keeps teaching. The Gulf keeps reminding. And in Lee County, the memory of that year lives not only in photographs and reports, but in the way we now carry ourselves when the satellite image turns our home into a swirl. We step into the choreography that no one claps for, and we do it anyway, because all the applause we need is the quiet of a house that holds, the reappearance of power lines humming in the night, the first mango of the season pressed into a neighbor's hand with a smile that says: we're still here.

Rituals of Care

I used to think self-care sounded like a spa brochure—soft music, soft lighting, soft voices saying soft things. In 2025, I learned that care is often sturdy and unsentimental. It is the act of editing the calendar with the same confidence I edit a paragraph: this stays, this goes, this moves here for clarity.

Mornings began earlier, not to do more but to be less hurried. I walked the block before sunrise and let the air talk sense into me. I stretched on the porch while the kettle boiled. I turned off notifications on my phone in the middle of grading to give my mind the uninterrupted stretch it deserves. I recommitted to the unglamorous pillars: water, sleep, laughter, prayer. When guilt tried to frame these as luxuries, I reminded myself that exhaustion is not a virtue; it is a leak.

At school, I protected the margins around my classroom the way a gardener protects roots. I closed the door during planning and breathed in the quiet. I put a "Welcome, Come Back in 20 Minutes" sign in the window so that my open-door policy did not become a door I could not close. I mentored still, but from a place of fullness rather than depletion. The difference was subtle and saving.

On Saturdays, I kept a standing date with a book that had nothing to do with my curriculum. Sometimes I read history, sometimes mystery, sometimes poems too strange for lesson plans but perfect for reminding me that language has more rooms than we use on weekdays. The mango tree became my reading partner, its shade adjusting itself over my shoulder like a patient friend.

502

Seeds We Scatter

The mango tree does not ask where its seeds land. It releases them to the grass, to birds, to the hands of children who run sticky and laughing across the yard. Some seeds sprout where they fall; others travel. I tried to live that lesson in 2025 without controlling outcomes.

In class, we built more projects that left the room. Students recorded mini-podcasts about family sayings and the wisdom hidden in them. They designed broadsides — illustrated quotes — with lines that mattered to them, then taped them to the corridor walls like small, stubborn billboards. We mailed a bundle to a partner class two counties away and received theirs in return. For a week the hallways felt like a festival of borrowed courage.

Seeds went other places too — into conversations with younger teachers about boundary-keeping, into emails to parents that did not wait for a problem to say, your child shines in this way, and into my own notebook

503

where ideas queued up like birds on a wire, waiting their turn to lift off.

Sometimes the seeds circled back. A graduate sent a photo from a bus stop two towns over: one of our broadsides taped to the shelter, rain-wrinkled but still legible. "Kept me from skipping class today," he texted. Another messaged a voice note at midnight—her grandmother's proverb in Spanish first, then the English she'd stitched with her aunt. I saved them both, not as proof, but as weather reports: look, something is moving through.

I began leaving chalk in my bag. On walks, I'd write a single line on the cracked sidewalk near the bodega—**Read something that argues with you**—and then keep going. At school, I put the students in charge of the courtyard bulletin board; they layered poems with science diagrams and recipes for Sunday rice and peas. The assistant principal walked by, slowed, then smiled without notes. Even the security guard started dropping off song lyrics. "For your seed thing," he said, shrugging.

There were boundaries too. I learned to end the day with my notebook closed, to let unfinished ideas stay unfinished until morning. The mango doesn't rip open its fruit at dusk to check on sugar levels; it trusts the dark to do its quiet work. So I tried to trust as well. I kept the door propped open during dismissal, waved students into the corridor, and watched them carry small, bright things I couldn't name. Not mine to name. Just mine to release.

Letting Go

Growth looks heroic in time-lapse videos. In real time, it feels like doubt punctuated by small confirmations. In 2025, I practiced letting go of outcomes I could not choreograph. A student I had worried over vanished from my roster when a family moved suddenly. Another, whom I had almost given up on, arrived one morning with a draft so luminous it made me re-see his grin. A workshop I hoped would be full drew only six people; hours later, a single message from one attendee described their classroom shift in a way that justified the entire night.

The mango tree sheds what it no longer needs. I started doing the same. I retired a beloved unit that had stopped serving my students of this season. I let an old ambition set sail without me, seeing it for what it was — a younger man's project that the current man didn't need to finish. I held a long, quiet goodbye to the part of me that believed I could rescue everyone if only I worked harder. I kept the part that still believes love changes futures.

Letting go did not diminish me. It clarified me. The tree remained a tree whether or not every blossom became fruit. I remained a teacher whether or not every plan landed, every heart opened on my timeline. There was dignity in tending, in showing up with clean hands and a willing spirit. There was power in the gentle insistence of again.

The Classroom Legacy

At school, I had entered my stride. Teaching wasn't new anymore, but neither was it routine. It was ritual. Every lesson carried the weight of memory and the fire of possibility. Students knew my classroom was different.

The walls weren't just decorated with charts — they were alive with stories. Poems written in patois. Essays that began as raps. Drawings that became metaphors. Every Friday, we still ended with *The Last Word*, but now students insisted on leading it. One boy, usually quiet, stood up and said:

"Sir, you always tell us we are writers. Today I believe it. Today I claim it."

I clapped until my hands ached.

Former students returned often. Some to say thank you. Some to say they got into college. Some to say they were still writing. One girl dropped by after school wearing scrubs. She had just completed her CNA training. She handed me a note that read: "You told me to write myself free. I did." I pinned it to the corkboard.

In Florida, my classrooms have been a canvas of cultures—a living mosaic of migration, memory, and dreams.

Haitians brought their Creole resilience.

Hondurans and Mexicans carried stories of border crossings and family separations.

African Americans bore the weight of generational trauma and inherited strength.

Dominicans danced between Spanish and English.

Puerto Ricans spoke in rhythms.

Jamaicans came with swagger and song.

Filipinos brought quiet determination and ancestral respect.

And every one of them brought a piece of the world that no standardized test could measure.

I met them where they were.

I didn't pretend to be color-blind or culture blind. In fact, I invited their full selves into the classroom.

Their accents.

Their slang.

Their songs.

Their struggles.

Their sacred rituals.

In my room, a boy could talk about his grandmother's tamales and link it to a poem about memory. A girl could write about her cousin shot in Bayamón and connect it to Romeo and Juliet. I once asked a class to write an ode. One student wrote about his uncle's machete. Another, about the smell of curry goat on Sundays.

I allowed code-switching in writing prompts, understanding that language is identity. I let them write first in their voice — their patois, their Spanglish, their soul — and then shape it into academic English, like a sculptor chiseling without losing the essence of the stone.

I said, "Your first draft is you. Your second draft is for them. Both matter."

I allow students to perform their narratives — spoken word, rap, skits, TED Talks — and clapped the loudest when a shy girl from Haiti belted out her trauma through a Creole-infused poem that left the room in tears.

I created anchor charts out of rap lyrics, analyzing Kendrick Lamar, J. Cole, Chronixx, and even Vybes Kartel.

"Look at this simile," I'd say, pointing to the board.

"Same thing Shakespeare did. Different beat. Same brilliance."

I placed Caribbean folktales alongside Edgar Allan Poe.

Anansi the Spider sat next to The Tell-Tale Heart.

Louise Bennett's dialect poems stood proudly beside Robert Frost.

The classroom library was a jungle of genres—*Dreaming in Cuban, Things Fall Apart, The Hate U Give, Old Story Time,* and yes, *Green Days by the River*—that childhood classic that once gave young me a glimpse of who I could become.

I encouraged debate—not just about literature, but about life. Immigration policy. Police brutality. Gender roles. Generational trauma. Colorism. The classroom was often charged, sometimes emotional, but always respectful.

There was always a quote on my whiteboard, scrawled in blue marker:
"Your life is a story. You get to write it. Make it bold. Make it messy. Make it yours."

To some, they were just words.

But to the students who felt invisible, voiceless, or defeated, those words were marching orders.

511

They weren't just invited to write their story — they were given permission to own it.

And sometimes, all a student needs is to know someone sees them.

I noticed.

Epilogue: The Fruit Still Grows

Sometimes, on warm Florida evenings when the air sits heavy and the birds retire early, I dream of Denham Town.

I dream of Tulip Lane, where time felt different—slower, richer. The scent of kerosene from lamps mingled with frying dumplings, the murmur of neighbors became a lullaby, and zinc rooftops clanged like old songs when the wind rushed through.

I dream of nights when blackout meant candlelight flickering on cracked walls, when laughter spilled from verandahs like gospel, and when my world was both impossibly small and unimaginably vast.

The wet earth after a sudden rain left a smell I could never quite describe — something between promise and memory. And even now, decades and countries later, I catch a whiff of it in a Fort Myers storm and am transported, instantly, to barefooted days and muddy trousers.

I remember the children skipping rope in the middle of the lane, their chants rising with the dust:

"Zing zang zung,

Mek di likkle gal run!" (Allow the little girl to run).

We'd play until the sun melted behind rooftops and streetlights blinked to life like tired eyes.

And always, there was my mother's voice — Mama's voice — sweeter than any lullaby and firmer than any belt.

"Come wash yuh foot before yuh come pon di bed." (Come wash your feet before you come on the bed.)

A command, not a suggestion. But behind the sternness was love — unshakable, unconditional.

There is no statue of Horatio Ward. No honorary degrees. No viral videos. But my legacy lives in the silence before a student dares to read aloud, in the scribbled draft of a poem that might never be turned in, in the eyes of a parent who once thought their child had no future — until they entered Mr. Ward's class.

I am a tree planted beside water. A storyteller who chose the long, hard, thankless road of transformation.

And in my three-act journey, I have proven what every great teacher eventually understands:

That to teach is to believe.

To believe in the child who doesn't yet believe in themselves.

To believe in words, and books, and messy essays and lunchroom drama.

To believe that somewhere beneath all the noise, a story waits to be written.

And so, I rise every day, coffee in hand, keys around my neck, walking past faded hallway posters and pencil-scuffed desks — to start Act IV: as I currently live it. Because though the boy from Tulip Lane now leads department meetings and mentors new teachers...

He is still climbing.

And the fruit, though still high in the tree, is sweeter now.

In Lehigh Acres, my yard is smaller than the lane that raised me, but the mango tree makes a cathedral of it. I stand beneath those broad leaves and hear the old neighborhood in the rustle — the iron gate creaking on Tulip Lane, the distant rattle of a handcart, the bassline of a sound system finding its courage after dusk. Florida holds new music, but Jamaica is the melody that threads it. The tree carries both: roots here, rhythm there, a bridge between boyhood and the man who shows up in a tie, a whistle, and a soft voice that does not always feel soft enough.

I carry my mother with me into every room. Mama knew how to braid order out of chaos — laundry lines tight as staff paper, a pot that could feed one more mouth without complaint, a look that made you pick up your shoes before she had to ask. When I teach, I am borrowing her power. When I write feedback in green ink instead of red, I am speaking in her tone: firm, hopeful, specific. I tell my students that love is not the absence of standards; it is the courage to hold them steady while standing close.

517

From my mother, I learned the long view. She did not need to perform wisdom; she lived it like a quiet drumbeat. She would point to a wall I could barely see over and say, *"Tek time. You'll reach"* (Take time. You'll reach.) In Denham Town, that meant stepping-stones across a flooded gutter, or the patience to shape a kite until the breeze agreed. In my classroom, it means holding silence long enough for a shy hand to rise or letting a draft sit for a day so its author can return with eyes that see what they meant all along. The long view is how mangoes ripen; it is also how people do.

Some nights I dream of the zinc fences painted in bright colors, the patchwork that turned scarcity into a style. I see boys racing bottle trucks downhill, and girls balancing buckets on their hips with the same elegance queens wear their crowns. I remember the first time I left the lane and realized the world could be both gentler and more indifferent; how the sea at Kingston Harbor taught me that distance can be a teacher, too. I carry those distances like coordinates stitched into my passport. They lead me back to the desks I arrange in a horseshoe, a small geometry of inclusion.

I have learned that a good classroom smells faintly of effort. Expo marker and warm paper, the copper tang of anxiety on test days, the citrus of a cleaned desk when a kid decides to start again. The best sound is not applause or even laughter, though both are medicine. The best sound is the quiet that follows a strong question. It is the sound of thinking shifting gears. When a student says, "Wait—so if the narrator is unreliable, why do we trust that scene?" the room tilts toward possibility. That tilt is why I keep showing up.

In Act IV, I mentor more than I grade. I sit with first-year teachers who think every bad day is a verdict and every good day is luck. We talk about pacing like breathing—how you cannot sprint the whole year, how you must build rest into the lesson plan. I tell them Denham Town taught me how to improvise: when the light goes, bring the candles; when the chalk breaks, use the shard; when the copier fails, teach from memory and make it look like design. Improvisation is not sloppiness; it is respect for the moment's needs.

Sometimes I bring tulip bulbs to PD as a joke only I fully understand. I tell my colleagues the name of my street and pass around the bulbs like tiny promises. "Plant them wherever you need color," I say. "Plant them where a hallway needs hope." We laugh, but I mean it. Schools are brick and schedules; they are also stories and seasons. In Florida we do not get spring the way the brochures show it, but we can still make bloom a verb. A bulletin board can flower. A binder can. A habit can.

I think of the children on Tulip Lane skipping rope, their rhyme beating time into the dust. Those children live inside the ones I teach now — their swagger, their quick-tongued kindness, their mischief that is mostly a shield. When a student back-talks, I hear a boy on the lane practicing for a world that will not always listen. When a student falls asleep, I see a girl who rocked her baby brother at midnight because her mother works the late shift. This is not an excuse; it is a context. In context, discipline becomes dignity. We correct because we believe they can rise.

On certain afternoons the Florida light drops just so, and the mango leaves shine like they were polished by old songs. I take a picture no phone can capture: my backyard holding two countries at once. The breeze moves and I smell kerosene and cumin and the clean, green bite of cut grass. Memory does not ask permission; it rearranges the furniture of the day and seats you where you need to sit. In those moments I write a few lines in a notebook no one will grade. The pages gather like fallen leaves. Someday, perhaps, they will be soil for something new.

Legacy is a word people use when they want to sound like they are not afraid of endings. I am not done, so I use quieter words: practice, witness, return. Practice is what I do when no one is watching — reading that chapter I avoided, revising the unit for the fifth time, choosing to rest. Witness is what I offer my students when they risk themselves on paper or in a sentence. Return is the way I keep walking back to the work after disappointment or praise. Practice, witness, return — three roots that keep a tree steady when the season wants to lean.

When I go back to Kingston, I drive past Denham Town with my windows down, slow enough to hear the lane hum. The zinc still shines in places, graffiti layered like palimpsest. Children still shout to each other across distances adults pretend not to cross. A woman sells bag juice near a gate that looks like one I once swung from until Mama bawled my full government name. I buy two coffees, cold and too sweet, and sit in the car to drink and remember. No camera can hold the tilt of my heart in those minutes. I am as old as the houses and as young as the chalk on the wall.

I have never believed that teaching saves anyone; it invites them. The saving, if it comes, is a collaboration between a child's stubborn heart and a community's steady hands. I watch a student in May who in September would not open his notebook now argue with evidence about a poem he once called foolish. I watch a girl ask for feedback like a chef asks for salt. I watch a parent come to school wearing fear and leave wearing relief. These are not miracles. They are mangoes: grown in ordinary weather, ripened by attention, offered freely.

Some evenings I sit with colleagues after dismissal and we talk like old people on a corner, swapping stories until the sun edits us into silhouettes. We argue about phones and phonics and whether grades measure anything worth measuring. We laugh at the child who called me "sir" in a tone that meant the opposite and praise the one who apologized without being prompted. When the custodian rattles his keys, we gather our bags and promises. I lock my door and touch the frame like a mezuzah. "Tomorrow," I say to the empty room. Tomorrow is a loyal friend to those who prepare for it.

Mama's voice follows me home. "Mind how you speak." So, I try. I call more parents to share good news than bad. I write fewer words on essays so the right ones ring. I leave space in conferences for silence to do its work. On the phone with my mother, I describe the mango tree and she laughs because she knows what I am really telling her: that I am still her boy, still listening, still washing the day off my feet before I come inside.

Horatio's lessons arrive when the car is quiet, and the stoplights stretch red. "Tek time." (Take time). So, I do. I choose the long way home. I turn off the news and let the road offer its own headlines: a heron stalking the retention pond, a child chasing his shadow, a neighbor wheeling a grill out with the reverence of ceremony. Tek time, and you will notice the life you almost left in your haste to improve it. Tek time, and you will see the fruit for what it is: not a prize, but a proof of patient labor.

Sometimes former students write from college or the service or a job two counties away. Their messages are a chorus of small, bright lines. "I used Cornell notes for my certification exam." "I argued with the rubric in my sociology class and won." "I read a book because I remembered your face when we finished one." I answer every message. I send a photo of the mango tree when the first fruits blush, and I tell them what I tell myself: keep tending. The world is noisy; attention is a rebellion.

In the epilogue I do not land the plane; I circle to see the coastline better. Tulip Lane, Fort

Myers, classrooms arranged like invitations, mornings that begin with coffee and end with calendars. The fruit still grows because the roots still drink. I am less interested in applause than in alignment—between what I say and what I do, between where I come from and where I am going, between the teacher I am and the man the lane would recognize. If I manage that, the rest will taste right.

So, if you see me under the mango tree at dusk cooking jerk chicken, know that I am counting blessings and making lists. I am hearing a skipping rhyme in a new accent. I am thanking women named Marva, Sharon, Pauline, Patsy, Dorrett, Esmine; men named **Hugh Valentine St Aubyn Ward** and Basil and another man named Horatio Lancelot Ward for their stubborn faith. I am forgiving yesterday for its crooked lines. I am promising tomorrow I will walk straighter. And I am whispering to anyone who needs to hear it—student, colleague, the boy I used to be—that the fruit does not ask how high you climbed to reach it; it only asks that you share.

As I live Act IV

As I live, Act IV begins without trumpets — only the steady drum of morning routines and the whisper that I am still becoming. I wake to responsibilities that once frightened me and now fit like a well-worn jacket: mentoring the young, honoring my elders, strengthening the circle at home. The work is quieter here, but deeper — repairing what was cracked, planting where I once only harvested, speaking with the patience I once admired in others. I carry the names that made me, and I make room for the ones still arriving. I move with intention, measuring my words, choosing which battles are worthy and which deserve blessing and release.

In this act I count success differently, not by applause, but by the peace that lingers after a hard conversation; not by the scoreboard, but by the smile that returns to a tired face. I practice forgiveness as daily bread — of others, yes, and of the impatient boy I used to be. I try to live the way I learned from Sharon. I write more, listen longer, and choose presence over speed. Act IV is stewardship: of stories, of health, of hope. I curate memories without becoming trapped by them. I prepare the table so love can sit down and stay awhile. And as I live, I choose gratitude, and I keep walking.

About The Author

I was born in Denham Town, one of the most impoverished communities in Kingston, Jamaica, and I have taught English and Religious Education across three continents. A graduate of The Mico University College in Kingston Jamaica and Middlesex University in London, I have spent over two decades as an educator, storyteller, and mentor. I currently teach in Florida, where I continue to inspire young minds through literature, culture, and creativity. A Journey in Three Acts: The Story of Horatio Ward is my debut memoir.

www.ingramcontent.com/pod-product-compliance
Lightning Source LLC
Chambersburg PA
CBHW021656120626
46545CB00004B/1266